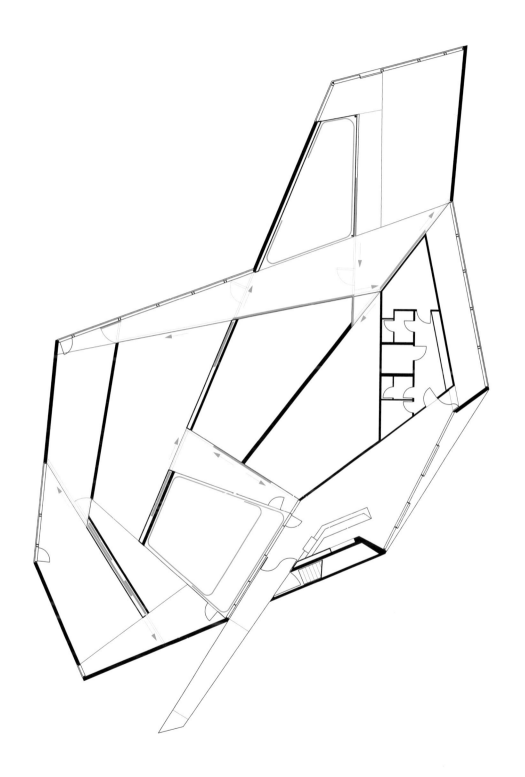

Editorial

The GfZK-2, the second exhibition building of the Galerie für Zeitgenössische Kunst (GfZK) / Museum of Contemporary Art Leipzig Foundation, was inaugurated on November 28, 2004. However, our collaboration began three years before that with collective reflections on the conditions imposed by the institutional framework, the act of exhibiting, and the scope of artistic/curatorial practice with regard to an increasingly heterogeneous audience or public. This process kindled vigorous exchange – between the specialized planners/technical designers, the GfZK team, and the members of the GfZK Friends' Organization – on possible forms of implementing a new building within a clearly limited budget. The project could be realized thanks to the concerted effort of all involved. Since its completion, the building has received a number of important prizes – the *City of Leipzig Architecture Award* (2005), an honorable mention of award at the *German Architecture Prize* (2005), and the *Bauwelt Prize* (2007), among others. One may well ask: why are we publishing a book on this building as late as five years after it was inaugurated? The architecture of the GfZK-2 resists concepts of a conclusively defined, unalterable architectural statement. Therefore, approriating the building by continually changing and redefining is integral to the architectural concept; the spatial structure is designed as being reversible, consequently demanding the negotiation of institutional and spatial parameters.

In general, conceptual demands can only be measured through utilization, and are thus best described in terms of how the building is put to use. Hence, the present book could necessarily be produced only several years after the building's inauguration. The architecture is not the only point of emphasis, but rather also the way in which architectural, artistic, and curatorial practices interlock. This book seeks to translate the intellectual position on which the building is founded; the publication, apart from our own texts, equally contains statements and contributions by artists, curators, theoreticians, and planners. We consider the exhibitions selected here as exemplary analyses of the architectural/institutional structure, context, and methods of display inherent to the GfZK – central issues addressed by this publication.

The book's graphic layout aims communicate this multiplicity of voices: reflections on individual exhibitions and the processes of planning and construction reveal the interaction and structural parallels between space and its utilization. The descriptions are interspersed with theoretical essays, marking a discursive area that opens up a further level of debate concerning potential forms of institutional and architectural agency. The selection of images relates to the process of construction, the finished building, and its use.

In the beginning, none of us expected that the preliminary concepts for the building would ever be realized – the mere thought of it seemed utopian. Yet, thanks to support by a number of benefactors – patrons, collaborating professionals, and friends – we could implement the project very much the way we had conceived of it at the outset.

We would like to thank Thomas de Maizière and Arend Oetker for their unabated dynamism, the local authorities in Leipzig for their continuous support, and all the planners and designers for their surpassing commitment and effort. Without this, the building could not have been realized! We also extend our gratitude to everyone who contributed to supporting the present publication, the GfZK Friends' Organization, and the graphic designer Tom Unverzagt for designing the book's layout.

Paul Grundei, Stephanie Kaindl, Christian Teckert (as-if berlinwien), and Barbara Steiner (Director, Galerie für Zeitgenössische Kunst / Museum of Contemporary Art Leipzig – GfZK)

The Architecture Has Become an Actor in the Process of Negotiation

Barbara Steiner (Director of the Galerie für Zeitgenössische Kunst – GfZK / Museum of Contemporary Art Leipzig), Paul Grundei, Stephanie Kaindl, and Christian Teckert (as-if berlinwien) in an interview with Leipzig writer and critic Arnold Bartetzky in February 2005, shortly after the opening of the building.

Bartetzky The idea for the new exhibition building of the GfZK Leipzig is based on a design process, which not at first, as is usually the case, arises from the appearance of the building or from the integration of the building to its urban environs, but rather from the curatorial practice, from the specific needs of the institution. What experiences did you gain in the process?

as-if The decisive point was to define the project agenda together and to find a common language for it, to transform it step by step in the direction of architecture. There were already common experiences with Barbara Steiner, in which similar thinking about architecture, about exhibition spaces, and about the politics of visibility of the institution emerged. That point strongly interested us, because the practice at work in an institution like the GfZK is very much about a strong reflectivity towards its own institutional mechanisms and the institutional practice as a whole. It is a way of working that is really about complex layering of diverse activities that are also permanently reflected and discussed in relationship to one another.

Steiner In contemporary art, there is an incredible multiplicity of possible positions and for these a screen is also needed – spatial conditions that can properly address these various challenges. These consistently new positions require a corresponding architecture that in the end allows for and responds to these changes in artistic positions. In our case, it was important to collaborate with architects who really have a strong awareness of the needs of contemporary art. The building owes itself at least as much to inspirations from artistic practices as from the history of architecture.

Bartetzky How are these premises for the actual building then manifested, on the one hand the wish toward visibility or articulation of a specific institutional profile and on the other hand toward changeability, toward a variable, should one say stage – set or a display for contemporary art?

as-if During the design process and in consultations with the GfZK, we tried to develop many moments of friction – between adjoining spaces with different uses placed next to each other, which might be brought into new relations with each other again and again through specific architectural elements. It also became important that the spaces themselves could change their functional meaning. At the beginning of the design process, the spaces had clearer functional assignments than they currently do.

Bartetzky So they were more clearly defined as rooms?

as-if Their roles were more clearly defined. They were still simply called "collection," or "cinema," or "storage," or "project space." That was then also a question for the GfZK, what type of definition is necessary and relevant, which definition is somehow bothersome, which variability of these usages is possible, and in which setting could the spaces be arranged together. The discussion over the design also dealt with the mode of operation of the institution, which is always connected to the power of defining art and viewing art, architecture, or the perceiving subject, with all mechanisms that are inscribed into every institution and that begin to exercise their power the moment someone visits an institution and crosses over these staged, clearly defined thresholds. The question was, how can one really critically reflect the perception of the visitor, of the viewer to create a setting that doesn't simply naturalize the interests of the institution, but rather shows it in its several layers or in the construction of these layers. That has also to do with how the building now actually looks, that there aren't even any closed off spaces, that there are always indications that suggest the specific function of a space, but this function is not 100 percent defined. These are negotiable spaces, which can be appropriated so that the institution can operate them. It's also an instrument, a "machine" perhaps to a certain extent, in which the institution may expose its mechanisms.

Steiner   In the interior, the singular architectural elements are partly in disparate relationship to one another. There are two display zones, one chunkier, the other sleeker, almost perfectionist in its appearance. By defining these spatial envelopes within the interior, certain zones are emphasized, which have a stage-like character. One could also speak in terms of "settings." Thus not only does the construction of an exhibition space unfold, but also the construction of the institution itself. And in the moment one doesn't encounter these constructions "naturally" they are still negotiable. Because one can imagine alternatives with respect to the "status quo," viewers are explicitly invited to confront the role and significance of art, but also architecture.

Bartetzky   Well, could one say that here the architecture has become an actor, an actor in the process of negotiation, that connects with the curatorial practice, with the creation of an exhibition, with the exchange of interests between curator, artist, and the public? The architecture no longer simply serves as building envelope, no longer as stage, as presentation space, as we know it from the "white cube," but the architecture operates as an actor that each curator and the artists who are invited here must confront?

as-if   "Must confront" is a good keyword, because the architecture of course is formulated this way, that one can never avoid it, as it often happens in museums or exhibition halls. What interested us very much in this project was to anticipate a lot of what would actually be specific exhibition design and to preconfigure elements to produce these specific spatial settings. There are these permanently visible surfaces of displays, creating spatial divisions – zones that cannot be overlooked in their appearance, but can be specifically altered. The meanings and functions of the spaces can be changed, just like the spaces in their relationship to one another through this setting of sliding wall elements and curtains are changeable. The building is basically understood as a play space, like a chessboard or a game that allows for the addition of more players: architecture, institution, curators, artists, visitors …

Steiner   In the field of art there is, in addition to the obvious, another layer of economic and political actors. And in the end, these all come together in such a place. Architecture is here essentially an instrument, a kind of "tool" with which to actively moderate this process of engagement between actors but also with what is displayed. One could also say: the architecture is supplying the basis for this debate, that in fact it is provoking it.

Bartetzky   One imagines that it must be a really big challenge above all for nonresident curators and artists, simply because the floor plan of this building is so tremendously complicated, even more so, when one tries to visualize the possible variations. How well has it functioned to communicate the possibilities of the building to nonresident curators or artists so far?

Steiner   Well there are two possibilities, that is, two reactions that have been prevalent. The one reaction is: one is shocked facing this situation …

Bartetzky   overwhelmed …

Steiner   At first perhaps. The challenge here consists of, ultimately, having to take into account the many relationships and therefore also levels of meaning. We also see the case that some artists have a relationship to space, namely the "white cube" that's been internalized and is difficult for them to un-think. And exactly this is necessary: one has to engage in new situations, in order to develop a concept for these spaces. We curators, already involved sometimes in the role of moderators, point out the qualities but also the limitations of this architecture. Of course everyone must interpret the space for himself or herself. We've also seen however, that the longer the artists are on site, the more the excitement grows with respect to the possibilities. For example visual relationships are utilized as relations between certain meanings, works are staged outside that are perceivable only from inside the building or also the façade is used like an interior wall. An enthusiasm has developed for a balanced engagement with the architecture, which doesn't dominate but is also not subordinate. I have problems with architecture that pretends not to be present at all, thus nevertheless unfolding an enormous effectiveness. We made the assertion from the beginning that there is no neutral museum space or exhibition design. That is, so to say, the first premise. The agenda was to expose and to put on display the mechanisms of architecture and the disruptive power of its meaning, as well. Furthermore, the building doesn't allow establishing a hierarchy in the relation between the architecture and the visitors.

as-if   There was a strong claim from our side to avoid producing clearly predetermined, controlled successions of orchestrated spaces. We were trying to avoid prefabricated narrations and scenarios carefully thought through and controlled, but rather create a field, that tends toward being horizontal and anti-hierarchical, and in which one can create distinct relationships.

Steiner   But it's obvious that it's not about losing one's point of view. This architecture clearly makes a stance; it formulates an attitude.

as-if   It's also not only about placing these inner spaces in relationship to one another, but also about the relationship to the larger context, for example to the outside: through the large glass façades, through overhead lighting and through smaller glass openings, spaces are connected that are actually physically separate from one another. There are distinct spatial features, like the interior glazing in the entrance area, that simply call for a specific reaction.

Steiner   Likewise it's also important, that there are specific things that you can't do. Insightful to me from the beginning was what the building doesn't allow. It doesn't allow for a certain awe or contemplation. It's not possible

to seal oneself off completely from others, because the building opens out on all sides through the large glass windows. And even if one were motivated to close off all the openings, it hardly would make sense and look quite forced.

Bartetzky   That would be counter to the concept, and totally apparent. It has to do with your specific institutional profile as GfZK, that you are not about showing or collecting art relying on a notion of aura, that you rather focus on the relationships between artworks and viewer.

Steiner   We think of ourselves as an institution, which finds itself in a specific context with a specific history. We are interested in engaging in social questions; to close oneself off would be counterproductive.

Bartetzky   Thus, transparency in the presentation of art, refraining from hierarchies, avoiding a frontal presentation of art, in the way the "white cube" would presuppose it.

Steiner   We're foregoing a patronizing presentation. Notions of participation, activation, and engagement are handled through architectural means on a rather abstract level here. Any literal signifiers claiming "attention: participation is possible!" won't be found around here.

as-if   In this project there is an interest in reformulating boundaries, which of course in modernity was always a theme. For museums built in the 1980s, it became important to incorporate foyers, cafés, bookstores, etc. in the museum itself – a kind of drawing in of consumerism. Thus the boundaries were shifted. What interests us now, is that these boundaries are no longer there, because this primary difference between inside/out, private/public no longer exists in such a simplistic duality. Even the first space you encounter when entering the building through the main entrance, isn't the classical lobby. It is actually already an exhibition space defined by an envelope of displays. It was also very important to us to think even about the façades as a conceptual part of the display system that could be continued almost endlessly.

Steiner   Today there are other kinds of boundaries that are of a more immaterial nature. Not everyone partakes, because they either don't want to or they can't – and this more and more for economic reasons. We do a lot to broaden the circle of those interested, and to remove the barriers to access, but it remains a challenge. Also in this sense architecture is important.

Bartetzky Perhaps a question in conclusion: the ideas of changeability and negotiability have already inspired artists that have worked with the spaces. We are currently sitting in the GfZK's *Café Neubau* that at night turns into *Club Weezie* and takes on a totally different character … that is actually a nice continuation of your concept. To what degree has this building changed you, your way of working, your habits?

Steiner It is a challenge to see, how one can handle this building, how one exhibits art, and this exhibiting then becomes a theme in itself – for the public, for the curators, but also for the artists. One might assume, that this is always the case anyway, but it is absolutely not always like this. The white exhibition space with all of its ideological implications has become all too self-evident. And with this room type, an entirely specific production of perception and meaning has also been established. For us, the exhibition itself as powerful instrument is the explicit theme.

INDEX of Structures, Activities, and Programs at the Galerie für Zeitgenössische Kunst (GfZK) / Museum of Contemporary Art Leipzig

The buildings GfZK-1 and GfZK-2   The GfZK-1 is located in a bourgeois villa, called Villa Herfurth, which was converted into an art institution by the architect Peter Kulka. The architect maintained the representative character of the *Gründerzeit* (late 19th century) but reorganized the spatial structure and extended the building. A gray annex forms a contrast to the old building's substance and offers additional space. Inside, Kulka pursued the concept of the "white cube." Large glass panels and a grid floor in one of the central spaces establish visual relationships but do not connect to the outside. This first building of the GfZK opened in 1998. In 1999, Kulka was awarded the *City of Leipzig Architecture Award*. So to initiate a debate about the role and function of architecture and its relation to art, the second building of the GfZK, GfZK-2, opened at the end of 2004. From the outset, the new building by as-if berlinwien was conceived in terms of a stark contrast to the villa. The idea of the second building is based on the attempt to define a spatial structure as a reversible set of relational elements, representing specific institutional functions and modes of production. As a whole, these segments form a changeable infrastructure for the contemporary practice of exhibiting and curating. In 2005, as-if berlinwien was awarded the *City of Leipzig Architecture Award*. Also in 2005, they received an honorable mention of award at the *German Architecture Prize*, in 2006 they were bestowed with the 3rd Prize of the *Austrian Architecture Award (aaa)*, and in 2007 with the *Bauwelt Prize*.

Café The concept of having artists create alternating interior designs was retained in the new spaces, with Jun Yang taking up the offer after Anita Leisz. His café is called *Paris Syndrom*. "Paris syndrome" is the term used to describe a type of psychological disorder suffered by Japanese tourists, whose longing for the fulfillment of their preconceptions about Paris is thwarted by the reality of the city. They suffer a kind of negative culture shock akin to trauma. The café name chosen by Jun Yang is indicative of the notion, whereby longing and disillusionment are experienced simultaneously upon encountering the reality of that which is desired. Emulation and replication create an image, a surface onto which unfulfilled longing can be projected. The chairs are upholstered with imitation Louis Vuitton fabric; grandiose chandeliers hang from the café ceiling, which is decorated with stucco elements. The chairs are reminiscent of designs by Charles and Ray Eames, and photographs on the walls show famous buildings from architectural history, which have been reconstructed in various places around the world. Magazines such as the French *Vogue* and *Wallpaper* are laid out for visitors to read; cover versions of famous songs recall the originals, only to reveal themselves as imitations. The café plays a significant role in the conception and mediation of the GfZK. It addresses audiences that are not typical museum visitors. A wide range of events takes place in *Paris Syndrom* each month; alongside established artistic programs, young bands primarily from the artistic scene are given the opportunity to perform their music. Moreover, screenings of films and literary readings are held, which attract various different groups of people.

The collection The GfZK dates back to the turbulent sociohistorical period after the fall of the Berlin Wall, which is reflected in the collection itself. Works by Rosemarie Trockel, Michael Morgner, Marcel Odenbach, and Günther Uecker were initially presented to the GfZK in 1990 as programmatic loans from the Kulturkreis der deutschen Wirtschaft im Bundesverband der Deutschen Industrie (BDI) e.V. (Cultural Circle of German Business within the Federal Association of German Industry). When the GfZK opened in Villa Herfurth in 1998, these works were donated. In late 1990, the director of the GfZK – at the time, Klaus Werner – chose works for the collection by Hubertus Giebe, Hartwig Ebersbach, Werner Stötzer, and Friedrich B. Henkel from the Center of Art Exhibition in the GDR, which was on the verge of closure. In 1992, the Kulturkreis der deutschen Wirtschaft im BDI presented long-term loans of more than fifty pieces ranging from artists whose works were partly influenced by the Bauhaus and labeled

Designing and Building the GfZK-2

At the **beginning** of this project, as-if berlinwien was asked to develop strategies for new forms of presentation and display for the Galerie für Zeitgenössische Kunst/Museum of Contemporary Art Leipzig (GfZK).

The buildings of the GfZK are located just outside the center of Leipzig, on the border between the old Musikviertel (music quarter) and the extensive green space of the Clara-Zetkin-Park. Since 1998, the institution and its exhibition spaces have been housed in a late 19th-century villa, which is unusually positioned at a 45-degree angle on a corner of an almost square site.

"degenerate" by the Nazis – such as Hubertus Glöckner or East German and West German (mainly informal) artists of the 1950s and 1960s such as Willi Baumeister, Ernst Wilhelm Nay, or Emil Schumacher. In 2006, these works were also donated to the GfZK collection.

Nowadays, positions that were not permitted in any GDR esthetic forum are shown next to younger artists from the postcommunist era and artists from the western world up to the present. The collection is continually extended through donations from collectors and from artists who have exhibited at GfZK such as Horst Bartnig, Sibylle Bergemann, and Ilya Kabakov, along with works purchased by the GfZK Friends' Organization of Olafur Eliasson, Tobias Rehberger, Tilo Schulz, Dan Peterman, Franz West, Dorit Margreiter, and others. The new acquisitions have been closely linked to the exhibition program since 2001.

Since 2007, parts of the GfZK collection have been presented annually in an exhibition addressing questions rooted in the history and cultural context of the GfZK. For the concept of the museum does not so much follow the idea of a huge storage facility, but rather provides the ground for public negotiations about the museum and its social role.

Conservation   Since 2007, the GfZK-1 holds changing annual collection exhibitions of various durations. Apart from exhibitions of the GfZK collection, examples and cases of artistic restoration are exhibited as well as discussed in the exhibition series *The Conservation Machine*. These public exhibitions give children, young people, and adults an opportunity to gain close insight into the processes of art preservation and restoration in unconventional ways. It becomes a means of explaining why, among other things, art also requires maintenance and "nursing," and how best to prevent artworks from becoming "inpatients."

Cooperations   The GfZK maintains local and international cooperations – within Leipzig, with institutions such as schools, kindergartens, theaters, and cinemas, as well as with free initiatives and groups. All curators plus the custodian teach at universities and academies, taking this opportunity to connect their teaching with work at the gallery. The international cooperations are connected to various research projects. Past partners for more than one project were, among others, the Rosseum in Malmö, the Forum Stadtpark in Graz, the J.E. Purkyne University in Ústí nad Labem, the Bunkier Sztuki in Cracow, and the Institute of Contemporary Art Dunaújváros.

GfZK-3   The *GfZK-3* project was born in 2007 as a reply to the increasing importance of new technologies in

perception and communication. It is a project that seeks new ways of conveying art while, at the same time, respecting the selective interests of individuals. The first project of GfZK-3 is connected to Carte Blanche, the research project of 2008/2009. A comprehensive database will be gradually built up containing information about the selected artworks, their owners, and artists, as well as offering space for discussion. Reactions from the press, visitor opinions, and the views of curators are to provide different perspectives. The most diverse formats will be used such as texts, audio recordings, videos, and photography. All information will be arranged by keywords and can be downloaded.

GfZK garden   In the summer of 2006, parts of the garden were redesigned by the artist Jun Yang and transformed into a cultural and social meeting place. Museum visitors, students of the nearby academies, park visitors, and their children, as well as anyone seeking peace and quiet can make use of various special features ranging from a children's playground, rest areas, and platforms for individual use to a kiosk called *Hei Di* selling various goods. The individual elements are related to the tradition of the German corner shop, Japanese gardens, convenience stores, grocery stores, Bavarian beer gardens, and

Asia shops. The project takes the economic situation of today's museums into consideration, opening up a debate on the circulation and distribution of goods, branding, local, and global contexts.

Grants   The *Blinky Palermo Scholarship* was held until 2007 and financed until then by the Ostdeutsche Sparkassenstiftung/Sparkasse Leipzig. Artists were invited to develop a work that is specific to the local area, which was then presented in a large solo exhibition in the GfZK. Among the previous winners of the grant are Simon Starling, Francesco Vezzoli, Sofie Thorsen, Dorit Margreiter, and Dora García.

ROOM 107 is financed by the state bank of Saxony, Sachsen Bank, and supports younger artists from Leipzig. From 2008 onwards, four recipients each year will have their work displayed in *ROOM 107* of the GfZK-1. The *ROOM 107* exhibition series enables these artists to present their work to a wider public.

In 2002, the GfZK and the Cultural Foundation of the Free State of Saxony in Dresden established a grant program for young curators from Eastern Europe especially intended for scholars who wish to improve their skills by working in a contemporary art institution. Each year, a contest for applications is held, and a young curator

The property is characterized by a meadow that can be freely accessed from all sides and can be considered a continuation of the Clara-Zetkin-Park. The villa was converted into an exhibition building from 1996 to 1998 by Peter Kulka, after he originally won a competition in 1992 to design a new large museum on another location of the site.

from a specific European country is invited to Leipzig. The grant fosters an exchange of different experiences and cultural influences. The contacts made through this scheme and the resulting collaborations, which often extend over many years, flow directly into the program of the GfZK. Past trainee curators at the GfZK were: Ilina Koralova (Sofia) in 2002/2003, Lena Prents (Minsk) in 2003/2004, Oana Tanase (Bucharest) in 2004/2005, Andreja Hribernik (Gortina) in 2006/2007, Edina Nagy (Budapest) in 2007/2008, Joanna Sokołowska (Warsaw) in 2008/2009, and Nino Palavendishwily (Tbilisi) in 2009/2010.

Institution The Friends' Organization of the GfZK under its chairman, Arend Oetker, was founded in 1990 to promote the implementation of a contemporary art space in Leipzig. The director designate of the GfZK, Klaus Werner, therefore set up a series of activities in the city of Leipzig: exhibitions in vacant buildings, at the main station, or at the Völkerschlachtdenkmal (Monument of the Battle of the Nations). The aim was to test the concept of the future art space before it was given its own site. Bringing the Friends' Organization to life was a means of reviving the link with the tradition of civic commitment that had come to an abrupt end under Nazism, and the foundation of the GDR had made it impossible to resume. The early activities

of the GfZK were not only grounded in a reanimation of bourgeois commitment, but a connection was also made to independent forms of exhibiting in private apartments, which were brought outside and to the public.
In 1998, the GfZK moved to Villa Herfurth, which was architecturally converted into an art institution (see GfZK-1). The German name of the institution, "Galerie für Zeitgenössische Kunst," was chosen to distinguish it from the Museum of Visual Arts in Leipzig, the older museum in town founded in the middle of the 19th century. Since 2001, the proper English translation has been "Museum of Contemporary Art" to emphasize the fact that the GfZK is a museum, too.

Legal status The museum was founded in 1996 as a nonprofit limited company and, in 2003, it turned into a private foundation. The GfZK follows the model of the Public Private Partnership. Allocations come equally from the City of Leipzig, the Free State of Saxony, and the Friends' Organization. These funds cover the institution's running costs. The GfZK has neither a budget for its program nor for its acquisitions; the required budget must be fund-raised every year. The monies come from national and international foundations and, to a much smaller extent, from local companies. Fundraising for 2008/2009 was connected to the Museum's research on private commitment to art.

In a close dialog with Barbara Steiner, who was appointed the new director of the GfZK in 2001, our first goal was to develop **spatial strategies** aimed at strengthening relations and reciprocities between temporary exhibitions and the permanent collection of the GfZK. In this stage, concepts were developed for actively and critically integrating the existing collection as an essential part into the exhibition spaces with architectural means. These concepts were not yet bound to the possibility of a new building.

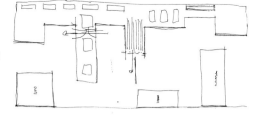

First concept sketches showing possible relations between storage areas, exhibition areas, and instituational areas (mediation)

Leipzig Leipzig is located in the east of Germany; the train line to Berlin is one hour. Around 500,000 inhabitants currently reside in the city. Prior to World War II, there were about 750,000 people living in Leipzig. Leipzig was a famous center of commerce (for instance the Leipzig Fair) and industry, which reached its peak of growth in the 1930s. When the country was divided into East and West Germany, Leipzig was still one of the three biggest industrial cities in the eastern part. Since the changes and until the mid-1990s, thousands of people have left Leipzig to move to the west or to the suburbs; recently, however, the situation has stabilized somewhat. The economic circumstances are still relatively weak but, since the past few years, large companies – for instance, Porsche, BMW, Siemens, and DHL (at Leipzig airport) – have settled and established themselves.

Library/Archive The library's holdings, which have primarily existed since 1991, comprise approximately 30,000 volumes. Their contents focus on the themes of the collection and exhibits of the GfZK, but also include primary and secondary literature on art of the 20th and 21st centuries. There is a programmatic integration of books from other fields of contemporary culture. The library also holds the archive of the GfZK, which provides insight into the institution's past and present programs.

From 2008, a series of exhibitions and projects engage with the theme of "the library" and research the possibilities of artists' library designs. Realized and fictitious, ideological and playful approaches and statements are juxtaposed, showing perspectives that may offer ways towards future libraries of art institutions. Artists who have been invited in the past include Michael Clegg & Martin Guttmann, Tobias Rehberger, Maria Eichhorn, Falk Haberkorn, Wilfredo Prieto, Clara Montoya, Gyula Várnai, and Till Exit.

Mediation/GfZK For You The GfZK mediation program caters for adults, children, adolescents and young people, families, kindergartens, and schools. Mediation for adults, children, and young people takes place at the exhibitions or outside – in the city or at other external venues. The themes and activities in the program revolve around the current exhibitions or the current focus of the exhibition program. Children and young people are encouraged to take self-determined action and engage in committed debate with their social environment. For a project period over the course of several months, for instance, children investigate and photographically document changes in their immediate surroundings such as the change of the seasons or advances in building work around them.
▷▷ 43

In an **initial study,** we examined the potentials of correlating temporary exhibition displays with methods of archiving or storing works of art in order to generate strategies for new concepts of dialog. The spaces of the collection were to play an active role by creating areas of friction and dialogs around the temporary exhibitions.
▷▷ 43

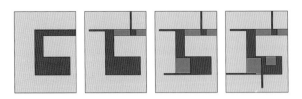

By connecting the storage area with the exhibition area, a variety of changeable spatial situations und zones of passage can be created.

■ storage spaces ■ exhibition area

Performative Architecture as the Basis of the Performative Museum[1]

Barbara Steiner

The analysis of performativity has been a staple in the GfZK program since 2004. The term was first used in the context of the exhibition *Performative Architecture*, organized in collaboration with the Siemens Arts Program.[2] The show was inspired by the construction of the GfZK's new exhibition space in Leipzig by as-if berlinwien. Taking this "performative" building as a starting point, BLESS, Monica Bonvicini, Angela Bulloch, Oliver Hangl, Jeppe Hein, Olaf Nicolai, Anita Leisz, and Pro qm were invited to create work dealing with the relationship between architecture and performativity. Since then, performativity has been extended to incorporate the concept of the museum as well. Both the terms "performative architecture" and "performative museum" seem to evoke a double contradiction, as neither the static concepts of architecture nor the museum appear at first to correspond with the notion of performativity.

According to John Langshaw Austin, a performative speech act is an act in which the speaker produces the thing (s)he names: I express myself by means of language and accomplish an action – because "saying makes it so."[3] Austin's concept was later reformulated, amended, and extended – drawing into account the patterns, possibilities, and limitations of the functions of language; the contexts, social structures, and the respective competence of the speakers; the rituals and stereotyping to which performative utterances are subject; and finally in consideration of the consequences and effects of the reality-constituting power of language. In this context, gender study assumes special importance, investigating the relation between speech acts and identity constitution.[4]

In the 1960s, the term appeared in art in a modified form as *performance* and primarily denoted a unique event occurring within time limitations, frequently involving a situation-based ad hoc action: particularly in the western hemisphere, performances aimed to challenge the prioritization of the static esthetic object and the "commodification" of art, and demanded a change of production and reception conditions.[5] In turn, the "white cube" – as the predominant model of the exhibition display in the postwar era – became the focus of critical attention, and was, like the object too, forced to undergo temporalization. The exhibition space no longer acted as a representative repository for immovable values and attributes, but as a place for temporary and changing spatial proposals: the space transformed into an event venue, assuring unrepeatable experiences and encounters in the here and now.

These developments affected the conception of museums: Willem Sandberg, director of the Stedelijk Museum in Amsterdam, even considered abandoning completely the old idea of the museum that holds a permanent collection. Seeking to render the museum more dynamic and acces-

1 Parts of this text have already been published in the essay "Performative Architecture" in: Angelika Nollert (ed.), *Performative Installation*, Cologne 2003, pp. 180–194

2 Under the umbrella title *Performative Installation*, the Siemens Arts Program organized a five-part exhibition series, which took place in various institutions in Innsbruck, Cologne, Siegen, Vienna, and Leipzig. Different aspects of the central topic were dealt with in each respective location: Construction & Situation; Narrative; Communication; The Body & Economy; Architecture.

3 Cf. John Langshaw Austin, *How to Do Things with Words*, Oxford 1962

4 Judith Butler, "Performative Acts and Gender Constitution. An Essay in Phenomenology and Feminist Theory," in: Sue-Ellen Case (ed.), *Performing Feminism: Feminist Critical Theory and Theatre*, Baltimore 1990, pp. 270–282; Judith Butler, *Gender Trouble*, New York/London 1990

5 Concentrating on the artwork's "material" substance was understood as an extension of capitalist logic and the need to overcome that logic. It was thus necessary to confront the autonomous esthetic object, seen as a crystallization of materialism, with a definition of work based on process. Cf. Robert Morris, "Anti Form" (1968) in: *Continuous Project Altered Daily: The Writings of Robert Morris*, Cambridge/London 1993, p. 68

6 Cf. "'Kann man hier Pingpong spielen?'
Johannes Cladders in conversation with Hans-
Ulrich Obrist," in: Jungle World 48, 11.24.1999, p.
2 (see also: http://www.jungle-world.com/
artikel/1999/47/29131.html)

7 However, this does not mean that the visitor
is supposed to physically move the walls, but
rather that he/she is constantly aware of the
walls' potential movability.

sible, he suggested putting the artworks in storage, taking them out only when needed for specific exhibitions. They should be placed in surroundings pertaining to leisure, so that synesthetic strategies, contrasts, surprises, and shocks jolt the spectator out of his/her passivity to kindle active confrontation with art.[6] Sandberg's emancipatory approach to the museum as a venue of experience, in which notions of space and display, the artworks and the viewer are conceived of as a correlative entity, later led – albeit unintentionally – to the rise of an event culture. While in his exhibitions, such as *Dylaby* in 1962 for instance, the mechanisms of presentation were still comprehensible, in later attempts to reinterpret Sandberg's concept, the visitor would be absorbed into the spectacle. Today, the performative no longer automatically denotes emancipation, activism, or even the critique of prevailing conditions, materialism, or consumerism, but rather collaboration between spectacle culture and neo-liberal demands. Performative expression may act affirmative and liberating by reinforcing dominant patterns and attitudes, but can also generate deviations, even so not always intended.

The new building designed by as-if berlinwien is based on a changeable spatial concept, allowing a range of different uses and functions. Large sliding partitions, revolving doors, and curtains make it possible to connect or divide the spaces as required, to create different spatial configurations, exhibition layouts and correlations of meaning. The spaces are to be experienced by means of movement: constantly changing, unpredictable views and connections confront the gaze. Perceiving the street, neighboring houses, and park through windows extending from floor to ceiling, makes the architecture appear to interlock with its urban surroundings. The slits along the base of the walls and the design of the surfaces guide the gaze, thus linking (parts of) the spaces with (elements of) the exhibition. Glass walls, transparent partitions, curtains, and reflective surfaces resemble huge screens. The operational concept of the building is geared to constant redefinition and shifting functions. The glass partitions act as display windows; the cinema can be used as a gallery or lecture room; the café and the exhibition area function as project spaces and vice versa.

Here, performativity is defined in terms of spatial praxis. The facilities, their layout, and fittings heighten our awareness of their perpetual movability[7] and potential functions, but also emphasize the spaces' physical boundaries, as well as their social commitment and embedment within society. Consequently, the building's variability and production opportunities intentionally impose certain restrictions; the construct's transparency is regulated. Not all the walls are movable and even the ones that are, cannot all be moved at the same time. The curators are required to decide on one option. To remove the walls is also technically impossible, as they cannot be dismantled. The curtains can only be fitted in designated places and some areas within the building cannot be readily darkened. Disruptions of visibility caused by low-lying slits in the walls or direct sunlight are intentional. Throughout the entire structure and facing the city, the interstices, apertures, and views inside and out of the building demonstrate that visibility and transparency adhere to specific regimes of vision: the subject is addressed as to his/her dependence on the immediate architectural and social context. The building is conceived of as contingent and fluid. Outside and inside merge, demarcation lines dissolve; the instability of spatial relations is programmatic. Thus, the concept developed by as-if berlinwien is directly opposed to the neutral, white exhibition space, devised as a (static) space with consistent, unaltered, and unalterable lighting, sealed off from the outside world, and thus removed from the context of society. Not for nothing, in his book *Inside the White Cube*, Brian O'Doherty speaks disparagingly of the "white cube" as "a kind of eternity of display."[8] as-if berlinwien refers to this sterile exhibition space, literally unfolding it to lay it flat against the floor, and intercept it with sliding walls, slit windows above and below, to mesh inside and outside, thus translating irreversibility into reversibility. This reference to the "white cube" is particularly apparent in the rooms in which a second, additional wall layer of plasterboard conceals the walls proper: seen from the right position, the space-within-the-space is clearly visible. The "white cube," thus transformed into a "gray cube," forfeits its universal ideality and authority.

At the most general of levels, architecture seeks to organize (the relationship between interior and exterior) space. The liberal, bourgeois subject insisted on a clear division between the public and the private sphere, satisfying a need for protection, but also for separation and exclusion. However, taken specifically to denote the production of cultural boundaries, spatial allocation, and representation, the "bourgeois domicile" – like the bourgeois subject, too – has increasingly seen itself in a state of crisis.[9] Distinctions between outside and inside have become indeterminate and ambivalent, and the modern subject is required to endure this uncertainty. While Le Corbusier still observes the "menacing" world outside from a secure, locatable vantage point inside – thus domesticating the outside world as a "picture" – the concepts of mobility propagated by the exponents of "nomadic architecture" literally mobilize the subject. Buildings no longer serve to locate – or localize – the subject, who becomes "delocalized" as a result. Deconstructive architecture pushes the instability of the subject further, consequently transposing this instability into architecture. The instability of spatial conditions thus parallels the "unstable" subject.[10]

Not only architecture, but also art is concerned with the problematics of the subject in terms of spatial relations. Various works by Dan Graham investigate the subject's position in space and, by extension, questions the constitution of the subject. In *Public Space/Two Audiences* (1976), consisting of a room bisected by a pane of glass and accessible via two separate entrances, Dan Graham examines processes of subject constitution by exposing the relationship between subject and object: the viewer looks and is looked at – thus alternately becoming subject and object. Mirrors on the back wall of one section of the room allow the spectator, very much in the Lacanian sense, to perceive him/herself as the other.[11] The spatially mobile (social) body is the place in which subject constitution is acted out: the subject is formed by means of confrontation with the other(s). The behavior of the visitors – acting to all intents and purposes on a stage, simultaneously observing (as spectators) and being observed (as actors) – at once discloses and displays as part of the exhibition the relationship between the subject and the external "gaze of the other." Later, in the pavilions, Graham addresses the relationship between inside and outside by means of the materials selected, such as glass, mirror glass, Plexiglas, and tinted thermal glass. The subject is put in the position of having to negotiate whether the space is inside, outside, or both at once.

8 Brian O'Doherty, *Inside the White Cube. The Ideology of the Gallery Space* (1976/1986), Berkeley/Los Angeles/London 1999, p. 15

9 Cf. Anthony Vidler, *The Architectural Uncanny. Essays in the Modern Unhomely*, Cambridge, MA/London 1992. Vidler investigates the "uncanny" and "homelessness" as constituents of the modern predicament. Moreover, in this connection it is interesting to note that coinciding with the first crisis of the "modern subject," the bourgeois museum was invented, very much as the expression and material manifestation of bourgeois identity and self-reassurance. Thus, the museum served as a sort of refuge for a crisis-ridden identity. However, an end could not be put to this process of gradual erosion, as demonstrated by the criticism of the museum in the 1910s, and later again in the 1960s and 1970s. Cf. Barbara Steiner, "Zwischen Widerständigkeit und Komplizenschaft," in: Barbara Steiner, Charles Esche (eds.), *Mögliche Museen*, Cologne 2007, pp. 9–21

10 In Mark Wigley's writings, the house appears as a figure of thought within philosophical discourse. Adopting Derrida's description of deconstruction as a "violent shudder" through a building – strictly speaking: "as the 'soliciting' of an edifice, 'in the sense that *sollicitare*, in old Latin, means to shake as a whole, to make tremble in entirety'" (Jacques Derrida, *Margins of Philosophy*, Chicago 1982, p. 21), Wigley writes: "If deconstructive discourse is anything, it is a form of interrogation that shakes structures in a way that exposes structural weaknesses. It puts structures under pressure, forcing them, taking them to the limit. Under a subtle but relentless strain their limits become evident and the structure becomes visible as such, but it becomes visible, precisely, as something unlike the culturally enfranchised image of structure." (Mark Wigley, *The Architecture of Deconstruction: Derrida's Haunt* (1993) Cambridge, MA/London 1995, p. 35)

11 In some works by Graham such as *Present Continuous Past(s)* (1976), the video camera assumed a function comparable to that of the mirror. Cf. Jacques Lacan, "The Mirror Stage, Source of the I function as shown by Psychoanalytic Experience," in: *International Journal of Psychoanalysis*, 1949; *The Seminar, Book XI: The Four Fundamental Concepts of Psychoanalysis* (1964), ed. by Jacques-Alain Miller, New York 1977

12   Cf. Barbara Steiner, "What Does This Text Do? About Distortion, Resistance, Dislike and Subjectivity," in: Jörn Schafaff, Barbara Steiner (eds.), *Jorge Pardo*, Ostfildern-Ruit 2000, pp. 22–33

13   Ibid.

14   Kaja Silverman, *The Threshold of the Visible World*, New York/London 1996, p. 2

15   Ibid., p. 195

In a similar way, Jorge Pardo is interested in motivating viewers to a more active approach, inviting them to interpret what they see. *4166 Sea View Lane* (1994–1998) neither gives clear information as to the status of the "object" – that is, whether it is a house, a sculpture, or an exhibition project[12] we are dealing with – nor offers a clear delimitation between inside and outside. Inside and outside perpetually switch positions: both interpretations are possible depending on where one is standing. Connotations become clear only upon ascribing a specific meaning to an object, and not as the result of visible distinctions. Pardo defines his objects as situated in a transitory stage during which meaning is processed and produced. His objects, pictures, photographs, and books are conceived so that "the subject runs through them,"[13] according to the questions and expectations (s)he incites.

In *The Threshold of the Visible World*, Kaja Silverman seeks to investigate the "psychoanalytic politics of visual representation."[14] She refers to the decisive influence of the screen in terms of subject constitution, an idea very much corresponding with works by Dan Graham and Jorge Pardo. In psychoanalytic theory, the screen defines a projection surface that regulates and depicts the subject's relationship to reality, and by extension, to his/her notion of self. Therefore, reality never appears in an unmitigated form, but is always conveyed as an image or projection requiring interpretation. Not only do social and ideological notions emerge on the screen; the latter also acts as a surface of reflection for the subject, who seeks self-realization and self-regulation in his/her mirror image. Silverman employs subjects that increasingly define themselves via "the logic of the images through which we figure objects and are in turn figured, and the value conferred upon those images through the larger organization of the visual field."[15]

They conceive the building as an architectural screen that serves to mirror conceptions of society, organize the visitor's gaze, and represent his/her relationship to reality, while simultaneously functioning as the visitor's reflexive plane. The subject is required to constitute the architecture, aware that both the edifice as well as his/her own position (within it) are prone to change – and thus becoming aware at all times of the instability of (the architecture's) boundaries, sociospatial functions and representational assignments. The outside can conceivably be the inside; the building's spatial stratification provides no information as to where the divisions between individual strata lie. The spaces are not designed to the ends of a single, specific function, but necessitate from the very outset the idea of possible reinterpretation. This puts the subject in an active situation, on the one hand by recalling the subject's potentially multiple position within space – as imago, reflection, and physical entity – and on the other, by continually demanding active participation in creating contexts of meaning. The space, its function, and the way it is charged with meaning are negotiable.

The artists Anita Leisz and BLESS have responded directly to the architectural concept forwarded by as-if berlinwien. Leisz's design for the museum café fused two types of locations without changing the furnishings – the daytime café *Neubau* and the bar *Weezie*. Leisz employed a kind of basic vocabulary, with elements derived from youth and club culture, such as tabletops painted over in black on the one hand, combined with references to traditional living room comfort on the other – such as armchairs upholstered in Scottish tartans. From the furniture to the crockery, the furnishings' connotations shifted according to the differing times of day or night, and their different uses and modes of appropriation by different social groups. The place's identity thus also shifted – *Neubau* became *Weezie* and vice versa. Even though *Neubau* and *Weezie* were allocated to daytime and nighttime respectively, both types of identity were able to coexist, triggered by the individual client and his/her expectations. Just as the building and café – designed by as-if berlinwien and Anita Leisz respectively – have demanded that possibilities be constantly redefined, the objects in the entrance area designed by BLESS also bear multiple alternatives as their functional (and esthetic) status continually changes:[16] The books in the foyer are not only meant for reading or purchase, they are also transformed into (temporary) display plinths and stools, while utilitarian computer and monitor wires are adorned, and thus visibly declared valuable (*BLESS N° 26 cable jewellery*). The *Perpetual Home Motion Machines (BLESS N° 22)* offer storage and presentation surfaces, one of the mobiles functions primarily as a coat rack. Some elements provide no clues as to their potential function; the user is required to work this out.

The building by as-if berlinwien and the projects by Anita Leisz and BLESS are integral and programmatic components of the "performative museum," a concept encompassing both space and time. In this context, the performative aspect denotes participating in the negotiation of art and its location. Annual exhibitions of works from the GfZK collection and research projects extending over several years, serve to formulate and visualize conflicting constellations of artistic methods, to the ends of publicly addressing and influencing the value systems within art and society. The respective mediation venues are provided by the buildings GfZK-1, a villa renovated by Peter Kulka, and the GfZK-2, designed by as-if berlinwien.

Before concluding this essay, I would like to mention one of our research projects, *Carte Blanche*, which exemplifies the principles of the "performative museum." In 2008 and 2009, the GfZK invited eleven private individuals, one friends' association, companies of various scale, and two commercial galleries, among others, to practically explain the reasons behind their engagement in the arts – in the format of exhibitions and hence also make it public. The participants were given carte blanche, i.e., complete freedom to interpret the project and to select the curator(s) with whom they wish to collaborate. In return, the former financed their respective part of the project. GfZK provided those invited with the institutional infrastructure and, if desired, curatorial and organizational support.[17]

With *Carte Blanche* the GfZK opened itself up to a span of interests from outside the institution, interests not necessarily in accord with the institutional or curatorial priorities of the museum. The nature of the project meant that modes of presentation and attitudes – diametrically opposed to the GfZK – often found their way into the exhibitions, expressed through the selection of artists or differing concepts of showing/mediating art. Rival approaches, viewpoints and attitudes were given space; they came side by side and were exhibited along with the works, through the works themselves, through their constellations or, the particular display, through discursive formats, and so forth. All the research projects of the GfZK (and *Carte Blanche* is, after all, merely the most visible and apparent expression of this research approach) have been planned in such a way that they offer potential frictions – a primary interest here being continually to challenge the system of art and its values.[18]

16 The foyer is designed by BLESS and may be continuously reconfigured and extended according to the ideas of the respective user. The mobiles have taken on various functions during the past years. Initially used as a counter, one of the mobiles is now in use as a visitor information platform. A picture of this area, specially designed for the GfZK-2, was transferred onto wallpaper for use during the book presentation of BLESS, *Celebrating 10 Years of Themelessness* in Japan in the summer of 2006. Since then, the wallpaper is an integral part of BLESS N° 29 *Wallscapes*.

17 The eleven chosen paid a basic contribution to the joint program *Carte Blanche*, including the costs of a joint exhibition, for communication and mediation, a final publication, and running costs for the spaces used. Project participants also took responsibility for all expenses associated with their own exhibitions. Those participating in *Carte Blanche* also undertook to acquaint the public with their motivations in the context of the series *Carte Blanche discursive*. In the case of an irreconcilable conflict between the project partners, it was agreed that the invited parties would get carte blanche. But the GfZK reserved the right to publicize those points and to discuss their impact on the institution.

18 Instruments by which frictions are deliberately produced – include not only the temporary research projects connected with the context of the GfZK, but also the annually changing presentations of the collection and our two exhibition buildings.

In the case of *Carte Blanche*, the exhibition spaces of GfZK-2 created appropriate conditions for the project, – one reason this building was chosen as the project venue. One important point is that while the design and equipping of the spaces do sensitize to the possible changes of the spaces and their functions, they also draw attention to spatial limitations. "Disturbances" of visibility by means of wall slots – or shadows on the walls – are deliberately factored in. Openings, inward and outward vistas through the building complex – and into the city – permit visibility and transparency to be recognized as phenomena controlled by regimes of view. Exterior and interior flow into one another. Boundary definitions blur. Thanks to these characteristics, the building was the perfect complement to *Carte Blanche*, a project in which private and public interests continually overlapped, and diverse interests and expectations were to negotiate within a given frame.

The principle of negotiating different claims and expectations within set parameters – of which architecture is one example – is the basis of our institutional self-conception. This demands that the museum adopts a clear position to mediate potentially controversial social and/or artistic issues for public discussion, "display" and negotiate the latter from different perspectives. This implies opening one's own position towards those of other – demonstrating how the institution may propose itself as the object of radical debate: in exchange with different groups, its legitimacy and orientation demands constant redefinition. The conception of the GfZK is thus less geared to preserving than to producing new contexts, correlations, and modes of vision, in awareness of the fact that speaking about the museum – that is, employing speech acts – indeed contributes substantially to the constitution of the museum.

Kids and teenagers produce their own video clips examining notions of role-play and self-image. *GfZK For You* cooperates with various educational institutions in long-term projects, whereby the perception and design of surrounding environments, presence in public, and media competence are areas of special interest.

Audio tours, guided tours, and information desks form the basis of mediation for adults. Short video introductions have been presented at all exhibitions since the fall of 2006, in which curators explain concepts, artists are interviewed, and videos of the installation of the exhibition are shown. The form of videos changes, as they adapt to the individual artist and exhibition concerned. Lectures, debates, and podium discussions introduce themes with which the GfZK is involved. Audio tours, documentary videos, and introduction videos to the exhibitions are also available at *GfZK-3* (see *GfZK-3*) and can be downloaded.

Moreover, there are additional mediation projects outside the regular program, which altogether strengthen GfZK collaborations. For example, an art calendar was produced with the Sachsen Bank presenting works of both the Sachsen Bank and GfZK collections. This calendar followed two additional collaborations between the Sachsen Bank and GfZK, *The Writing Station* and *The Corridor as Display*. *The Writing Station* gave bank employees the opportunity of sending postcards of works of their collection, and the addressees were marked with pins on a world map. In *The Corridor as Display*, three different proposals for the design and display of the corridors in the Sachsen Bank premises were tested and discussed in an exhibition at the GfZK. They were then realized in the bank afterwards.

Neighborhood   The GfZK is located in Leipzig's Musik-viertel (music quarter), which, in the late 19th century, was one of the bourgeois suburbs of the city. In the past, the quarter has accommodated famous institutions such as the Gewandhaus concert hall or the Supreme Court of the German Reich. Factory owners and Leipzig publishers commissioned respectable villas. The GfZK-1, too, is located in a villa commissioned by Carl Hermann Credner, who founded the Palaeontological Institute in Leipzig at the end of the 19th century. In terms of style, the building reflects the Italian Renaissance. During World War II, almost 50 percent of the buildings in the Musikviertel were destroyed. During the GDR, prefabricated high-rise buildings were erected, offering low-cost living spaces also in the attempt to break with the bourgeois character of the area. Today, the Musikviertel is once again a sought-after residential area. Close to both the Johannapark and the Clara-Zetkin-Park, it is a quiet place in close vicinity to the

---

The **first diagrams** that were developed during this process show how the different realms of the collection could be interwoven with the temporary exhibitions in such a way that the references and interchanges would be maximized. Here, we introduced a conceptual third layer, which we referred to as "mediation," and designates the level of the institutional presence, that is, the various activities of the GfZK and its staff in relation to the public.

The first conceptual diagrams show the interest in maximizing the zones of friction between the areas of the exhibition, storage, and mediation.

■ Storage Spaces   ■ Mediation Areas   ▪ Exhibition area

city center and with recreational amenities close by. The GfZK has organized projects in the neighborhood such as *High-Rise Fest* in 2003, a collaboration between the Leipziger Wohnungs- und Baugesellschaft mbH (Leipzig Housing Bureau) and the GfZK. Furthermore, projects by participating artists Marion Porten, Helmut & Johanna Kandl, and *GfZK For You* (see Mediation) offered children the opportunity to actively participate in the *Papperlapappstadt* (Balderdash City), a built cityscape out of cardboard, which they then painted. The *Papperlapappstadt* was exhibited at the base of the high-rise buildings, thus bringing attention to and encouraging greater popularity for the event. During two days, the GfZK café (see Café) was open on the roof of one of the buildings.

Prizes   Since 2004, the IT service provider alpha 2000 has donated EUR 5,000 every year to support artists from Europe with a prize entitled *The Future of Europe*. During the first five years, the focus was on artists from eastern, north-eastern, or southeastern Europe. In 2004, the winner was Kristina Leko (Croatia); in 2005, Rafał Bujnowski (Poland); in 2006, Jakup Ferri (Kosovo); in 2007, Ioana Nemes (Hungary); and, in 2008, Kamen Stoyanov (Bulgaria). In 2008, an exhibition with these five prizewinners took place in the context of the GfZK's *Carte Blanche* project. In the future, the prize will be extended to include other European regions in the attempt to examine the construct "Europe" and its ideological implications. From 2007 onwards, *INFORM – Award for Conceptual Design* represents an international prize awarded on a yearly basis. The prize of EUR 10,000 honors young graphic designers who in their projects, collabora-tions, and publications have come to adopt a singular standing in the world of graphic art. This expressly targets those working at the interface of graphic design, artistic publications, and contemporary art. An exhibition in the new library space of the GfZK is to accompany the award. The first winner in 2007 was the London-based graphic designer Laurent Benner. In 2008, the prize went to Julia Born based in Amsterdam, and in 2009 Rebecca Stephany, also based in Amsterdam.

Research projects   In 2002, the GfZK launched *Cultural Territories*, the first almost three-year-long research project, which involved a series of exhibitions and discussions on the role of art and culture in post-communist countries. Since then, the GfZK has taken on multiannual research projects on the heritage of modernism (*Heimat Modernism* and *Shrinking Cities*), and on the role of artistic ctitique/criti-cality in capitalist and communist countries (*againstwithin*). The focus in 2007 was on collective and individual cultural

---

We worked on the question of how we could develop a spatial setting in which one is conscious of being an integral part of a stage-like space on the one hand, but can also reflect on the mechanisms of perception within an institutional space on the other hand. The **theatricality and perfor-mativity** that are implied in the act of visiting an exhibition were themes on which we worked, with a strong reference to artistic strategies that call upon the viewer to become an active agent in a politics of the display.

By using slideable or foldable wall elements, the same **space should be transformable** in a way that produces completely new relations between the elements in the space each time. We were interested in developing models for spaces that were **program-matically underdetermined**, as well as spatially ambivalent. The elements of the collection should be able to define the spaces on the level of content, but they should also be capable of altering the visitor's paths.

memories and, as a corollary, the social conception of art
and its means. In 2008/2009, the focus was put on private
commitment to art. All research projects lead to a series of
solo and group exhibitions, discussions, publications, as well
as educational activity. The programs are planned two or
three years in advance and the subjects are chosen in relation
to the particular situation of the GfZK – be it the role of the
museum within a post-communist or global context.

Working structures   All themes come out of the context
of the GfZK and are interpreted by the (guest-)curators, the
custodian, the librarian, and the mediators. The departments are interconnected and in permanent exchange with
one another. The mediation department (see Mediation)
runs its own exhibition space. Its exhibitions are curated by
the children and teenagers and supported by the mediators.
A group of graphic designers works in various forms and
configurations for the respective departments.

The programmatic collages demonstrate how an area could be
transformed in order to produce
different forms of relation between
the collection and exhibition. The
permanent presence of the spaces
"behind" was an issue bound to wall
and display elements that could be
moved in order to change the spatial
relations fundamentally.

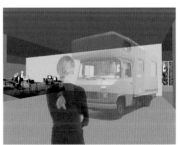
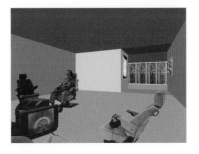
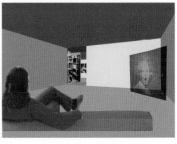

After this first conceptual phase, it became clear that we would consider the design of a **new separate building** that would represent a different model from the spatiality of the existing villa, where the temporary exhibitions had been housed so far. After the confirmation from the Free State of Saxony for the financing of building costs within a clearly defined financial framework, the first concepts for the site were developed.

The early conceptual plans were continuously adapted in order to specifically deal with the conditions, needs, and **options of the site**, with its rather complex arrangement of trees and its potential of various references to the surrounding area. We wanted to leave the borders of the site as open and accessible as possible. We appreciated the potentials of the meadow, which was positioned in the urban fabric like a

carpet, enhanced by the open corners of the site. Also, the positioning of the villa at a 45-degree angle to the roadside contributed to a reading of the site as a homogeneous surface on which spatial elements seemed to be placed like islands.

GFZKLEIPZIGbless.

perpetual home motion machine cashdesk and perpetual home motion machine wardrobe

Steiner   You came up with two draft sketches for the design of the GfZK-2 entrance area.

BLESS   Usually we don't make any sketches for our products – at most, a couple of "doodles" to visualize our thoughts and thought processes, mostly to make us remember things. But we usually do this in verbal form. After all, we don't design houses but products – precisely because we can do that "directly." We have always seen ourselves as "doers."

Steiner   However, in this particular case, properly formulated plans do exist: were they a result of the planning process?

BLESS   For things that are bigger than a piece of clothing, a carpet, or a lamp, then a drawing is always helpful. As soon as things are manufactured by a third party, then a technical drawing is usually indispensable. But it's probably more our nature to exchange thoughts verbally, to bounce ideas off one another, and then simply to try something out.

Steiner   More of an empirical approach …

BLESS   Yes, exactly. This turned out to be quite difficult in terms of the furniture, which explains why we had to build models to attain the final forms. Christoph Degenhard, an architect from Berlin, also helped us to communicate our ideas to the executing crafts and trades, thus supporting the project "dynamically."

Steiner   What is great about the entrance area is that it's in a permanent state of flux and improvement – a situation fundamentally due to permanent shortages and deficiencies, leading to new modifications time and again.

BLESS   That's because of the enormous challenges that we were faced with. We had improvised with all the various solutions possible (reads from old notes): "securing the cash desk mobiles using a pulley system every evening – the idea that one secures things as on construction sites, for instance, fastening of a tool bucket on a crane; railings as delicate as possible; cash desk mobiles above ramp attached to the railing; benches suspended; seats rigged to

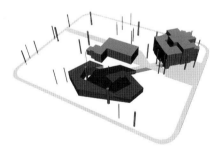

First design sketches, 2001

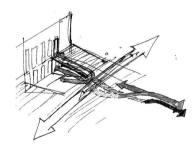

First attempts were undertaken to directly connect the buildings, either with a bridge or underpass.

the railing; signal points in the radius of movement of the cash desk mobile."

Steiner And yet you didn't quite meet the demands entirely.

BLESS Yes, but it's still productive to get several people involved. The visitor services played an important role. I still remember how bemused I was, for instance, when the visitor services personnel spread themselves out with coffee cups, lunch packs, and the like. Your collection manager, Angela Boehnke, called my attention to the fact that people didn't have any space for their personal belongings. I asked myself: which personal belongings? But then we came up with these boxes that can be filled from the top. They are not as convenient as a cupboard or a locker, but in this way we were at least somehow able to accommodate the needs and requirements of the visitors and staff.

For us, work on the GfZK project was very important. I mean, when does one really have the opportunity to design a handrail for the entrance area of a new building?

Steiner … and which is then even authorized by the building authorities! The debates were definitely exciting: it is probably not very common to vehemently discuss esthetic questions in the context of a construction work acceptance. I was asked, for example, whether we really

wanted such an ugly solution for the entrance. Such different perceptions and evaluations rarely meet, and seldom does one so quickly determine whether things are ugly or beautiful. These absolute categories do not tend to have their place in contemporary artistic debate. But your work actually motivates the spectator to voice his or her opinion and to discuss it with others. The controversies culminated in the umbrella stand, incidentally, closely followed by your solution for the handrail.

We defined the main programs which we would have to accommodate in the new building and then worked on defining other possible programs that could take place within these areas. We also positioned these main programs with regard to their potential for creating dialogs within the urban context of the building. The aim was to keep the level of the **functional determination of the spaces** deliberately low, so that they could also be interpreted in different ways. However, all the spaces in the

building had to be capable of being used as possible exhibition spaces. We tried to **eliminate the hierarchies** within the building as much as possible and to make movements and determinations as fluid as possible. For us, this was a way to deal spatially with the complex and continuously shifting conditions of present art institutions and their multilayered and interrelated activities.

The conceptual goal was the **development of a dispositiv**, which

makes it possible for the institution to negotiate and display its own methods and politics.

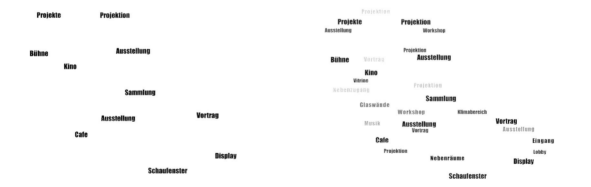

Conceptual diagram showing the basic
programs and their possible interpretations

In order to create a maximal amount of interchanges between the different programs of the institution, we produced a horizontal spatial structure in a polygonal arrangement.

Koralova   To be honest, I also thought that the umbrella stand was dreadful. But I have my reasons – in Bulgaria you find these horrible large ceramic works, and when I saw your umbrella stand for the first time, I thought, oh my goodness, was that thing imported from Bulgaria?

Steiner   Whether one finds something pleasant or unpleasant, beautiful or ugly, essentially has to do with socialization. Maureen Pailey's assistant, in turn, was crazy about it. Maybe London would be ready for your umbrella stand …

Koralova   As curators, we constantly need to do a certain amount of convincing so that your foyer is not always taken apart. I mean: in a traditional museum interior, one would not even dare to ask. But I guess that the flexibility and facility of the furnishings and installations probably encourage the act of dismantling.

BLESS   Thankfully. Imagine if it were one of those "slick" foyer areas of one of those MoMa-MiMu museums – that would be terrible!

Steiner   You can clearly see the fact that it can be potentially dismantled and, in certain cases, we do just that. However, the furnishings also have to fulfill certain functions that cannot be ignored: we need cupboards, a wardrobe, a place that provides information, a cash desk. And due to the building code, the handrail is requisite in any case. Most people strangely tend to overlook it. Again, the reason here is an esthetic rather than a functional one.

Koralova   Were the architectural premises difficult for you?

BLESS   Finding a connection between the building, the glass, and the transparency – namely, something that adapts, is useful, and simultaneously autonomous – was not easy.

Steiner   Your solution addresses a number of notions that are applied in the building: convertability, hybrid functionalism, and the constant necessity of new definitions. But you definitely succeeded in creating a striking contrast,

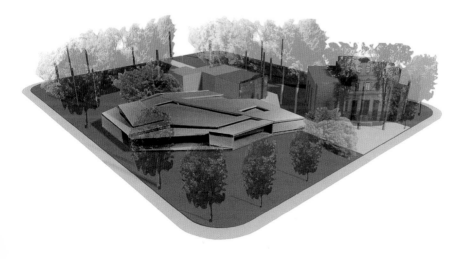

especially in terms of the esthetic of the materials employed. I also like the fact that one can virtually overlook the entrance area, as if it didn't even exist …

Koralova Exactly, it's not representative enough.

BLESS Which is good. If I remember correctly, we actually found the place so suitable back then precisely because we thought that it could also be a shop.

Koralova As it is, the foyer already looks different. Your boxes were moved around inadvertently, because Jürgen Boehnke, the house and exhibition technician, painted the wall and was forced to dismantle the parts without making any notes. So now they are positioned differently and, at the last conversion, I thought, "just leave them like that! – it's an interesting interpretation."

Steiner Incidentally, we have many more plants in the foyer during wintertime to protect them from the frost.

BLESS These modifications are great. The people can just pull up the chairs in whichever way they need them.

Steiner I kept thinking that we would never be finished, would never reach a final point. And precisely that's what I find most exciting.

BLESS Exactly, we will never finish: that's work for us!

In this stage, the design process was still based on the assumption that artists studios and the collection had to be an integral part of the new building. The different areas of the collection defined those zones that were initially hidden, but could be opened and accessed at several points. Additionally, they were the instruments for creating changing pathways by using large sliding walls.

Four exemplary configurations showing different spatial connections and relations by using sliding wall elements, 2002

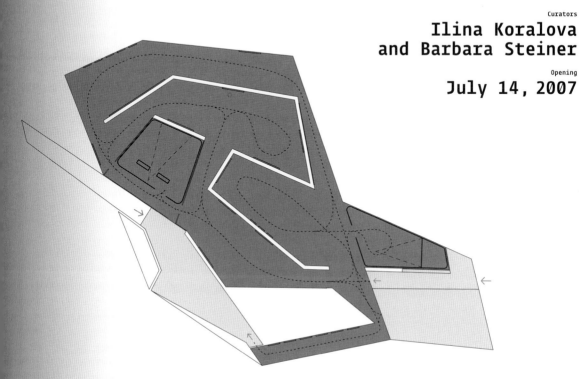

Title
Make Death Listen

Artists
Muntean/Rosenblum

Curators
Ilina Koralova
and Barbara Steiner

Opening
July 14, 2007

The **positioning of the building** (which at this point had a footprint of 1,250 square meters) was finally conceived as a kind of docking to the existing footpath, which runs through the center of the property. The space generated between them should represent the connection between the old mansion, the studio houses in the center of the property, and the new building.

The design had to be **revised and changed** after a very early initial cost estimation which indicated that 1,000 square meters would represent the maximum size of an affordable framework. Additionally, the attempt to include the collection as an integral and active part of the building gradually turned out to be an overcomplicated spatial definition that would have also placed too many limitations on the future possibilities of the building. It was therefore decided that the collection remains in the villa and will be shown occasionally.

Early design stage,
1,250 square meters footprint, 2002.

The images shown by Muntean/Rosenblum in their large-scale, figurative paintings, drawings, and films are familiar from art history. Gestures, poses, and colors are used dramatically to heighten emotions – a formulaic pathos that is employed by the advertising industry today in order to market products and services (even) more effectively. The artists' works manage to establish a connection between the artistic traditions of past centuries and the present day, dominated by the mass media. They explore the different cultural codes, social conventions, and ideals of beauty that conflict with our longing to be individual but simultaneously influence how we construct our identities. The artists make conscious use of this contradiction, rejecting the claim for a clear boundary between authenticity and artificiality, between true emotions and the deliberate use of contrived, emotive language. (Ilina Koralova)

In order to generate a spatial situation in which the perception of the artworks would be closely linked to the perception of their spatial framing, we decided to avoid the creation of a perfectly closed exhibition space. We introduced horizontal window openings that operated in part as light sources from above, and also in part as so-called glass slits, so that a visual connection to the neighboring spaces was always maintained.

We also worked on the production of spatial situations that would evoke **reflections and ambivalences** between inside and outside, above and below. The building should continually establish newly configured visual relationships through a continuous, horizontal flow of movements. The establishment of a simultaneous perception of several self-similar spaces on a horizontal plane was crucial, thereby.

Steiner I would like to discuss your exhibition's color concept. What made you choose colored backgrounds?

Muntean/Rosenblum First of all, we should say that we already presented our pictures on colored walls in an earlier exhibition at the MUSAC León in Spain, albeit with a completely different concept. We had the idea because our pictures have white frames and they seem more powerful on a colored wall than on a white background. On white walls, the white frames "extend" out onto the wall. In Leipzig we were pleasantly surprised, because we initially thought that it would not be that easy to display our pictures in this building. So we were even more amazed to see that they work really well here. The concept of the concrete walls and partitions is convincing. We wanted the colors to respond to the concept of the exhibition space and to match the grey concrete. Which is why we chose two colors as complementary colors: one is really bright, the other really dark. We ultimately opted for cold phosphorous yellow and blackish-green.

Muntean/Rosenblum At the MUSAC, we wanted to allude to the typical shades of wallpaper in the museum. In Leipzig, that would have been inappropriate and uninteresting, because of the space's architectonic guidelines. Indeed, cold phosphorous yellow is not intended to connote the

The design was deliberately developed from the inside out. The external features of the building follow the conceptual logic of the principles inside the building.

Early design stage, collage, 2002

An additional theme was then introduced to the design, which can be seen in close relationship with the **adjustable walls**: a thin layer of **display elements** seems to fold itself into the spaces in order to define those primary, staged areas of exhibition, thereby creating border-lines on which the **negotiations of the space** should take place.

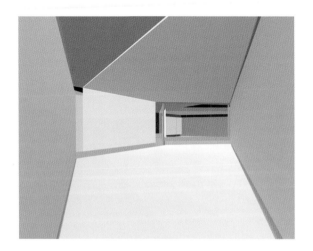

Interior view of a typical exhibition space, 3d model, 2002

coloration of the traditional museum. It was important to rule this out.

Muntean/Rosenblum   And then we decided to use all the walls except for those of concrete. That made the concrete walls all the more visible. It was important not to use these walls, to thus "exhibit" them as part of the overall display.

Steiner   You use colors to structure the space.

Muntean/Rosenblum   The priority was to use the space's segmentation and emphatic interruptions in order to re-establish a flow.

Steiner   Viewing the exhibition greatly relies on movement, which is also a crucial aspect of the architectural concept from the very beginning. You positioned the pictures in such a way that the viewer is practically drawn into the following area. This is due above all to visual correlations guiding the gaze.

Muntean/Rosenblum   You also forget the feeling of stepping into a new space. Before you know it, you're already in a new part of the building, because there are all these gaps and angles. That was a compelling starting point for us.

Muntean/Rosenblum   What's also interesting is that the traditional wall hanging is equally possible. We didn't take this for granted at the beginning, but we're glad that it works.

After a process of reworking the design, adapting it to a reduced scale, and defining the parameters of the inner varability we came to a final design solution, which will be explored in detail in the following pages.

Birdview collage of the final design stage on site, 2003

Steiner You seem to transpose into the space the disjointedness at work within the pictures. Your paintings constantly thrive on fragmentation and ruptures – both in form and subject matter …

Muntean/**Rosenblum** Yes, there are parallels between our works and our use of the space. Also implementing colors as a means of quotation works in that direction. We also seek to do that in our pictures.

Muntean/Rosenblum The white frames, the texts – serve to break up the autonomy of the image-as-object. Consequently, the picture is built up through various superimposing layers and levels. In Leipzig, the architectural component offers an ideal supplementary layer, offering an extension of the characteristics inherent to the works.

Project Management Report

Upon being asked to contribute a text to the present book, I immediately accepted the offer. But then I wondered for some time about whether an essay on cultural project management methodology was right in the context of this publication. So I decided to report on this unique project by compiling a record of how I experienced it, providing information pertaining to my profession – such as costs, deadlines, standards, and organizational facts and figures – wherever appropriate.

It was Arend Oetker (GfZK co-founder and foundation committee chairman) who asked our office to collaborate with the previously constituted team as project manager. We met the client, the architects, the construction supervisor, and the building services engineer in February 2003.

▷▷ 69

New Spaces, Other Visibilities[1]

I was pleased but also a little surprised when Barbara Steiner approached me about speaking at the opening of the new building of the GfZK. I was surprised because it seemed unusual to me that an artist was being asked to speak on this occasion. But then the question occurred to me: why should that be unusual? Why shouldn't an artist have something to say about the space in which he/she – in the broadest sense – also works. Why is a gallery or museum only rarely understood as a place in which an artist takes up a position, not only for the presentation of their art, but also through how they place themselves and their work in relation to the space and thereby articulate their "contemporary-ness."

I would therefore like to use this evening as an opportunity to speak about "the contemporary," for which this institution is also named, the Museum of Contemporary Art. What actually is "the contemporary" in art, and how do artists define themselves as contemporaries? There are a great many clichéd answers to these questions. We are all familiar with them, they are quoted over and over: for example, that through the avant-garde, through artists, other areas are opened up which one does not experience in everyday life and which therefore make new perspectives possible. I would like to present another version of "the contemporary" to you, perhaps a more austere one, but no less interesting, I hope.

The French philosopher Jacques Rancière once called the museum a place where the invisible becomes visible. Museums are for him those places in which culture defines where the invisible and visible come in contact with, but also distinguish themselves, from each other. What did Rancière mean by this formulation? First of all, he surely meant museums in the sense in which the past – which for us is no longer so visible – becomes visible, or those museums which refer to newly discovered, unknown territories. But what Rancière refers to above all, is the meaning of this process, that is, the meaning of this defining of boundaries, because the specifics of a culture are defined by how these boundaries are formed and presented. Cultures are thereby described by how they define their relationship to the invisible, how things are allowed to become visible. In this sense, a museum is not an extra, surplus, or luxury item that a society allows itself to have, but rather, a place where culture defines itself. On the basis of this thesis, Rancière also postulated that the museum is a place in which social hierarchies are formed. It is a place where it is decided what does or does not have a meaning, what is important to us and what will become important to us. And this consensus on what is visible or invisible not only works its way into society, but also creates and differentiates it.

The late art historian Stefan Germer put this point more succinctly: "The artistic and the social production of art go hand in hand." That is, in what the artist does, he/she is always already contemporary, and museums are the places in which this contemporary-ness becomes visible. Now you would probably think to yourself, "but that's obvious just by looking around at the artwork here," however, I mean this in a more fundamental sense: it's not so much about the content as it is about the connection between the ways in which art presents itself and how this is experienced by its viewers, as well as the way in which art is produced.

1 This text follows the transcript of the speech which was given on November 24, 2004, on the occasion of the opening of the GfZK-2.

I would like to cite a historical example here that illustrates the aforementioned points. Using the example of Piero della Francesca, Michael Baxandall examined which compositional principles can be found in the artist's paintings. Few people know that della Francesca had also written economics guides. He wrote mathematics books for merchants, in which the then innovative application of geometry played a crucial role in the recording of quantities. This basic commercial knowledge provided an enormous advantage during the Renaissance for merchants in the southern part of Europe over those in the north. Baxandall then proved that one can also detect these geometrical formulas in the compositional principles of Piero della Francesca's paintings. He does not argue that a viewer at that time simply saw an application of set theory in the pictures. He is more concerned with showing that the modes of perception cannot be separated from the modes of production, that the ways in which a society is produced also determine the ways in which it is perceived and sensed. The mathematical knowledge is effective in the physical presence of the paintings: the clear arrangement, the carefully chosen proportions, the construction of geometrically even patterns to intervals – this is what we then notice on the visual level. It is then not simply about translations, but rather about configurations of sense within the sensual.

In terms of the growing re-orientation of museums, which was occurring at the end of the 1970s, the American art historian Rosalind Krauss investigated a similar dialectic. In one of her key essays, she speaks of "the logic of museums of late capitalism." She begins with a description of the expansion of the Guggenheim Museum from a small independent museum to an international company. Her analysis of this phenomenon discusses the connection between the economic changes and the growing presence of minimal and conceptual art in museums. Krauss does not place the critical potential of the artwork into the foreground, but rather asks to what extent their physical presence refers to other connections. Minimal art, as demonstrated by its prominent representatives such as Donald Judd and Dan Flavin, works with industrial materials. Donald Judd built aluminum cubes which measured 1 meter × 1 meter × 1 meter , and constructed them with colored Plexiglas. Dan Flavin used commercial lighting tubes to illuminate spaces. Industrial products and production methods were the focus here. There is the casual theory regarding the disappearance of the collection in museums – one actually only sees the spaces. If the viewer gets involved in these experiences, then he/she experiences what he/she cannot experience so directly in everyday life – the space as a three-dimensional, fundamental, sensual experience. It is an experience that one did not attribute at this time to the working sphere. Rosalind Krauss brings attention to the fact that it was exactly in this time that these shifts had also been emerging in the workplace since the 1960s, and in a phenomenological sense, seemed to be occurring simultaneously. For example, in the 1960s, the gold standard came to an end, and television started intensifying advertising in such a way that we speak today about a product more in terms of its symbolic value – meaning to what extent it is distinguished by its appeal due to advertising – than we do in term of its use value.

For Krauss, the aforementioned artworks are indications – as much through their physical features as they do through their means of production – of a new economy, which represents a new stage of capitalism. And this is not only in terms of the transformation of spaces, but also in terms of a new form of production: sensual experiences and situational events obtain a commodity-like character and become new elements of a post-Ford economy. Krauss pessimistically views this development as a movement towards event politics and Disneyfi-cation. She argues that the consumer is actually only a consumer in a postmodern world who is in search of experiences that allow one to experience him/herself intensely. Even if I do not share this pessimistic perspective, I find Krauss's critical questioning of the utopian potential of art admirable. These potential worlds sketched out by artists are less preparations for future spaces in the context of positive utopias than they are actual and direct references to transformations in the here and now.

The question that follows is: keeping this background in mind, where would an artist begin who does not only want to take part in the reproduction of what already exists? This building provides a very good occasion for envisioning how this could be possible. Charles Esche spoke today on the occasion of this opening about the function of the museum, and Barbara Steiner spoke about the concep-tion of this building. It is a museum which makes a permanent dialog possible, which makes many new insights possible, which provides the most diverse perspectives. The architects see it as a stage for perpetual debate.

I would say that this museum is actually a performative space. It is a space that was designed with cinematic precision in mind – films have different camera perspectives and editing techniques – the difference being that the building offers a three-dimensional experience of this precision. The space makes various scenarios possible through which fiction can be experienced as reality. This idea of different scenarios had already emerged in the 1960s. Dan Graham made a very small drawing in 1967 that hardly attracted any attention at the time, but today seems very prophetic. The drawing shows a tree diagram in which the points provide local and numerical data. Graham was simply noting the process of options which result from decisions made through binary logic. Depending on which process one chose, different movement samples resulted. At the lower end of the drawing, there is a multiplicity of possible constellations, which are contained at the top of the tree graph. Place and time contain an infi-nite amount of possibilities of movement. Graham's drawing is an example of a reflection on the multiplicity of events, also alluding to a multiplicity of construc-tions of the self.

A well-known example of architecture that demonstrates such processes is the mirror hall of Versailles. This hall was not just set up as an infinite setting of reflections in tribute to the Sun King. The mirrors also had a significant organiza-tional function for the royal household and the visiting audiences. The centraliza-tion of the royal court created an entirely new phenomenon: the noblemen had to leave their own estates and live in the court if they wanted to exert any influence. It was only possible to gain influence there. In these social plays and their means of communication, it was important that one's own intentions did not become outwardly clear or recognizable, that one had achieved one's goal without the others noticing it too early on. For this diplomacy of behavior, the mirrors were indispensable.

In 17th-century French painting, an intensive study of gestures and expres-sions was required. Manuals of facial expressions were provided in academies and then applied. The portrait was shaped by the vocabulary of these pattern books. One could already recognize here those forms of self-reflexivity that Dan Graham's contemporary constellations explored in his pavilion architecture. These pavilions are not only small labyrinths of glass and mirrors, equipped with cameras and monitors they also become active, usable spaces in which one's behavior can be rehearsed, altered, or perfected through repetitive enactments. We also practice these feedback loops in everyday life, the difference being that we are not aware of our repetition. We have internalized these behaviors. This is what I would like to describe as performance and what I mean when I am referring to a performative space/architecture in terms of this location, the new building of the GfZK.

This kind of performance is not only found in museums. The most extreme example of it is the frequently-cited "Big Brother" phenomenon. These same media techniques also shape everyday social relations. Only in concrete situations do contextualizations and utilizations form differentiations, which do not in fact exist separately from each other. The British sociologist Dick Hebdige speaks of the fact that forms of adaptation do not simply face "negations" and forms of resistance, but are actually all synthesized together. Sharing these techniques does not mean there is no other way around given standards, but rather concerns the question considering the options of other possibilities that can be articulated through them. The utopian would therefore not only be possible through another system: the investigation of the potential of the given methods of production through other applications, hybrids, and rewordings takes the place of the demands for the invention of new methods.

The Slovenian philosopher Slavoj Žižek expressed this idea in such a way: he believes that today it is more important than ever not just to talk continuously about wanting to change the world, but rather to continually interpret the world. He is convinced that we do not really know what is going on at the present and that it is time to reflect upon ourselves again. He then introduces the term of repetition – a repetition, when translated into the spatial-sensuous, forms spaces that are similar to those scenario rooms for reflections. Repeat is not return. Through repetition, paths are opened up and other directions become possible, which seem to be already laid out but have not yet been realized. This presents an option in which the past and present can be reflected on and thereby made negotiable. I feel this personally as my contemporary-ness in these spaces.

Applied to the distinction mentioned earlier between visible and invisible, one could make the argument that the new cannot turn from the unknown into something that is seen simply through an addition to what has not been seen, but only through a change of the matrix, which is the basis for the visible. To work on this change is what is important. I hope very much that these spaces are used as a laboratory for the contemporary, for which they hold promise today.

Title
Homezone

Artist
Via Lewandowsky

Curators
Heidi Stecker and Barbara Steiner

Opening
March 04, 2005

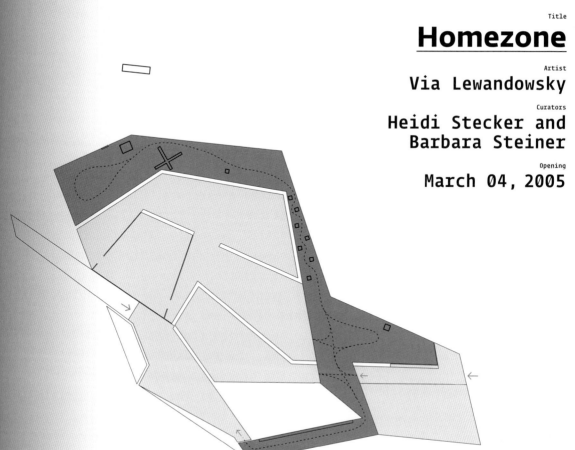

After introducing ourselves, we openly discussed the option, given the tight budget, of reducing costs. Could the additional fees of the project manager not be amortized by his direct involvement in the design and construction processes? I wanted to gain the trust of all participating partners, as I was to control and supervise all stages of the project – from the ambitious initial design to the final completed building. Within this process, the project manager's main job was to support and verify the technical feasibility of the client's conceptually clear ideas.

We had at our disposal a property under hereditary lease and a budget of precisely EUR 2,500,000 gross. This had to cover everything: the complete cost of construction from the foundations up, including the building's complex services technology. Furthermore, the budget had to cover fees for planning and building permits, connection of the utilities, and, naturally, the payment of our own fees.

When we joined the project, the conceptual design was already complete – the building's outline, functional areas and related locations had already been specified. Subsequently, based on the convincing design, it was our job to draw up a plan of implementation, intelligible to the construction workers. This phase of the project was marked by lengthy, yet ultimately productive discussions with the architects. In collaboration, our team was able to achieve the goal of completing each planning phase

In his exhibition held in the outermost areas of the building, Lewandowsky explored the contradictory nature of the two concepts – "Heimat" and "Utopia," the familiar and the radically new – in the light of apparently everyday situations. He focused on the moment in which the great plan – for example, a glorious future for everyone – becomes isolated and a parody of itself, and when the pleasure in its downfall can be enjoyed. The gallery spaces appeared deserted, as if after a house move, an event, a temporary use, or an alteration. The objects left behind were scattered like traces, connected visually from space to space; their material presence seemed unreal and inappropriate. Passing by empty, destroyed, or deformed show-cases, squeezing through a wall that pierced a wardrobe, hearing the buzz of a housefly – the exhibition's spatial concept reflected Lewandowsky's general interest in an absurd and disjointed normality. The artist's decision to work with the outer spatial perimeter of the building promoted a direct communication with the public. He positioned the neon slogan Der Sozialismus siegt (Socialism wins), blatantly visible, in the display window of the GfZK's new building. This slogan was once prominent on a high-rise building in Dresden only to be removed from its position a year before the GDR collapsed. On the one hand, the reframed version caricatured the utopian promises of Socialism; on the other, it stood for loss – of a society's promise, belief, or hope. At the back of the building, visible both from the outside and inside, Lewandowsky installed another light installation which flashed the word WOW in regular intervals, referring to a sensation that itself remains invisible. (Barbara Steiner)

within the respective deadlines. While planning the facility's technological system, we discussed various alternative ways of heating, ventilating, and air-conditioning the exhibition spaces. We also had to consider the fact that the GfZK annual budget did not include supplementary resources to cover the operation costs of the GfZK-2 exhibition building. Therefore, the planned air-conditioning system was not aimed at fully regulating the humidity and temperature levels of the entire exhibition space. To provide for the climatic demands imposed by the wide variety of materials of differing sensitivity used in contemporary art, we were able to create separate atmospheric zones within the building.

To ensure optimum fulfillment of the project's financial and conceptual aims, the building's potential for a modular structure was closely examined so that extensions could be made if necessary – without restricting business in the interim. One such option was the café's roof terrace, which may be erected at a later date. The stairs, railing, and wooden deck were estimated to cost a total of EUR 35,000. This amount was originally reserved as a backup budget, but was expended on other measures during construction. All the necessary preparatory fixtures (staircase stud frame, impact resistant thermal insulation) already exist so that the terrace may be added to the café as soon as funding is available.

A central issue discussed by the client, the architects and the other parties was the surface quality of

Steiner Via, some time has passed since your exhibition, as well as the inauguration of the GfZK-2. Do you remember what it was like seeing the GfZK-2 building for the first time? Did you think engaging with it would be easy or difficult? And did anything change during or after your working with it?

Lewandowsky When I saw the building for the first time, it was still a construction site. I had to piece together the visible fragments to imagine what the spaces would be like in the end. But I already knew then that there would be sliding walls with which spaces could be opened up or closed off from one another if desired. And I also saw that a lot of glass was being used in the construction of the building. That's basically good – but also demanding for the staging of artworks. Too much light and fluid transitions from space to space also create a lot of disruptions – and that means that not every spatial concept is going to work.

Steiner The aspect of visibility – and invisibility for that matter – is certainly an issue. Also, the building itself deals with questions pertaining to the limits and limitations of the visible. In any case, it calls for a response in terms of a clear position.

Lewandowsky Exactly. The building requires the artist to tackle the architecture – and to think about it more than is necessary in, say, the "white cube," where the architecture seems to disappear almost completely. Here however, there is no tacit agreement on clearly defined laws to keep the outside world at bay.

Steiner At least that seems to be the case. I think the same also applies to a "neutral" exhibition space, albeit differently. This is often overlooked, particularly because of what I would describe, beyond all of its advantages, as the "white cube's" greatest flaw: the "white cube" appears natural, as if there are no alternatives, no other options available whatsoever. In precisely this matter our building is fundamentally different. It always offers a variety of spatial options.

Lewandowsky And that is exactly why it naturally appeals to me. I really like the idea of "distracting fire" – it can serve as an interpretive aid. And on closer inspection I really liked the overall lightness of the architecture – the feeling that it hovers above the ground, its pavilionesque layout, subtly reminiscent of the German Pavilion in Barcelona … I found that really compelling.

Steiner The building makes a number of references – it even quotes the "white cube." This also introduces a number of allusions in terms of content. Moreover, the limitations it imposes in terms of visibility, transparency and flexibility allude to central themes of 20th-century

the ceilings, walls, and floors. The concept of subdividing the building into so-called display and non-display areas by means of differences in surface structure and material ply was tested and specified in one of the GfZK studios on a 1:1 scale model of a sample exhibition space. A surrounding skirting profile of approximately two centimeters, also at floor level, was to underline the impression that the display areas are inserted into the shell of the building. Deliberation concerning the planned tripping edge

preoccupied the whole project team over a period of weeks. In view of legal liability, we expressed our doubts about the architects' conceptual demands. We were afraid that such a pronounced edge would later have to be clearly marked out with black-and-yellow safety stripes, thus ruling out liability toward visitors, but not employees. Ultimately, the threshold was reduced to a height of a mere 4 millimeters. A clearly visible profile now defines the intended caesura between the two display areas.

The planning process was integrative. The client, the architects, and those in charge of construction (especially the construction supervisor and project controller) extensively discussed ideas to resolve issues concerning the building's variability, esthetic, and functionality. This took place on the basis of regular meetings between the respective planners, to consider individual points and coordinate subsequent steps.

The lighting system was planned in detail early on. This ensured that the

architecture history. You were obviously able to accommodate these ideas in your exhibition. At least you
responded to them.

Lewandowsky Yes. Rather than competing against the
architecture, I tried to make use of it. I wanted to
specify the available options, and so I incorporated the
free-flowing configuration of the spaces. For instance,
the vitrines looked as if they had been deposited in no
particular order … I'm interested in what is imperceptible,
transient and generally taken for granted – as a means of
generating irritation.

Steiner Indeed, although the vitrines seem to have been
deposited haphazardly, their positions are deliberate. And
this accounts for the quality of your work – the productive
consideration of inconveniently arcane irritations, the
effects of which are only exerted later when the need for
reflection arises.

Lewandowsky I define it as construction through deconstruction, as making things visible by keeping them
imperceptible, and so on. I like the ambiguities and
misunderstandings that arise as a result, the fragility of
the message. After all, it is not my aim to reveal (a) truth
in the original sense of the word – that is, as a definitive
entity. I am looking to achieve quite the opposite!

Steiner What I really like about your work is that you

deal with and within contradictions, and play with
multiple meanings. Nothing is ever completely clear or
unambiguous. That's also how I felt while seeing your
exhibition at the GfZK. Your chosen areas of focus –
Heimat (home) and utopia – are already ambivalent.

Lewandowsky With regard to ideas of utopia, I was
particularly interested in nostalgia. It's strange, but when
we think about utopias, we suddenly become nostalgic.
That relates to the fact that utopian imagery is extremely
powerful and pervasive – and also to our experiences of
that imagery's decline. For instance, beyond the many

---

customized light components could be
delivered in good time, and also that
the fixture points could be specified
while planning the shell building.
An instruction manual documenting
the customized light fixtures was
compiled by the lighting designers,
Studio Dinnebier. As a repository
of the information and knowledge
acquired during construction, we
continue to refer to it in our office
as a successful example of practice-
bound documentation.
A museum has to be safe. The alarm

system was thus a central concern
from the beginning. In order to bring
it up to the necessary standard, we
sought advice from several insurance
companies. Also the functional
requirements had to be clarified early
on, because the alarm system was
integral to planning all other systems
(façade, doors, electrics) integrated in
the building. The building is divided
into three separate security areas:
the exhibition space, the cinema,
and the café. Timely and intensive
coordination and planning with the

insurance companies proved worth-
while. Shortly before the building was
completed, the alarm system was
inspected and approved by the same
insurance company under contract for
GfZK-1. We were thus able to negotiate
that the new building could be
insured at no additional cost.
The uninterrupted black surfaces of
the building's exterior walls are a
dominant design feature of GfZK-2.
These are exposed to considerable
strain due to temperature fluctuation
between summer and winter. That

images one experiences during childhood, the grandiose architecture of the TWA terminal at New York's Kennedy Airport often appeared in the movies I grew up on – and such stunningly new places were related to promises of the future. Then, when visiting these locations many years later, I suddenly realized that nothing was the way I believed it to be. Nothing promising was left, the building was in ruins, and the place was buried beneath the banality of the present. It was quite a pitiful sight really …

Steiner   … Well, that's what the past consists of – remnants. I remember the description you used to announce your exhibition in our museum: "Similar to the sight of a marooned whale, we can now recognize the real extent of now defunct magnitude. Failure can be quite a hilarious matter – and we relish the sight of it." The neon work *Der Sozialismus siegt* (Socialism wins), which you installed in the display window facing the street, strikingly demonstrated this reversal, as the exhibition in its entirety also ventured to do.

Lewandowsky   The work *Der Sozialismus siegt* deals with an exemplary case. It demonstrates the revaluation of a big utopian image as a simple slogan, a clear neon sign, with the elegance of commercial lettering – like company logos or disused advertising captions found in shop windows. Nowadays, slogans such as *Geiz ist*

geil (Scrounging is sexy) would run there instead, but probably not in such a static form.

Steiner   When recontextualizing the text, location and timing play a predominant role. Naturally, the slogan's original position – on the roof of a high-rise apartment building in Dresden in the 1980s – worked to quite a different effect.

Lewandowsky   Though back then I already thought about how I could incorporate it in my work. The slogan was sufficiently inspiring in its original state. For instance, it was always a moment of vindictive glee whenever the neon letters glitched, because that was not supposed to happen to slogans of such importance. The slightest fault could change completely the message of the sovereign phrases. Similarly, it never ought to have been allowed to switch them off. Switching them off is like installing the eternal flame somewhere, without subsequently seeing to it that it constantly burns. All this makes you conscious of the innate fragility of signs, and of how difficult it really is to proclaim such pervasive symbols.

Steiner   Twenty years later, these words are inevitably going to be read differently, particularly if the work is exhibited in the context of a building, which obviously does not aspire to nostalgia. Though the work, on the one hand, refers to socialism in the German Democratic

---

is why most buildings do not have extensive black façades, and why dark façade usually consist of floating cladding. The exterior walls of GfZK-2 are made of rubber, a product usually used for sports flooring. Initially, our experienced construction workers harbored great reservations about this material. To test its features, a sample cladding of 2.5 square meters was fastened to the outer wall of the GfZK studio building. On the basis of our observations, we were able to accurately define the scope of

installation and put the construction contract out to tender. As black rubber is rarely used, the minimum quantity in this customized color that could be produced and delivered by the manufacturer was approximately twice the amount of cladding actually required. The construction has proven to be resistant, bearing no major flaws after more than four years. We embarked on the project in March 2003, and we aimed to complete construction in September 2004. Four weeks before the topping-out

ceremony, all that was visible on the construction site was the slightly elevated floor slab. When our client anxiously inquired whether there would be anything visible to top out, we smilingly replied that there would be, though we had our secret doubts. But in the end, the prefabricated walls of reinforced concrete could be rapidly fitted on the floor slab, so that on the occasion of the ceremony, the "flat-pack museum" (as one tabloid put it) was discernible and could be presented to the public.

Republic, on the other, it cites emancipatory social theories that are much older. Thus, a cynical reading of it seems to owe a lot to the conditions prevalent in the GDR. At any rate, the neon work occasioned much debate in Leipzig.

Lewandowsky   Unfortunately I wasn't aware of these debates at the time.

Steiner   Many of the works included in your exhibition explicitly refer to issues relevant to the outside world, which certainly serves to foster heightened attention.

Lewandowsky   I explicitly intended to articulate opinions and statements pertaining to the outside world. I was interested in ways of utilizing a building such as this one, in terms of the relationship between inside and outside. I wanted to emphasize the significance of the direction of the gaze, and movement through the space. For instance, it was particularly important to establish an overarching connection between the slogan *Der Sozialismus siegt*, visible from outside, and the flashing slogan *Wow* on the other side of the building. *Wow* could only be seen, flashing intermittently, if you were inside the building.

Steiner   I see the exhibition's power as a result of its specific dramaturgy. The visitor had to go past the casual arrangement of vitrines, practically squeeze his/her way in through the work *Schrankwand/Wandschrank (Wall unit/unit*

However, there were some delays and we were forced to improvise. The opening exhibition had already been scheduled. Although we didn't manage to complete construction quite on time, the first exhibition could nevertheless take place in a functioning building. Although the floor finish was still missing, the occupants could test the building before the final acceptance inspection. The flooring was then added later during an extended exhibition break.

In conclusion, we were able to remain within the budgetary limit of EUR 2,500,000 gross. Due to timely agreement on priorities of expenditure, we could also meet the varying expectations of the participating parties. Finally, compiled on December 15, 2005, our funds utilization statement was approved without further inquiries or additional demands by the Free State of Saxony. The construction project was thus implemented within the limits determined by the budget and

time schedule. Looking back over the past ten years, GfZK-2 was certainly my favorite project.

wall), which was wedged under the ceiling of the museum, to finally wind up in front of a white picture – the *Moor-soldaten* (peat bog soldiers). This designated a trail, which was unsusceptible not only in terms of space, but also with respect to its position within time. Were we looking at the past, the present or at a glimpse of the future? The viewer was never quite sure.

Lewandowsky   I wanted these temporal jumps – they were there all the time. They served to evoke feelings of ambivalence: What is an instant? How long is "forever"? What does it mean, if something flashes on and off, but does so incessantly? Imagine what it would be like if the hands of the clock would turn faster, if time would pass more quickly, and thus if more time would elapse in a single instant.

Steiner   And imagine a baseball bat on the verge of striking, jerking endlessly, without it ever carrying out the strike, just endlessly drawing back, ready to …

Lewandowsky   Well, it's about constant tension, a willingness to act, and potential action. I asked myself if this could work. What constitutes this state of tension? But I was also interested in specifying both the object and the context. What makes something meaningful? And when does it become meaningless? Ultimately these questions are always raised when anything is concluded or a specific time period ends.

Steiner   Again that reminds me of the texts you ascribed to each of the spaces. They were a bit melodramatic at times, weren't they? (*reads*) "Work: time had an agenda and spelled the present as an illusion – bodiless." "Everyday life: between daydreams and awakenings gazes glare at the passing clouds – endless." "Faith: certainty became as insubstantial as the ash of a love letter – powerless." "Heritage: abandoned places, the scenery of exile in the new land – worthless." "Leisure: naked brothers corner the sun while singing 'Schni Schna Schnappi' – tasteless."

Lewandowsky   I have to admit today these lines seem rather soppy and overly poetic. They are solemn and overladen with meaning. But the language is supposed to allude to the GDR socialist regime and the reversal of meaning often conducted by that regime: work destroyed the body; everyday life became a misery; faith became vacuous; inheritance became valueless. Even the free time you had was more of a punishment than it was pleasurable, because you didn't know how to spend it properly. There were really hardly any interesting things to do apart from reading, having sex, and drinking alcohol … which led to the emergence of abstruse phenomena such as cowboy clubs.

Steiner In my opinion, this predicament also engendered moments of heightened creativity. I don't share the widespread assumption that the GDR regime generated absolute passivity.

Lewandowsky Just recently I heard about a Russian who had painstakingly constructed a mini-submarine over a period of many years, which he can now actually operate. That reminds me of the prison inmate who insists on digging his escape tunnel although the guards left long ago. I'm not convinced that this doesn't pose mortal dangers. But precisely that's what it's about – namely the ambivalence of every single image, of all images.

Steiner Many mental images still remain, one of which cannot completely be erased.

Lewandowsky That's what the white canvas alluded to. It is not blank. It cannot be blank. Rather it is a projection screen for hopes, desires and ideas. In a way, this is quintessentially an anti-utopian image, and also explains why the song of the peat bog soldiers can be heard when one stands in front of the picture. This is, as it were, the memory of a partisan song, created in the most despicable of circumstances and sung in times of greatest want and desperation. Utopia consisted of singing this song, as this was the only hope of escape from the situation. I wanted to depict an image, which is not a visual image, but

simultaneously consists of an infinite number of images compressed a hundred thousand-fold. Ostensibly, this resembles a black hole.

Steiner Recourse to the perceiving subject was also a constant theme in the exhibition. I remember the constant sound of flies buzzing – sometimes it was barely audible, at other times it was enough to drive you mad. Neither was it possible to not hear the sound, nor by any means to put up with it. You were continuously forced towards an awareness of your physical presence and perception.

And these processes of perception also incorporated an awareness of the context. This was just as difficult to get rid of as the buzzing sound was.

Lewandowsky   Exactly. This becomes all the more evident if you consider that the fly, also featured in a show of mine in China, was even less welcome there. In China, the fly is historically considered as being an impure creature that must be combated. And there was even a time when Chinese citizens were paid for each fly they killed! Understandably, the ridiculousness of such methods is blatantly obvious today, and the Chinese prefer not to be reminded of them. But because of its ideal conditions for the distribution of acoustic waves, the museum building in Leipzig lent itself perfectly to this audio installation.

In a phase of **intense discussion** with the GfZK, examples of present institutional working models were discussed and their possible spatial strategies were analyzed. We wanted to develop a building that represented these increasingly complex and overlapping levels of institutional work, while also making them negotiable and visible. The building had to be able to **accommodate various programs** such as temporary exhibitions, film programs, and a café, but these spaces also had to be usable on a temporary basis for other specific functions such as presentations of the collection, lectures, and workshops. We developed a system of spaces in which the **individual areas cultivate strong visual and contextual relations**. They are mostly functionally underdetermined in such a way that they can be reformulated and reinterpreted.

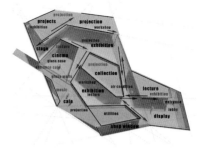

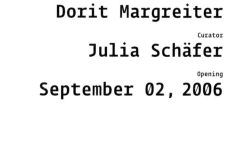

Title
Analog

Artist
Dorit Margreiter

Curator
Julia Schäfer

Opening
September 02, 2006

For example, two rear exhibition rooms can be detached from the rest of the building as a project space (1+2). The screening room can be integrated into the exhibition as a showcase (3). A middle exhibition space can become a storage space (4) and a narrow, glass-paneled area by the entrance can be used as a small seminar space (5). In turn, both of these areas (4+5) can be combined to accommodate delicate collection items that require an air-conditioned environment.

Analog comprised a survey of Dorit Margreiter's artistic exploration of architecture and interiors, in which she was concerned with what these represent, or have represented, and how they are used. The exhibition was divided into three spatial sequences of equal size. Central to the first work was a late modernist house by the architect John Lautner, 10104 Angelo View Drive (2004) (see p. 81). This was followed by several works grouped close together, which connected the first and third part of the exhibition. Here the artist focused on the effects of artificiality and its construction in film and commerce. The work zentrum (2006) (see p. 82–83), created in Leipzig, concluded the exhibition and showed Margreiter's attempt to reanimate the legacy of socialist modernism – or, more precisely, its neon lettering. All the works combined an interest in images from print media, film, and entertainment. The artist investigated the influence of these images on the collective and individual social memory, asking how they create or hinder identification or, indeed, produce reality itself. "Only film can make the new architecture comprehensible," commented Siegfried Gideon in 1928 in reference to buildings by Le Corbusier and Pierre Jeanneret. He thus sought to explain that film is the only medium suitable for documenting and describing modernist buildings, an approach Margreiter also took in her filmic debate with architecture. The parcours of the exhibition was planned as a "dead-end path," in which the visitor started in the area of western modernism and ended with eastern modernism. After all, in order to leave the show, he or she was compelled to walk the circuit back again, hence passing each work anew from a different perspective. (Julia Schäfer)

In the design phase, within the financial parameters for the project, a room schedule with twelve exhibition spaces measuring between 30 and 120 square meters, a café, and secondary rooms seemed to be appropriate. As the rooms developed, it became clear that they would remain functionally open, yet and also more similar to each other. At the same time, the ways in which the spaces could be interconnected emerged as a priority.

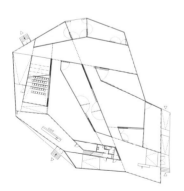

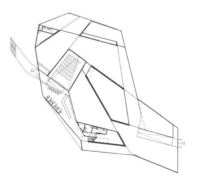

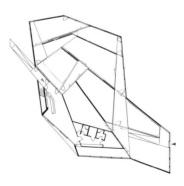

Design stage late 2001, elaborating the contrast between a floating exhibition space and inserted collection islands.

Design stage early 2002, quite close to the final design, including a bathroom in the rear in order to temporarily host an artist in the studio space.

Final design stage late 2002, focusing on creating a series of functionally not determined exhibition spaces.

The resulting system of spaces is a combination of trapezoid-shaped areas. These have a strong spatial and geometrical relationship to one another – thereby forming a **relational space structure**.

In traditional exhibition buildings, rectangular, static spaces do not refer very strongly to one another when considered in a purely geometric sense, and are therefore more autonomous. At the same time, visitors can clearly define their position in relation to the building and exterior surroundings and are therefore able to orient themselves.

We wanted to consciously challenge this orientability with this polygonal space structure. We were concerned with reflecting upon and questioning conventionalized and naturalized modes of perception in art spaces.

I have known the GfZK since 1998, and my frequent visits to Leipzig, several exhibitions, and a work produced during the *Blinky Palermo Scholarship*, not only connected me with the museum, but also stimulated an inspiring dialog with those people who, in very different ways, are involved with the conceptional work for the exhibitions as well as the institution itself – above all, Barbara Steiner, Julia Schäfer, and Christian Teckert. The astounding thing about these various ongoing discussions was and is that they always extend beyond the respective exhibition project at hand, thus enabling a continuous exploration of issues concerning the creation of space, ways of dealing with historical modernity, or the formats of diverse media with regard to architecture, space, and urban space.

When Julia Schäfer and I began to prepare my exhibition entitled *Analog* in the GfZK-2, she was already very familiar with the museum's architecture as an exhibition venue, having curated numerous solo and group exhibitions. I loved her drawings, which resembled models that had been folded apart – creating planes or surfaces out of three-dimensional space. The drawings were not only spatially legible but were, above all, highly practical tools to use for the planning of an exhibition. For me, at least, they were essential insofar as I was virtually unable to

imagine the architectural space of the GfZK in my mind – a circumstance hitherto new for me.

I almost always plan my exhibition projects with a concrete idea in mind for the particular location: a mental model that is probably the result of engaging with the discussion of "site specifity," which influenced me when I began exhibiting in the context of contemporary art in the early 1990s. Although the exhibition rooms of the GfZK-2 reflect aspects that are fundamental to my artistic approach – as the architecture itself mirrors the theoretical parameters of the production of space – they did not offer any simple guidelines for the concept of the exhibition. On the contrary, this turned out to be much more complex than initially conceived. It was as if I had to reassess my previous approach two or three times over, in order to position works all addressing themes similar to the architecture itself, which explores the interaction between constructed space and its function as a model.

Julia and I decided to adopt a radical approach, namely, to exhibit works that had either been intended for a different space or ones that describe a particular or specific place. We arranged the exhibition in such a way that there was no linear or narrative exhibition circuit with a beginning and an end, but rather that the visitor had to walk back through the same rooms again to reach the exit. This aimed at revealing both the respective artwork's conditions of production as well as drawing a parallel between the latter and the construction and principles of the new building.

The spatial arrangement of the building is not only functionally adjustable, but the spaces can also be combined in a variety of ways. This is facilitated by the single-floor structure of the building with two main entrances and two additional side entrances that can be activated at any time.

The café can thereby operate and generate revenue independently from the schedule of the exhibition spaces. The screening room next to it can be used independently as an external event space, and the exhibition areas can be divided up into several exhibition and project areas.

Curating in Models

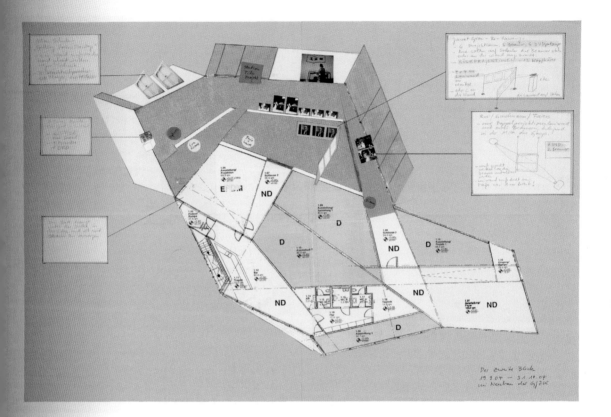

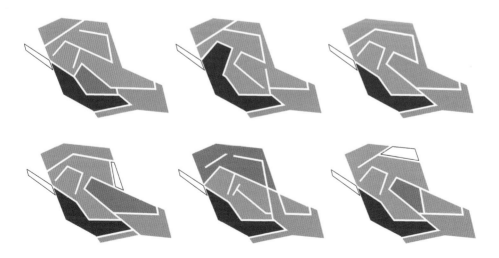

Six exemplary configurations of programming the building

■ Exhibition 1 ■ Exhibition 2 ■ Exhibition 3 ■ Project space ■ Bar/cinema

1 The old building – the GfZK 1 – was originally a residential house. In 1998, the GfZK was opened in this villa converted by the architect Peter Kulka. The conversion is guided by the idea of the "white cube."

2 Many details reveal that the villa used to be a residential house: visible radiators are, for instance, found beneath the windows. The house generally has lots of small-sectioned windows, niches, and skirting boards, and a progression of differently sized rooms with many openings. Above all, however, there are only two possible routes to take through the exhibition per level.

3 The lighting system initially required getting used to; the lights or rather lighting tubes, seemed too dominant. But, in contrast to the system prevalent in the GfZK-1, the advantages of this flexible lighting system quickly become apparent: the lights are individually dimmable, removable, and pivotable. The option of dimming is very important for me, since light, being manually determinable, is incorporated into the curatorial planning right from the beginning of an exhibition. Other lighting systems require daily readjustment, which often leads to "unfavorably curated" light.

4 This is the title of my essay published in: Leonie Baumann, Sabine Baumann (eds.), *Wo laufen S(s)ie denn hin?! Neue Formen der Kunstvermittlung fördern*, Wolfenbütteler Akademie-Texte, vol. 22, Wolfenbüttel 2006, pp. 141ff.

The Second Glance, one of the two opening exhibitions for the new building in 2004, addressed the processes of perceiving art as the subject for artistic work. Without having ever curated in a venue similar to the new building, it became apparent how the architecture was semantically feeding into the concept of my exhibition that led to a very exciting dialog with regard to the theme of artistic perception in relation to the surrounding architecture. This more or less had to do with the notion of chance back then. Planning the exhibition **(Fig. p. 85)** confronted me with challenges which, as a curator, I had not been faced with before. Over the course of three years, I had become accustomed to the old building[1] of the GfZK-1. Yet even if there were idiosyncrasies intrinsic to the architecture[2] that had to be overcome, the new building offered a kind of openness that I had to learn to work with. This openness has meanwhile revealed itself as a great opportunity. Initially, however, I asked myself whether the spatial concept of the new building was really so open and free, or whether it might limit me in my exhibition planning.

For example, was it truly advantageous not to have any fixed exhibition routes or locked rooms, but to have high and low ceilings and be able to slide and change walls, to turn lamps by 360 degree and dim them individually,[3] to consider different flooring, work with upper and lower light slits, with manifold views and light flooding in from the outside through large windows, to incorporate exposed concrete walls, and so forth? Curating in the new building undoubtedly had to abide by a new and different model which, like the building itself, also literally explodes perspectives in order to overcome the conventional forms of artistic presentation – or, at least, to question them. When I speak of "mediation as curatorial practice,"[4] I am specifically referring to the "curatorial mediation adapters" that I use for exhibitions – different ones, in fact, for each show – ranging, for instance, from a color concept or a particular form of light to installations and fixtures that bridge somewhat unfavorable spatial configuration and allow integration into the flow of the exhibition, as well as many others. I believe that these adapters are particularly

---

The negotiability of the exhibition spaces is enhanced not only by allowing for a variety of programs, but also by developing a **specific spatial variability**. In the design process, we developed strategies for creating more radical forms of spatial changeability. The development of the spatial concept was based on working on a series of interior models built with the viewer's perspective in mind.

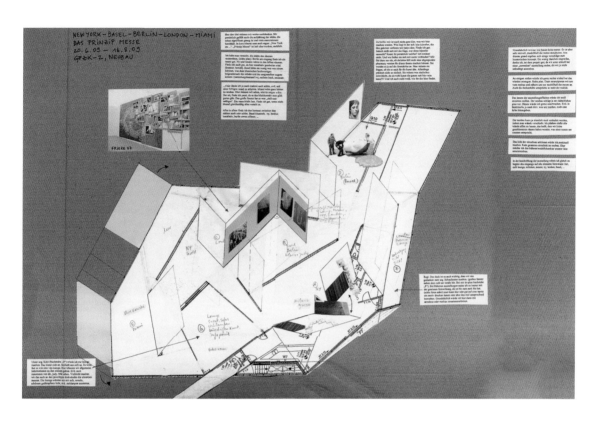

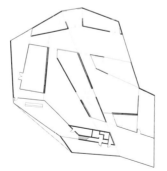

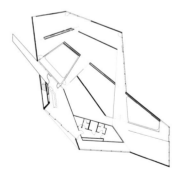

At first, our primary focus was on creating possibilities of different routes through the building and the development of selective extensions to secondary areas through a series of sliding and revolving doors. As a result, the spaces would fall even more clearly under a hierarchy and become more functionally defined, with larger and higher exhibition areas, and smaller, lower secondary areas for special uses.

Design stage late 2001   Design stage late 2002

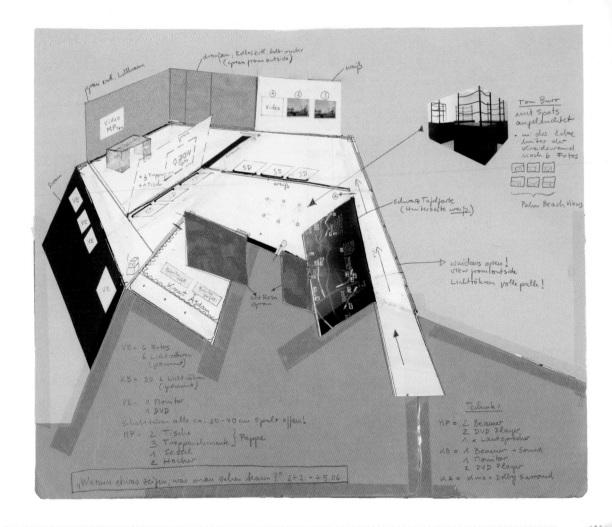

After further development, the spaces became more similar to one another, less functionally determined, and the spatial hierarchy between main and secondary areas was decreased. We increasingly experimented with altering spatial relations by using sliding walls, some being very large. The range of options for connecting the spaces in this way became the key factor for a variable exhibition design.

5 The DJ principle refers to the act of curating transitions in a way similar to the DJ when the samples that he/she is mixing melt into one long musical set.

Julia Schäfer   Curating in Models   89

important for the old building, as group shows constantly run the danger of turning into cabinet-like exhibitions that follow the so-called "staccato" principle: that is, one room comprises one esthetic position, without any smooth transitions. In the GfZK-2, relations are established within an exhibition yet without the need to create them artificially, according to the DJ principle.[5] The geometry of the rooms and their smooth transitions produce situations that take the visitor from one wall to another wall of a room, into the next, and back again to the start – as if one were following the path of an invisible billiard ball (see overview of exhibition routes in this book). This, among other factors, is the great attraction of working with these rooms, since other adapters are required – ones which are perhaps less physically constructed but which are made available, as has already been mentioned, by the building's range of fittings and configurations.

My exhibitions evolve in two stages or phases: initially, as a two-dimensional model in a scale of one to a hundred and, later, in a scale of one to one. The planning models are conceptual models as well as spaces to play and unfold. The more exhibitions I plan in the new building, the more the latter influences my ideas.

In the exhibition entitled *New York–Basel–Berlin–London–Miami*, which took place in summer 2009 and focused on

art fair strategies of the gallery owner Gerd Harry Lybke, the spatial layout was consciously kept as open as possible so that there was no predetermined circuit through the exhibition. Parts of the new building were kept empty on purpose in order to make semantic connections to the current crisis of the art market **(Fig. p. 87)** whereas, in the Sachsen Bank collection exhibition, done in November 2009, a fixed parcours led, for instance, to dead ends or closed doors. Moreover, a room "disappeared" in regular intervals through sliding walls that were changed once an hour to create ever-new spatial configurations. This was a ludic reference to the fact that, in the building of the Sachsen Bank itself, rooms remain shut and only those who demand special request are granted entrance. This play

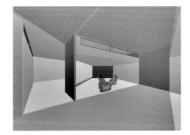

with the inside and the outside is to provide the formal parameters of the exhibition. In the GfZK-1, I would not be able to apply this curatorial principle.

For the exhibition *Why show something that one can see?* **(Fig. p. 88)**, all sliding doors were kept open twenty centimeters each so that visitors were able to look into the room that lay behind but not to enter it.[6] As the exhibition dealt with the methods of involvement and exclusion of gender-related (corporeal) spaces, the architecture again provided the supporting structure for the show's semantic concept. Via large color surfaces at the center of the exhibition,

This development also occurred in the context of keeping utility costs low. Although the museum had means for an extension of their exhibition spaces at their disposal, the operating budget was not raised accordingly. Ultimately, we designed nine ceiling-high **sliding walls**, with the addition of curtains, which provide the option of regulating the transparency of the wide glass walls in the interior space. This changeability offers a variety of possibilities to perform within a set of given rules.

We wanted to develop a spatial system that avoids the requirement of the production of a new exhibition architecture for each show. The variability is also deliberately limited, in order to make changes between shows readable. With each additional visit, the set of rules for the space will gradually become comprehensible to the viewer.

There are different categories of sliding walls. Some can disappear into wall alcoves, others, however, remain deliberately present and require a firm placement. A third category of sliding walls with integrated ceiling-high jib doors enclose an inner exhibition space that can accommodate special climatic requirements.

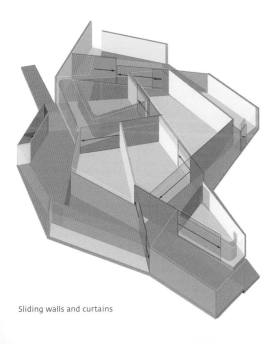

Sliding walls and curtains

I tried to create additional links so that the five artistic positions (Brooke, EXPORT, Porten, Asdam, and Burr) stood in constant relationship to one another **(Figs. p. 90, 91)**. One of the so-called display windows was also used to showcase a wall painting by Kaucyila Brooke. On a wall 9.60 meters long, she constructed a city map of Los Angeles consisting solely of lesbian bars both present or meanwhile closed down **(Fig. p. 93, above, left)**. Indeed, the display window became a way for the exhibition to communicate with the outside world. This was also the case with Dora García's exhibition, in which the artist, using huge film stills from her work Rooms, Conversations exploited the display window as an announcement platform, writing the title of the film on the outer wall **(Fig. p. 93, above, right)**. I had introduced the dual principle "display window plus outer wall = exhibition wall" at the exhibition entitled *What If*. The Berlin fashion label, Frisch, had used the window as a kind of store display and Terence Gower had used a light box to turn the façade into an exhibition wall **(Fig. p. 93, below)**.

The pictures of the preliminary planning ideas for the 2010 collection exhibition show the individual spatial zones of the new building as various puzzle pieces **(Figs. p. 94)**, which also explains the working title of *PUZZLE*. I came up with the idea for the exhibition through the notion of form and the play with spatial "splitters." People from various professions are invited to engage with the GfZK collection on a number of levels: students, artists, art mediators, art restorers, curators, and members from the GfZK's Friends' Organization will express their own understanding of the collection, thus helping to form the exhibition in parallel.

Every time a new exhibition is planned in the new building, a small dose of the unforeseeable and incalculable remains, which makes the arrangement of the exhibition exciting. Only at the opening can we see the way in which the concept of the exhibition is displaced through the act of engaging with the architecture. Thus, I regard the new building as a challenge to constantly reconsider the art of exhibiting anew. If one doesn't work "with" the building, then the architecture can very quickly become a form of limitation.

I would like to end on a comparison. If we characterize a building as the contextual parameters for an exhibition, then the new building is a very flexible frame that adapts to a given exhibition with all the "mediation adapters" available. The quality or nature of the GfZK is that it offers two models of exhibition architecture which, according to each exhibition, ideally make us consider which architecture is in turn fitting for which content.

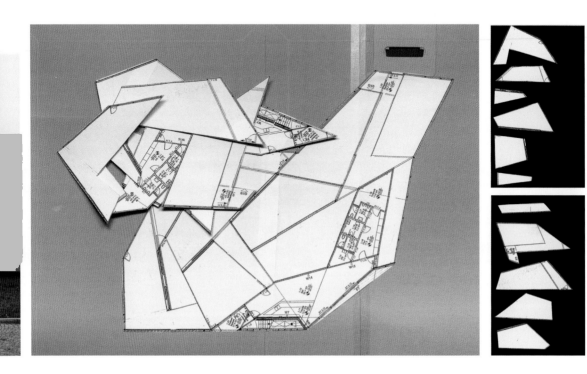

The sliding walls were made with hidden fittings and with paintable wood surfaces so that they could operate as exhibition walls. They can only be distinguished from the adjacent, bright display wall surfaces by their slightly darker coloring. In the planning and execution of the sliding walls, there was no prior experience to call upon. At the same time, they had to be reasonably priced. Everything from the construction to the fittings depended on a complex collaboration between the planning team and the carpenter. The hanging sliding walls had to be considered early on in the planning of the roof structure, since they added substantially to the structural load. Along the track of the largest sliding panel, the roof structure needed additional support to reduce sagging in order to guarantee a consistent gap between the sliding wall and floor in all positions.

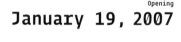

FORMSCHÖN

Artist
Tilo Schulz

Curator
Ilina Koralova

Opening
January 19, 2007

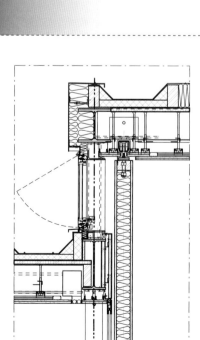

Detail: vertical section, showing the
construction of the roof, the skylight and the
mounting of the silding walls

FORMSCHÖN by Tilo Schulz deals with two central paradigms in the history of 20th-century Europe – formalism and socialist realism – reflected and interpreted from today's perspective through the artist's personal history and experiences. Tilo Schulz was born in 1972 in the German Democratic Republic, and the change in the political system took place when he was seventeen years of age. Thus, his understanding of culture and society has been characterized by two antagonistic ideologies, those of socialism and capitalism. The artist sees the ideological warfare between formalism and realism in art as a fruitful metaphor for the times of the Cold War. The exhibition – bound conceptually to the specific architectural context of the GfZK-2 – not only looks back to the times of the modernist utopia and ideological struggles, but also opens up a discussion on the representation and re-contextualization of contemporary art, and its conceptual and formal aspects. (Ilina Koralova)

The substructure of the sliding walls – wood and steel frames – was manufactured in the factory. These were installed on location, sided with wood panels, seamlessly taped and spackled, and painted with wall paint. Economical heavy-duty tracks and rolling mechanisms normally made for agricultural buildings were used for the suspended walls. All fittings used to operate the panels were either placed on the edges or installed to be removable in order to use the sliding walls as display walls in the best possible way.

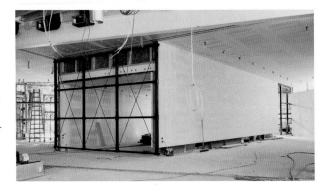

A particular challenge in the planning and execution was presented by the two sliding walls, which are used to close off the space with optional air conditioning. One must be able to enter and exit this sealed area, therefore, ceiling-high revolving doors were integrated into the sliding walls. The stationary parts of these sliding panels are only connected by a flat steel bar at the top. They are fixed into the floor with strong mortice deadlocks in order to provide a stable lateral bracket and stop for the integrated revolving doors.

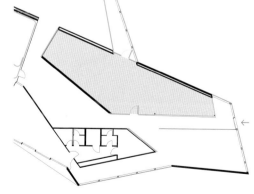

The on-site construction of the large sliding walls presented another challenge. The lateral joints of the sliding panels had to be small and consistent, therefore, all the connecting parts had to be accordingly precise. The sliding panels cross an already geometrically complex building like guidelines, connecting distant sections of the building to one another, requiring a dimensional precision that had to be constantly monitored in all phases of planning and building.

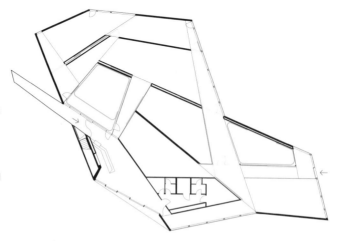

I have to admit that I underestimated the new building when it was still an architectural model. It was only when I later walked through the actual building that I came to realize what it could provide in terms of space for exhibitions and events. This realization is still alive today, as I come to appreciate the multifunctional nature of the building at every exhibition anew. However, the many possible spatial constellations that it can offer are not really what interest or surprise me. Instead, it is rather more the constant new interpretation of interspaces and perspectives arising between the fixed and movable walls: the skylight strips along the walls' upper perimeter, the floor-level windows, the vertical apertures, and the views through and out of the building.

In his conversion of the Villa Herfurth, Peter Kulka was already keen to emphasize the notion of the gap or the interstice, thus enabling a felicitous dialog between the late 19th-century style of the old villa and its extension. However, the new building of the GfZK goes a step further still and, in an apparently marginal way, incorporates the concept of the gap not as a connection, but as an opening instead. Thus, the architecture affords a formal solution that reflects the semantic and strategic work of the museum: the overlap of perspectives as well as the connection between various themes and artistic approaches.

It was important to us that the variable room system could operate with as few fire safety restrictions and costly technical constraints as possible.

With this space concept, different sliding-wall schemes required different fire escape routes. Accordingly, the visitors must leave the building in varying directions, indicated by the placement of illuminated fire exit signs, which must be repositioned for each setup. This **fire escape concept** was possible due to the single-story structure of the building, numerous exits, and relatively small spaces under 100 square meters that require only one fire exit.

The fire safety expert classified the building as a "contiguous exhibition hall with minimal fire hazards." It has only one fire compartment and therefore does not require fire-retardant partitions. On a technical level, the construction has no fire rating requirements. Only an objection from an art insurer led to the fireproofing of the supporting walls and roof structure, which would allow the building to be entered during a fire.

Whereas I was still reacting to the open structure of the exhibition space in my work shown in one of the opening group exhibitions for the new building in 2004, I increasingly started to focus on the idea of modules and a clear critique of modernism when realizing *City Fear/Origami Version (Module I–IV)* for the exhibition *Untitled (City IV)* in 2005.

I only began to make proper use of the aforementioned interspaces, perspectives, spatial rifts, and apertures in my solo exhibition entitled *FORMSCHÖN*, in which these elements became subjects – or rather, a means of utilizing the architecture. I designed a linear *parcours* through the rooms, which ran contrary to the open structure. Thus, the visitor had to walk from room one into room two, from room two into room three, and so forth; paths were blocked and views opened. Visual shortcuts could only be taken through the upper skylight-strip windows, floor-level windows, and partitions. Otherwise the visitor had to take the entire circuit from beginning to end and back again in reverse – which was crucial in order to read the exhibition. I chose to challenge the seemingly democratic principle of the architecture's flexibility by determining a rigid order throughout the exhibition rooms, which also paralleled the rigid *parcours* along my exhibited works. Yet a clear structural decision motivated this authoritarian gesture: the exhibition was designed like a novel. *Fahne/Flag* (room

one) introduced all elements of the exhibition, which were then parsed and examined from different angles in the following rooms, placed into various different contexts, and modified. The *COLD WAR* curtain made of 64,000 wooden beads functioned as a kind of transition or elucidation space, after which the exhibition took a different turn. At the end, the visitor was confronted with a choice between two rooms – that is, one was forced to read the story from other points of view. The idea of the gap or interstice as an opening (raised by the architecture) and the partition as a division (which I added) introduced a

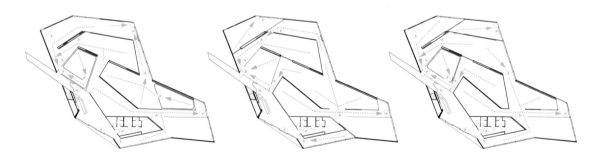

Some of the fire escape scenarios

speculative element into the game. Walking through and seeing the exhibition is complemented by visual curiosity and the spectator's additional thoughts.

The *SASHA* curtain in the museum's display window brings a further aspect into the discussion concerning visibility and speculation: it domesticates the doctrine of transparency in modernism. The simple gesture of a bourgeois net curtain illustrates the idea of perpetual access and, thus, control. At the same time, occupancy and the act of taking-into-possession shed light on the fact that an idea inevitably mutates as soon as it enters the reality of everyday life.

The freestanding wall of frosted glass bricks – *ART HAS BECOME ABSTRACT* – picks up the theme of the exhibition once again, moving it into the direction of staging and theatricality. I resisted the architecture in many places and in others it served me well. Then again, I never conceived of the new building as a final architectural statement, but rather as an architectural structure that I had to engage with; this meant that it was at once friend and foe. As a result of my on-site presence, I could constantly transfer my ideas into the exhibition space, and test and verify them there. However, I did not view this as a process in which I had to adapt my work to the architecture or, conversely, align the architecture with my work – rather, I would describe it as a form of mutual acquaintance-making.

In the design phase, alongside the development of a both programmatically and spatially fluid, strongly relational configuration of the spaces in the building, we gave more and more consideration to the role of the **display surfaces** in the exhibition spaces, that is, the architectural framing of current curatorial and artistic practices.

It was crucial to us that the display would not only operate as a neutral background for the exhibited items, but that it would also become perceivable as an active tool for organizing the regimes of vision within this exhibition building.

We wanted to highlight this usually inivisible element of museum design in the building concept. We worked on display shells that are composed of thin envelopes of bright, yet slightly colored surfaces – floors, walls, and ceilings – and placed them in the raw spaces. In an indirect way, these display shells reference the so-called white cube, which has become the cultural norm in museum design; that is, naturalized beyond recognition, yet still powerful in its invisible production of aura.

In our conception, the spaces – in contrast to the "white cube" model – are never completely closed off and the edges of the display surfaces also remain visible as signifiers of their physical presence. At the same time, the display surfaces themselves remain to a large extent free of distractions like technical components or door joints.
We thought of the display shells as stage-like settings in the exhibition space. The visitors may feel as if they are on a stage, in a certain way on a pedestal, which not only emphasizes the artwork, but above all, brings attention to the relationship between the perceiving subject and the exhibited object.

▷▷ 113

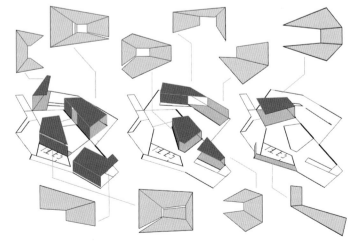

ARCHITECTURE IS THE ULTIMATE EROTIC ACT
CARRY IT TO EXCESS

Nothing Is Safe in the Museum

During the 1990s, cultural edifices, above all museums, offered one of the few remaining niches for architectural experiments. Hoping for the "Bilbao effect" to occur caused a slackening of public funding worldwide at a communal level. Yet barely inaugurated, severe criticism was fired at the formal ostentation of the new museum buildings, which were seen as serving the ends of their own superficial spectacles rather than those of art. The moment of restoration had come, with art and architecture returning in lockstep to models of a classical modernity. Although already considered obsolete on the grounds of its universality and aspired neutrality, the "white cube" has since seen a continuous revival. Art is to take precedence over architecture again, in one more attempt to salvage the autonomy of the artwork, a status that was already believed lost. Yoshio Taniguchi, architect of the new MoMA in New York, promised his clients, "If you spend really a lot of money, I will make the architecture disappear."[1]

At the GfZK in Leipzig, one is skeptical about the current trend toward a "lightweight modernism." Rather than retreating into the sanctuary of bourgeois canons of modernity, the GfZK refers in its work to still unresolved, experimental strands of modernism. Directed by Barbara Steiner, the GfZK focuses on contextual, performative, and political artistic practices. This also involves placing the GfZK's permanent collection in dialog with temporary exhibitions. The urge to increase – also in terms of space – such challenging configurations, led to the architects from as-if berlinwien being commissioned to design and build the new part of the museum. At the same time, it was intended to create additional space for the library extension and public programs in the GfZK main building, which was renovated and extended in the late 1990s by architect Peter Kulka. GfZK-2 provides a new spatial structure serving the programmatically enterprising institutional objectives of the GfZK.

Whereas Peter Kulka's extension largely retains the basic form of the existing late 19th-century villa (GfZK-1), as-if berlinwien erected a freestanding structure in the adjacent park as an extension of the existing ensemble, comprising the museum and auxiliary buildings. Compelling from an urbanistic perspective, the building dispenses with any geometric or formal references. Nestled against the existing stock of trees, the low, self-contained, one-story building appears as an irregular pavilion reminiscent of a random conglomerate of crystals. With its recessed base, the building seems barely in contact with the surrounding park, looking more like a raft adrift above the ground. The structure's accidental outer form accounts for its unspecified and disjointed appearance, further emphasized by the staggered elevations of the roof. Although it has a floor area of some 1,000 square meters, it conveys the impression of being a lightweight, perhaps temporary, pavilion, offering a refreshing contrast to the monumentality of much museum architecture. Inside, the fragmented volume serves to improve the lighting situation in the maze of smaller, interconnected galleries. While a desire for daylight generally results in large, sweeping exhibition spaces of uniform appearance, as-if berlinwien seeks to generate as many different spatial effects as possible, ranging from intimate situations to public display windows. Skylight

1 Cit. from Michael Freund, "Die Leichtigkeit eines Monuments," in: *Der Standard*, Vienna 11.20.2004

2 Le Corbusier, *An die Studenten. Die "Charte d'Athènes"* (1942), Reinbek 1962, p. 29

3 Ibid., p. 29

4 Beatriz Colomina, *Privacy and Publicity. Modern Architecture as Mass Media*, Cambridge 1996, p. 235

strips along the walls' upper perimeter, as well as floor-level slits at the base of the walls, provide natural light in even the innermost rooms, which are air conditioned to protect potentially fragile collection stock.

The structure's complexity really unfolds from the inside outward. Polygonal spaces, of which not one is quite identical with another, mutually adjoin, surround or interpenetrate each other. There is no single standpoint from which the visitor is able to see the overall arrangement of exhibition spaces. Now and then, when a sequence of rooms extends to the building's outer limits, a segmented view of the city or parkland outside suddenly appears. A subtle, rhythmic order of glass surfaces is sporadically interspersed with solid wall areas. Views out of and into the building are especially appealing because they are unpredictable. Perception remains unadulterated, one could say – following Le Corbusier who distinguishes between "dead" and "living" architecture, "depending on whether it disregards the law of the meander, or conversely obeys it brilliantly."[2]

According to Le Corbusier, architecture needs to be experienced by moving through it, in order for those who use it to perceive its forms and lines, its geometric relationships, rhythms, and proportions. Le Corbusier's "architectural promenade" incites a correlation between outer movement and inner motion with a "close succession of tremors."[3] The promenade becomes the symbol of a multilayered reality – consistent with modernism's preoccupation with relationships between space and movement. The modern subject is conceived of as being mobile, be it within urban space, technologically accelerated by means of modern modes of transport, or indoors, as the "architectural promenade" gives way to the (shopping) promenade. The window evolves from an illuminating instrument to a picture frame for the gaze, establishing a relationship between inside and outside, and as a means of staging this relationship. Notions of permeability, transparency and the threshold between private and public become central issues. New visual habits introduced by the medium of film boost the dynamism of the human gaze even further. Moving past extensive ribbon windows, the interlocking of inside and outside, now in the center of attention, appears as a filmstrip. The camera perspective seizes the eye: "The screen undermines the wall."[4]

With the GfZK-2, as-if berlinwien rejects the architectural model of the classic, modernist exhibition circuit. Here, neither the modern subject is addressed, whose position is substantiated by means of "edifying" circuits through, and clear overall views of the exhibitions, nor the flaneur, who lets the colorful bustle drift by as in a movie. In the GfZK-2, the confluence of spaces is repeatedly disrupted, just as continuities between interior and exterior are broken up. There are no panoramic views of the surrounding landscape or city. And also, inside, there is no vantage point from which the visitor may gain a comprehensive view over, or through, the whole building. In this almost labyrinthine structure nothing is ever self-evident. Rather than reaffirming him/herself while moving through the building, the visitor's sense of certainty is increasingly undermined.

However, the GfZK-2 functions differently with respect to the second paradigm of modernism, namely the mobilization of the gaze, which as-if berlinwien seeks to rigorously transpose to the 21st century. To the inhabitant of the 21st century, "the film" no longer unravels only as one moves through passages of spaces or lets the gaze roam over the ribbon windows, but also just as much through interaction with visual screens. Not only are the body and gaze fixed upon the screen in the collective black box of the cinema, but also in the private, everyday domain, while spatial sensation is temporalized in successions of image sequences. Similar to the way in which spatial experiences are layered in images, functions are not only accessible by following physical paths, but can be activated on visual surfaces or interfaces. The world appears on, and as, a display. And precisely this is what the GfZK-2 demonstrates. This also involves addressing the wall as the supporting structure or background of art. The technical structure, volume, and differing materialities of the walls are repeatedly left visible along the seams and edges of the sliding walls – not as a reference to their construction, but rather to the task and "activity" fulfilled by the walls, floor, and ceiling within the disposition of the exhibition. Many elements prove to be large sliding walls, by means of which the geometry, size, and order of the spaces can be changed. Movable in manifold ways, the display segments – as if on a three-dimensional image screen – can be rearranged in any number of new configurations. On this "screen," new correlations between gaze and projection, as well as alternative spatial solutions can be activated. Like the versatile operating system on the computer desktop, most of the spaces in the GfZK are not tied to a fixed program. A video screening room may transform from a black box to a vitrine, a gallery to a seminar room, the seminar room to a studio for artists in residence, and effortlessly back to an exhibition space.

This flexibility, which is naturally also economical by reducing the complicated reconstruction work in preparation for specific exhibitions, could easily drift to becoming a "redundant multifunctionalism." In this connection, the architects' impressive and somewhat confusing diagrams illustrating the building's possible spatial configurations and programmatic shifts seem to offer little help. The range of spatial possibilities is illustrated more appropriately by a video produced by as-if berlinwien for the exhibition *Ornament & Display*:[5] One can anticipate the atmosphere of the resulting spatial configurations, observing, from the fixed vantage point of an imaginary viewer, demonstrations of the sliding walls and textile partitions being moved back and forth by hand and locked into different positions. For flexible architecture is more than just a precise, functional instrument. Changing proportions and materials foster concentration in every specific situation, as nothing is suggestive of multifunctional arbitrariness. Alongside exposed concrete, glass, and cladding in various colors, unconventional materials, such as the rubber flooring found in sports complexes, occasionally crop up on the floors, ceilings, interior and exterior walls. From a distance, the partly rubber-clad outer walls can hardly be distinguished from basalt, which is widely used in traditional museums. Moving closer, the walls' monumental solemnity gives way to a sportive lightness. This is complemented by specially designed low-tech details, such as the mechanisms of the sliding elements and the slatted ventilation ducts.

Notwithstanding its partial roughness, the GfZK-2 is a noble space, indeed a museum. In spite of the institution's predilection for political discourse, both the client and the architects successfully avoided coquetting with the esthetic of the off-space. In fact, the differentiating esthetic of the surfaces deployed in the GfZK-2 is as distant from the sham neutrality of the "white cube" as it is from the quasi-naturalization of "critical display," which – characterized by the increased use of set pieces such as trestle tables and haulage pallets, and citing scaffolding and drywall – tacitly established itself during recent years. Quite contrary to this, the performativity of the GfZK-2 display structure exposes these unassuming conventions. Thus, marked by an "esthetic of anti-estheticism," the exhibition

5 *Ornament & Display*, curated by Angelika Fitz, kunsthaus muerz/steirischer herbst, 29. 10. 2005 – 26. 02. 2006

6 *Shrinking Cities – International Research*, KW Institute for Contemporary Art Berlin, 09. 04. 2004 – 11. 07. 2004; *Shrinking Cities 2 – Interventions*, curated by Philipp Oswalt, Barbara Steiner, Walter Prigge, and Nikolaus Kuhnert, GfZK Leipzig, 11. 26. 2005 – 01. 29. 2006

Shrinking Cities[6] worked well at the KW Institute for Contemporary Art in Berlin. The part of the exhibition shown in the GfZK-1 villa also diffused a discreet charm. In the context of the new building however, the same display appeared "demonstrative" – relinquishing its background function the display became an exhibit in its own right.

Nothing is safe in – or rather, from – this museum. The GfZK is a matrix of uncertainty, whose complex performativity offers resistance in many different directions, constantly guiding attention from the objects displayed to how they are displayed. The surfaces are already performative in multiple ways – as self-reflexive instruments of exhibition practice, as operative interfaces for programmatic shifts, and as atmospheric parameters. Therefore, this art space's nuanced esthetic is by no means mannerism. Or, as artist Olaf Nicolai writes in his essay Show Case, "Matters of form, mood, attitude and style are not luxurious little games with surfaces. They imply questions as to forms of organizing."[7] Given the current museum-building boom, these questions urgently need to be posited anew, if we are in future to demand more choice than is currently available between museums that are either amusement parks or sacral temples of art. The GfZK offers intelligent solutions to this dilemma.

Shrinking Cities 2

Curatorial team

**Nikolaus Kuhnert,
Philipp Oswalt,
Walter Prigge,
Barbara Steiner**

Assistant curators

**Friedrich von Borries,
Kathleen Liebold,
Heidi Stecker**

Opening

November 26, 2005

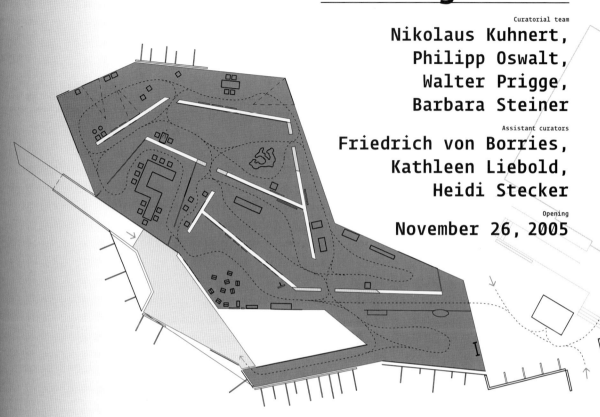

In addition, the display shells support the connections and interplay between the exhibition spaces, as some of them run from one area into the next, led by floor-level glass slits. The display shells create zones and define borders within the fluid space, making the dialog between architecture and exhibition design necessary.

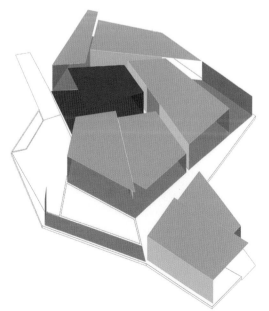

This exhibition presented concepts for action and intervention in shrinking cities that focused specifically on eastern Germany. It took place in the two buildings of the museum, the GfZK-1 and the GfZK-2. The thirty-five works ranged from artistic intercessions and self-empowerment projects through architectural, landscape, and media interventions to new legislative provisions and draft utopias; they were developed in close cooperation with local citizens, groups, and institutions. The projects were conceived by architects, designers, geographers, graphic designers, journalists, artists, landscape architects, local initiatives, philosophers, urban planners, political scientists, sociologists, and entrepreneurs from Denmark, Germany, Great Britain, Croatia, the Netherlands, Norway, Romania, Switzerland, Slovenia, and the United States. Alongside the newly developed projects, material on existing practices illustrated possibilities for action regarding the following issues: "negotiating inequality," "self-governance," "creating images," "organizing retreat," and "occupying space." The exhibition design reflected the topic of shrinkage: plywood panels covered the windows of both GfZK buildings; plastic sheets covered the rubber walls of the GfZK-2 and the café windows were painted white, while the ticket sales booth and wardrobe were installed in portakabins. From the street, the buildings looked abandoned – like many others in town. From the rear, however, it became apparent that the entire construction was meant to be a setting, which clearly showed its nature as a construction. Inside, movement through the building was blocked through the huge plywood constructions and scaffoldings that functioned as a means of displaying posters and texts. (Barbara Steiner)

The walls and ceilings of the display shells are made of lightly painted gypsum board with strong, visible edges measuring 2.5 centimeters. On the floor, they are defined by an epoxy resin coating of the same color, 4 millimeters higher than the adjacent floors, in order to emphasize the stage-like quality of these spaces, and to bring attention to the displays as a "physical layer," without producing a potentially hazardous step.

Fence between GfZK-1 and GfZK-2

– Fence built with twenty (1220 × 2440 × millimeters)
  plywood boards
– Supporting frame made of concrete blocks (existing
  fence block) and 4"/4" pillars strained to concrete block
– Gate supporting frame made by 2"/4" a regular stable
  door hinge
– Joints are bolted or screwed together
– Personal wagon dimension:
  half size of small container = 3010 × 2440 × 2440 millimeters
– Main intro sign frame made of concrete blocks and 4"/4"
  pillars strained to concrete block.
  Dimensions – Total height: 4200, Surface: 3660 × 2440
  millimeters

GfZK-2 / Façade

– Black plastic sheet (big rolls) roof dropping – held in
  place by sandbag and on front by used 2"/4" wood lath
– First window from left covered with 11/2 plywood board
  mounted on 11/2 / 2" skeleton frame facing window,
  reducing friction in oder to secure existing main façade
– The other windows smeared with *buttermilk*
– Black plastic sheet (big rolls) roof dropping – held in
  place by sandbag and on front by used 2"/4" wood lath

GfZK-2 / Ramp / Café Entrance

– Main bearing frame constructed with 4"/4" wood
  and 2"/7" wood.
– Pillars strained to ground with "horseshoe" metal
  fittings. Twelve × (1220 × 2440 millimeters) plywood
  boards needed for covering
– Joints are bolted or screwed together

Inside wall construction principle

– Tech info:
  2400 × 1200 millimeters plaster boards mounted on
  skeleton 1.5" × 2" wood lath
– Material info:
  For all indoor constructions GfZK1+2 (walls, tables,
  signs): 180 pieces. 4 meters (11/2 × 2")
  Forty pieces. plasterboard (1200 × 2400)
  Thirty pieces. plywood (1200 × 2400)

Additional material

– Tech info:
  Black & white plot is used for additional material in
  printform: 900 millimeters in width — perpetual length.
  Large images / wallpapers can be obtained with the use
  of additional columns of plotted matter.
  Mounted with colored tape.

The execution of the display shells
was a challenge, because wide-
stretching and all-encompassing
three-dimensional edges were
defined, built up on the rough work,
which was not cohesive at first. We
produced a large quantity of two-
dimensional detail drawings, but
these could only be communicated on
the construction site with additional
three-dimensional sketches.

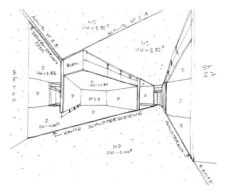

The material schedule of the display shells is supplemented in the design of the interior by the "non-display" materials – raw surfaces such as bare prefab concrete walls, cast cement floors, and drywall ceilings with rougher, light-gray plaster.

The choice of reinforced **concrete** as the material for the load-bearing **walls** only emerged in the course of the design process. Originally, we were imagining a temporary, light, raised pavilion, built to last for ten years, as a clad steel skeleton with many small steel feet and spot foundations. But the building ground proved to be extremely loamy and uncertain, laden with unknown remnants of the cellar of a former mansion, which would have made the spot foundation difficult. As a result, the structural design leaned towards a floating foundation with a reinforced concrete slab.

At the same time, the management of the GfZK was expressing the desire to be able to put more service load on the exhibition walls, which would not have been possible with a conventional skeleton. Meanwhile, a project manager who had been called in at the time questioned the estimated lifespan of the building: ten years for a temporary building was considered unfavorable, too long to deal with the restrictions of the temporary situation, but too brief to invest in a more long-lasting building with all the technical demands of a museum. The new estimated lifespan was set for twenty-plus years. Thus we moved from a skeleton structure to a cast concrete floor plate and supporting walls.

The concrete walls are left visible where no display shells cover them. We wanted them to be precisely made and seamless, but capable of being incorporated into the exhibition

design as surfaces to be exhibited on, leaving traces of usage instead of being seen as sacred fetish objects. We ultimately decided on prefabricated walls measuring up to 12 × 4 meters with an individual weight of up to thirty-six tons, because the quality of precast concrete in this region is substantially higher at the same cost as cast-in-place concrete. This also allowed the construction to be conducted during the winter. The walls were positioned in one working day in February with a 300-ton crane.

▷▷ 132

Title
Spermanent Instability

Artist
Monica Bonvicini

Curator
Ilina Koralova

Opening
February 25, 2006

Topping out ceremony,
march 2004

The critical examination of the subject's physical and intellectual relationship to his/her constructed surroundings plays an important role in
Monica Bonvicini's artistic practice. Furthermore, she explicitly refers
to the relationship of control and oppression to spatial dominance and
spatial restrictions by using various strategies – from subtle irony
through destruction to the use of gestures with a sadomasochistic charge.
The artist permanently challenges common, historically accepted norms and
conventions such as social marginalization and intolerance, or the role
of museums and art institutions for society, in particular. In Monica
Bonvicini's works, the architectural space loses its ideal conception,
authority, and claims for eternity, and stands in contrast to images of
decay, despair, and melancholy. Destructive sexual power, love and hate,
dominance and deliverance perforate – if not dissolve – the very foundation
of supposedly fixed definitions about (post-)modern society. (Ilina Koralova)

Construction Planning

With only a limited budget and a very short construction period at our disposal, a "dynamic spatial system" was to be designed and constructed. The numerous sliding walls, devised to ensure maximum functional flexibility, were a predominant feature of the building. The preliminary planning phase was extensive and closely linked with the activities of the other planners. Optimal solutions could thus only be found with perseverance and lateral thinking.

The construction site presented an unexpected challenge: a plot of poor soil with low load-bearing capacity with the basement of a villa destroyed during the war and filled with packed rubble, now protruding into the planned floor area of the new exhibition building, accounted for considerably unfavorable cohesion conditions, in view of the intended

Steiner   What were the first things that crossed your mind for your exhibition in the GfZK-2?

Bonvicini   The first thing I remember were the foundations of the building, which were all I could see upon my first visit to Leipzig. The building's dimensions were easily discernible through the snow; that was actually very inspiring. I was able to imagine what the whole thing was going to turn into – no walls to obstruct a virtual stroll through the edifice foundations. When I received the architectural plans for the building, I immediately thought that it would not be easy to exhibit in this building. I still think that it is rather difficult for sculptures and installations, as the architecture itself is already quite installational. The building does not really have one proper large room, the floor is painted in different colors, the ceilings are not that high, and the walls not really straight. Indeed, it is not the "white cube" whereby the standard, classic "white cube" is sometimes not such a bad idea for sculpture. The new building of the GfZK quickly makes one feel somewhat displaced, since it is all so "crooked" – that is, literally, crooked … I quickly realized that I did not want to exhibit sculpture.

Steiner   You decided upon drawings.

Bonvicini   Yes, drawings and other works. The exhibition views help to illustrate the effect of the drawings in the room. They look a little like stamps and, thus, almost make the architecture function like a model.

Steiner   Here, the question of scale arises. The drawings go beyond or explode the architecture.

Bonvicini   Standing in this central room or space, you got a true feel for its size. At the same time, it resembled a model room: the perspective, the sharp vanishing points … As you probably remember, it was not easy to design the room like that. We had to erect a wall, in order to limit the space and to give it a focus; that was essential and actually already visible from the plans. Back then, we spoke about the fact that the works go beyond the classical drawing in their size and in the width of their frames; they become objects, receive a body … they are, of course, quite heavy.

Steiner   One might also say that the drawings resisted the architecture. Yet this was due not only to the drawings, but also to their presentation.

Bonvicini   Some of the pictures were hung, others simply lay on the floor and leaned against the wall. I think that this even helped to highlight the existing architecture … I wanted to leave the architecture just like it was although I naturally felt the need, as it were, to correct it. Personally, I think that it is important to deal with spaces and to see what a space is built for, why and how my works can find

"floating" raft foundation. The latter was to consist of a load-bearing base slab on a fortified bed of compacted gravel.

Therefore, it was crucial to devise a cost-effective alternative for a suitable foundation, in order to avoid deformations due to the inconsistent soil conditions of the building plot, which could potentially damage the structural shell. As soil investigations revealed that strata with a potential carrying capacity were only to be found at a depth of seven meters

a place in them. If you construct a building like this one, you probably already have an idea at the back of your mind about the sort of art that you're going to exhibit in it.

Steiner No, I didn't. I am more interested in how artists work with the space they are given. Of course, I also ask myself: what can it be used for? The building and its functions still surprise me today.

Bonvicini Well, the building is not necessarily made for classical painting. It would be difficult for visitors of such an exhibition to forget the open crack in the wall while contemplating a Vermeer ... Indeed, it is a rather particular building that presents itself very strongly.

Steiner You just said that you wanted to leave the architecture like it was: that is both true and not quite true. Even though you did not convert anything, I believe your exhibition nevertheless challenged the architecture. This unmitigated engagement with space and with what it represents is something that permeates your works as a whole. One does not have to rebuild anything – that is far too obvious, too facile a thought perhaps.

Bonvicini The art critic Harald Fricke once said something very interesting and incisive about my works, something along the lines that they influence one's perception and recollection of the rooms in which they are exhibited to such an extent that the room is experienced differently

below ground level, we chose a foundation supported by compacted settlement-reducing piles as the most economical solution. In cohesive soil resistant to dynamic compaction, vibrating machinery was used to create a hollow shaft with a diameter of sixty centimeters in the ground, which was simultaneously filled with coarse material.

The reinforced concrete base slab with a thickness of thirty centimeters fulfills various functions. Firstly, suspended between single support points, the

slab is designed to transmit the traffic loads equally to the gravel friction piles. Secondly, the cantilevered base slab above the edifice's circumferential thermal barrier makes the building appear to hover above the ground. Applying the principle of concrete core conditioning, the concrete base slab is fitted with heating pipes embedded between its upper and lower reinforcement layers, thus serving as the building's underfloor heating system.

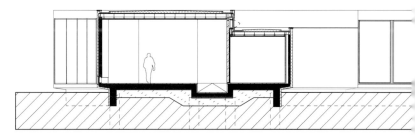

Since the load-bearing walls had to satisfy a series of requirements – such as allowing for an effortless securing of heavy artworks, the demand for durable multipurpose surfaces, and the idea of prefabricated component construction – we selected prefab reinforced concrete wall panels early on as a viable solution.

Some of the walls are not mounted directly on the base slab, but rather above "light slits" with a height of forty centimeters. These were designed as two-point self-supporting shear walls. The dimensions of the prefab concrete wall components remaining visible measure a maximum of 3.6 × 12.0 meters, with a wall thickness of a mere twelve centimeters. As three of the loads had to be channeled to the foundation through two support points consisting of flat vertical steel girders with a dimension of 14 × 3 centimeters, the walls had to be paneled in an oblique-angled manner. A considerable number of steel fittings had to be inserted along the walls' upper rims, on which the roof is mounted – no ordinary challenge for the design and manufacture of the prefabricated reinforced concrete components. The upper corners of the reinforced concrete walls are fastened to welded steel girders – the primary construct supporting roof slabs and fastening the upper edges of the walls – following the staggered roofline and rails of the interior sliding walls. After installing the steel girder framework, the oblique-angled, tiered structure of the roof was clearly visible. Due to

afterwards. I think he was referring to the installation *Never Again* in Berlin's museum, the Hamburger Bahnhof. There, too, I left the architecture like it was, but then again of course I didn't. When I say "left the architecture like it was," I mean that I am not using my works to manipulate the architecture, hide it, or even make it disappear. I believe that the need to leave something as it is primarily applies to rooms which, through their exhibition history or their claim to the artistic display, I consider unpleasant or unsuitable. With *Never Again*, for example, I clearly sought to express this discomfort about the room that was allocated to me, with its high ceilings and inelegant proportions.

Steiner   In the Hamburger Bahnhof exhibition, the room itself was a subject, because your installation made it impossible to simply cross it.

Bonvicini   Yes, I have interesting photos of the vernissage showing the discomfort that *Never Again* created within the space.

All the visitors seemed to be constricted in the entrance of the room and needed a few minutes to overcome their insecurity and dare to enter the room. I found your building in Leipzig highly "designed." Do you remember how much the lights annoyed me, because they were so present …

Steiner   Perhaps this was the reason for the exhibition's success, no? I found it exciting that the lights – or, rather, the light bands – could be seen reflected on the glass surfaces of the drawings so that parts of the architecture visually entered into the drawings. At the same time, the drawings – the text and image fragments – established connections to their surroundings. It was impossible not to make these connections in both directions. No matter how problematic the situation, something very productive ultimately results.

Incidentally, I once showed photos of your exhibition at a lecture. A lighting specialist in the audience was extremely vexed by the reflections on the glass surfaces. He said, roughly: "What you are showing are extraordinary drawings, but the lights can be seen reflected in the glass; did you know that this can be avoided today?" I personally find these disruptions, generated by means of the architecture, significant. It is not gratuitous that they took place – in other words, it is not a design error. Disruptions deter the phantasm of an ideality (in whichever form) from emerging. As for us, we should ask: what is actually ideal for the presentation of art? And above all: does this ideal even exist?

Bonvicini   Challenges are always welcome. From my point of view, the extent to which the works allow themselves to be influenced by the surrounding space is always more

---

the polygonal configuration of beams and bracing walls on the floor plan, we were able to avoid a plate roof construction.

Unlike the comparatively straight-forward choice for the load-bearing walls, constructing an "optimal roof" was far more complicated. Due to the staggered heights of the individual roof surfaces, it was necessary to employ a statically disadvantageous system of single-span girders as the load-bearing roof support compo-nents. We had to consider the higher

interesting – that is, whether or not it makes sense to work in a site-specific manner. Would it be possible to exhibit a site-specific work elsewhere? That is a question with which I have always been preoccupied. I have several works that have different effects according to where they are exhibited. In fact, they are always new works somehow "contaminated" by earlier exhibition sites, contexts, and situations …

Steiner The model-like appearance of the central space in our building was taken up again by your small glass cube with the neon lights entitled *White*. It seemed to resemble an architecture model itself.

Bonvicini *White* was a little lost in the room, framed by a wider glass vitrine – namely, the entrance area of the building. By the way, I also visited the architects in Berlin, which was very interesting, although I felt that the architects' interests stood in conflict with the needs of the artists.

Steiner Yes, that's right, one cannot simply just exhibit; but, then again, where is that possible? I think that we need to respond to the architecture in whichever way. The "white cube" only seemingly makes it easier; we are very familiar with this model, as most of us were socially brought up with it. I am interested in different modes of exhibiting. We are lucky insofar as recourse can be made

to two models – the villa and the new building. I believe that you have really engaged with the architecture. I would even say: you have resisted it.

Bonvicini I think that this is inevitable when one works in such an installational way as I do. What does "resistance" mean? The series of large-format drawings, for instance, evolved from the question concerning the idea and experience of revolt, and how this urge for revolt can be expressed from a feminine point of view. The quotations that can be seen in almost all of the drawings come from three female authors who have explored this theme in their poems, essays, or books. This can be interpreted in the context of the building's architecture. The three smaller drawings that share the space with *White*, by contrast, cite Le Corbusier who determined the ideal ceiling height using the yardstick of a man with an outstretched hand. These drawings show three construction workers with their hands in their pockets (a very "enthralling" motif …) – an expression of passivity and a pose of self-satisfaction.

Steiner Your deep interest in feminism weaves itself through all your works.

Bonvicini Recently I was invited to a symposium on feminism – in Spain. There was lots of avid discussion, which at times also became very emotional … The art

---

loads resulting from the building's integrated housing technology and roof terrace, as well as the changing loads caused by positional variants of the sliding walls, in order to ensure a smooth operation of the suspended sliding walls, and to keep the deflection resulting from these loads down to a minimum. The most economical solution proved to be mounting prefabricated rib panels (Kerto plywood boards laminated with shear strength onto lumber beams) with a breadth of up to

seven meters on the steel girders and reinforced concrete walls. The oblique-angled prefab rib panels had to fulfill static stability and a flush fit. However, we also had to adjust the geometry of the lumber beams to the construction demands of the sliding wall mounts as well as the omni-axial grid of the ceiling light apertures. The sliding walls are individually suspended from two mounting points, that is, roller devices, in response to potential deformations caused by roof elasticity,

thus ensuring static stability and consistency of pressures exerted on the mounts during sliding. The underlying truss frames of the sliding walls were custom-made; depending on the dimensions of the respective sliding wall, these are constructed of rectangular steel tubing or timber. The truss frames of the larger walls – of which the largest, weighing approximately one ton, measures 3.8 × 10.0 meters – were assembled on site and aligned using turnbuckles upon suspension from the rails. Once suspended, the world is more positive and more open to women than it used to be, but there is still a lot to be done in this respect. For instance, it is often said that my works are aggressive. I am not sure that this precise word would be used if I were a man. Of course, this is mere speculation, but I sometimes find it a little too facile to pigeonhole particular works by female artists as representing those of the "angry" or "aggressive woman." I interpret my works in this context rather more as a recurrent critique of institutions. For me, incidentally, other works of art are aggressive – such as bad painting.

Steiner I find it interesting that your works always show a perspective; in my eyes, they are hardly destructive!

Bonvicini Indeed, one wants to create something by destroying something else! Or as I often say: "no construction without destruction."

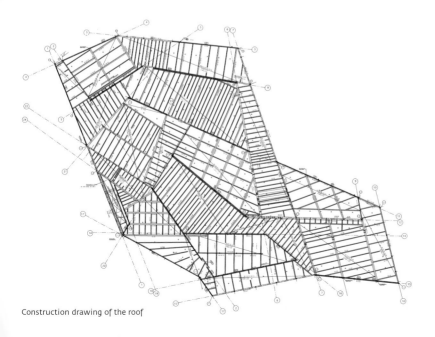

Construction drawing of the roof

walls were paneled with composite wood boards and their surfaces were finished. As several of the sliding walls were designed with sections that can be rotated vertically to create full height apertures, we had to take into account the resulting loads when planning the walls' underlying framework and their suspension from the joisted ceiling plates.

Finally, with regard to the building's outer window system, the glass-bearing supporting struts of the extensive glass façade also carry the roof loads in an unusual system of load interaction and distribution. This is possible solely on account of the relatively low roof load, and the fact that the supporting girders are restrained in the base slab.

The bottom of the load-bearing steel façade frame, including power supply outlets

An Ambiguous Beginning

Following the entire construction process of the new GfZK building – from the first concepts and architectural models to its inauguration in 2004 – I was initially, as paradoxical as it may sound, primarily aware of its limitations. In my little experience with museum architecture at the time, I was struck by the gray color of the walls, the lack of strictly rectangular and clearly defined spaces, and thus of a clear *parcours*. Strangely enough, my impressions were also shared by some of the artists, despite the fact that (or rather precisely because) their artistic practices involved a critique of the classical exhibition space, the "white cube." It took some time observing, reflecting, and simply "exploring" the spaces to get acquainted with them. The sense of being limited was gradually replaced by the excitement of discovering new possibilities.

The first time I had to deal with the entire space of the new building of the GfZK was in 2005 when I curated two exhibitions at the same time: the group show called *Untitled (City IV)* and the solo exhibition by Sean Snyder. Both were part of the *Heimat Moderne* project (Heimat Modernism), which addressed the legacy of modern socialist architecture, its impact on and consequences for the city of Leipzig – a theme that marked the GfZK's activities throughout the year. Although the group exhibition as well as Sean Snyder's presentation took the aforementioned issue as a starting point, the projects presented by the participating artists reached beyond the local context. The social and related architectural history, including the contemporary urban development of Leipzig, was taken as a point of departure. The city is in constant flux and change; it is a place where different tensions, ideologies, and desires clash, thus producing new spaces for negotiation on the subject of its future. The artists invited for *Untitled (City IV)* – Ebru Özseçen, Matthijs de Bruijne, Tilo Schulz, and Wolfgang Thaler – chose Leipzig as a site for their reflections on the topic. In the works shown, a somewhat emotional approach prevailed over detached scientific analysis, as the individual depictions charged concrete locations with metaphorical meaning.

Sean Snyder's projects explore aspects of the urban space and architecture as signs of economic and political structures. At the center of Snyder's solo exhibition was an analysis of visual perception. It showed how a picture's meaning can change over the course of a process of mediation and communication, in which various modes of technical reproduction are applied. The media as symptoms of cultural domination were put on display. Although both exhibitions were related by means of political and economic concerns manifest in the art works themselves, I was still dealing with two different spatial

1 Due to the specificity of the architecture, the "mediated"
gaze, as well as the mirror-effect multiplying certain
objects on display, have often been thematized in exhibitions in the new building of the GfZK ever since.

concepts that had to be presented within the architectural premises of the new GfZK building.

As a curator, I tend to compare every exhibition space either to a blank sheet of paper or a stage. The exhibition shown there is a "story" or narrative that the artists and the curator "write" together – and it can be written anew each and every time. As a stage, it allows for permanent change through its particular constructive elements or in the way that it functions as the backdrop for each respective exhibition. I used the architecture of the GfZK as a "tool" to connect the two presentations, allowing me, as it were, to "enframe" them.

I imagined that the building was a compressed model of a city or, more precisely, the core of a city, its historical center (traces of which are still found in many European cities) and the "ring road" surrounding the center that often follows the outlines of the old defensive moat. Sean Snyder's works were presented in the outermost area of the building premises, reminding me of a city ring. All spaces opened to the street and park, respectively. The fact that the projects presented by the artist could be seen from outside through the building's large windows added a new dimension to the perception of his works. The glass became a "membrane" – a physical equivalent of the invisible (ideological) lens through which the media see and make us see the world. Indeed, the glass has the double function of allowing the gaze to penetrate the building, but also – by means of a mirror effect – to obstruct it or give only a limited, often distorted idea of what is taking place inside.[1]

The "city center" – namely, the inner part of the exhibition spaces – was at the disposal of the four artists of the group show. By means of the sliding wall, which closed and either partly or completely opened spaces, I was able to create a circuit that evoked the impression of discovering a city when visiting it for the first time. The works of each of the artists represented different "sites." The symbolic "journey" started with the urban structure perceived by the stranger arriving in a new place. It essentially consists of horizontals and verticals. This simple structure was Tilo Schulz's starting point for developing his modular system, *City Fear/Origami Version (Module 1–4)*, which he integrated into the architectural structure of the GfZK-2. The second "station" was the fictitious city of *Mep'yuk* created by the photographer Wolfgang Thaler. It is constructed of various examples of modern and postmodern architecture – or, more precisely, of the interiors of public buildings. However,

119 ◻▷

We wanted to avoid visible heating elements in the exhibition area. The mechanical engineer suggested **core heating**, which functions like floor heating but is installed directly in the reinforced concrete floor slab, capital-izing on its heat storage capacity.

Various possibilities for the **power supply** were considered and discussed with the client. The display surfaces on the floors, walls, and ceilings were to stay free of distracting technical components. Floor tanks seemed too expensive, inflexible, and complicated to use. The side edges of the exhibition walls and hidden horizontal surfaces were equipped with electrical outlets, and the light fixtures on the ceilings have additional outlets.

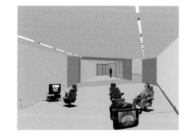

Thaler's photographic series rarely reveals the actual places where the pictures were taken, but is rather an observation on the uniformity and anonymity of contemporary architecture under the ideological pressure of the globalized world. Globalization, and its consequences for the organization of life, in general, was also the topic in Matthijs de Brujine's research project on real places in Leipzig and Buenos Aires. It provided information on sites where the "general plan" of socialism as well as capitalism had failed (*A Place I Dislike*). The journey through the exhibition came to an end in the projection room transformed by Ebru Özseçen into a "video lounge." The idea was to recreate the atmosphere of a nightclub where official and underground cultures are often seen to intermingle. This is the place in which the "vertical" structure of a city – that of regulations, as well as economic and political power – meets its "horizontal" counterpart – that of chaotic, unregulated growth. The installation entitled *City* consisted of armchairs upholstered in red velvet and designed by the artist, alluding to the futuristic interior design of the 1970s. The video projection – the insides of computers and PCBs transformed into a Sci-Fi cityscape through camera close-ups – evoked the anti-utopian vision of Ridley Scott's *Blade Runner*.

I understand the act of curating an exhibition as a two-phase process. The first phase is one of intensive communication between the artists and curator, in which initial thoughts take shape, new ideas are born, and others have to be sacrificed. Alternative solutions are thereby taken into consideration alongside a growing awareness of certain spatial and budgetary limitations. I have always been fascinated by the way in which an abstract thought becomes a "text" (to come back to the metaphor of the exhibition as a form of narration), and how artists are capable of unfolding the manifold layers of that text. The second phase concerns the mediation of the project to the public, which I regard as the curator's main responsibility: he or she must negotiate the space and its potential with the artists, displaying the works of art in such a way that they do not lose their complexity. And, at the same time, the curator must link and create associations between them so that the narrative that ensues as a result of the arrangement becomes readable for the visitors.

Early in the design phase, we began to develop a **lighting concept** together with the Berlin-based lighting design company, Studio Dinnebier. The spatial concept required a flexible lighting system that could support the different space configurations and be variable in itself in order to be able to adapt to different exhibition requirements. At the same time, the connected surfaces of the display shells should not be disturbed.

A lighting system was developed that features linear light fixtures along the walls equipped with dimmable fluorescent tubes inserted into small luminary mounting points that can be rotated in every possible direction. Each fixture can also be replaced by light spots or totally removed.

▷▷ 161

Title

Bad Female Painters Are the Better Artists

Artist

Anna Meyer

Curator

Barbara Steiner

Opening

November 28, 2006

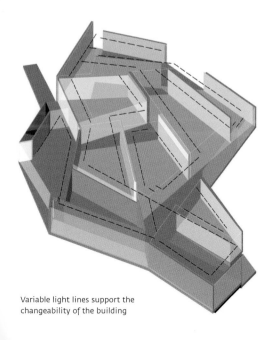

Variable light lines support the
changeability of the building

Anna Meyer's exhibition entitled Bad Female Painters Are the Better Artists, united paintings, models, and applied art. Images of decaying industrial buildings, of leisure parks, pictures of friends and role models, of glittering metropolises, shopping centers, homeless people, modern and traditional nomads, and, time and again, images of the artist herself are seen juxtaposed in single pictures and in work series. The use of advertising motifs, lyrics, Meyer's own invented words, and pictures as well as autobiographical elements produce hybrid pictures in which texts or individual words, torn out of their context, are placed in contrast to the subjects or are used to create paradoxes: "better is worse," "now is then," "right is wrong." The exhibition reflects Meyer's artistic approach of making themes, styles, and attitudes clash. The architecture was considered intrinsic to the entire concept. The transparent screens that Meyer painted blocked one of the spaces visually; another space offered a path through paintings spanned between two poles. In between these, there were models shown on pedestals. The models consisted of discarded cell phones, empty perfume bottles, and toy figures, which had all been painted over and resembled models of cities. Painted, small-sized acrylic panels were displayed on the floor in one of the central spaces, simply fixed by glass holders. The visitors had to move carefully so as not to destroy the setting. Moreover, the "glass box" in the building was transformed into a shop display featuring products of the collaboration between Anna Meyer, the artist, and Edwina Hörl, the fashion designer. However, it was not only art and fashion that merged, but also the painted screens, garments, as well as the surrounding space. Large paintings of street scenes from various cities were shown in the building's outer areas, thus referring to city life. The exhibition extended to the café facing the street. Again, the painted scenes were mirrored by the street life outside. Consequently, the external walls were used for Anna Meyer's large-scale paintings, too. (Barbara Steiner)

The Lighting System

The fact that the lighting design was considered unusually early on during planning allowed us to devise a lighting system for the GFZK-2, which closely responds to the specific demands of the architecture and its occupants.

We began the project by visiting a number of galleries in Berlin with the client and the architects. Based on these visits, the museum's specific demands clarified, and possible lighting concepts with directional ambient lighting were discussed. Barbara Steiner and the architects came to a clear decision: dimmable, fluorescent tubular lights were chosen to ensure consistent illuminance in all areas of the building. Additionally, the fluorescent tubes were to be optionally replaced with spotlights to accentuate individual objects. Conventional track lighting systems were ruled out due to the dominance

My work focuses on the inversion and interaction of space and concepts, the play with spatial perception, and an idea of space that is contingent upon it. For my exhibition, I chose a spatial concept that I called *Outside is Inside – Inside is Outside*: the inner walls of the new building of the GfZK were turned outwards, which subsequently forced the outside to shift inwards. Initially, this was nothing but the reversal of the functions of familiar spatial elements: the actual exhibits – the pictures – were hung on the building's outer walls, in the glass corridors, and in the rooms themselves on pillars or hanging freely from the ceiling. The centerpiece of the exhibition was a glass cube – often used as a "black box" to show films – in which, like in an inaccessible shop window or an aquarium, Edwina Hörl's dresses and my pictures were suspended on rubber springs that hung from the ceiling. The actual walls of the building remained empty.

Instead of disappearing, however, these otherwise relatively inconspicuous aspects of the room moved into the foreground: the walls themselves were exhibited.

of the slots in the ceiling. Forwarded by the architects, the concept of treating the walls, ceiling, and floors equally was to be emphasized by avoiding or reducing visible fittings, as well as by minimizing the distance between luminaire and ceiling. This led to our designing a customized lighting system, which, with regard to the museum's schedule of changing temporary exhibitions, had to be flexible and easy to operate.

The implemented light design, derived from lighting schemes

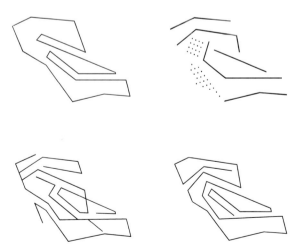

Early design stage: variation of exemplary light configurations

traditionally utilized in museums, employs luminaires positioned along the edges of the spaces. Each individual luminaire, mounted to the suspended ceiling at one point only via a metal shaft, can be turned or dismounted according to the different spatial configurations. Running parallel to the walls, the resulting circumferential rows of lights may variously emphasize closed spaces or create connecting lines between the individual galleries thus marking the building's open-plan layout.

Depending on the position of the sliding walls, the resulting rows of lights can be adjusted to delineate different circuits through the building. The recurring elements of the ceiling lights afford the viewer a sense of orientation and proportion within the building. Individual luminaires can be rotated horizontally into a position at right angles to the direction of movement, to thus interrupt the dynamic of continuing lines. If no lighting is required in one of the galleries, for the purpose of a

At the same time, the reversal of inner and outer also influenced the differentiation of work and architecture; in other words, the boundary between art and exhibition area began to dissolve.

The way in which I hung the works heightened the effect of a smooth transition between the rooms – that of the "sliding-glass-door-architecture" intrinsic to the building. I wanted it to emphasize the sheer permeability of the architectural space, both designed and designable, as well as its diversity of perspectives and visual correlations. The non-rectangular inner rooms proved to be ideal for my see-through transparencies and Plexiglas images, thus enhancing the transparency that, in my eyes, characterizes the building.

Following a spiral-like path through the building, exhibition visitors were led to the works; starting from the outer walls, they moved through the middle area of the glass corridors to the inside. However, the innermost area was itself no longer accessible, which not only influenced the way in which the art works were perceived – unattainable, they naturally aroused even more interest – but also made the path taken through the building more conscious, yet again drawing attention to the idea of space. In this way, a particular dialog emerged between my work and the architecture, as well as among the works themselves.

This nuanced method of arranging and hanging the works, and the prospects it offered, came to me simply: it was the first idea I had when I saw the building. Paradoxically, for me it is the ideal architecture, precisely as it does not follow the concept of the "white cube": it touches upon it, dismantles it, and thereby opens up an entirely different, highly innovative container that addresses the dissolution of the "white cube," rather than historicizing it. As a result, the architecture gives my painting exactly what the latter can and seeks to make use of.

screening for instance, the luminaires can be removed altogether so as not to remain in the space in the off state. The luminaire system comprises a flush mount ceiling fixture, the base plate of which is fastened to the supporting frame of the suspended ceiling, and pluggable fluorescent tubes and spotlights. The mandatory emergency lights consist of three LEDs respectively, mounted into the luminaire mounting point behind a ring of matte finished plexiglas. The dimmable fluorescent tube lights consist of a vertical housing of aluminum and a luminous tube of translucent plastic.

In order not to interrupt the linear arrangement of ceiling lights throughout the space and to ensure omnidirectional light emission, the electronic components necessary for operation are not mounted in line to the luminous tubes, but rather concealed within the vertical housing of each individual luminaire. The space between the light tubes and the ceiling – besides being beneficial in terms of light distribution – serves to emphasize the disconnectedness of the lighting from the architecture. To ensure that the distance between lamp and ceiling is not too large, the ballasts are recessed into the ceiling, extending in as far as the timber framework. Since the spacing between the timber beams is very small, the precise positions of the lamps had to be verified by the structural engineer. In addition, mechanically swivelable reflectors made of perforated metal can be mounted

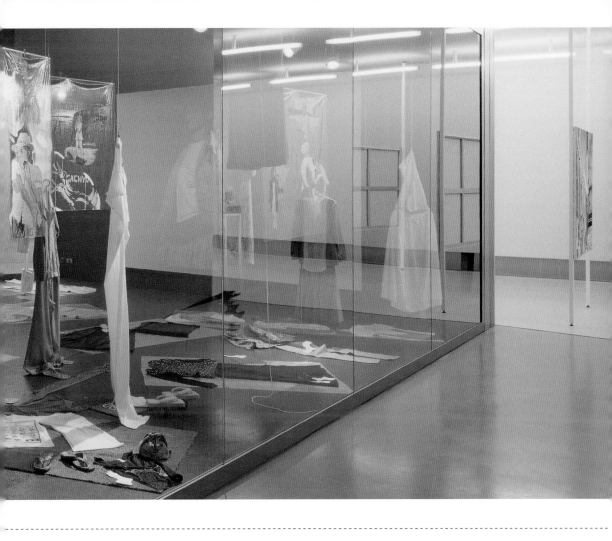

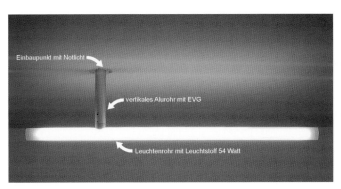

Einbaupunkt mit Notlicht

vertikales Alurohr mit EVG

Leuchtenrohr mit Leuchtstoff 54 Watt

LED - Notlicht

Dimmung /Scala

Drehgelenk

Steckdose

Dimmung im Kühlraster

on the light tubes – for instance to reduce ceiling glare.

Given that emergency exit routes out of the building may vary according to the different spatial configurations due to the positions of the sliding walls, an adaptable signage system was specially devised in collaboration with the fire department. The emergency exit lights consist of removable Plexiglas panes on which the emergency symbol is printed. The relevant sign can be removed or replaced as required.

Besides providing light, the luminaires also have incorporated power supply outlets (for instance, for video installations) so that the deployment of floor sockets could be avoided. We were thus able to install the entire power supply circuit in the suspended ceiling. While serving to reduce costs, this was also beneficial to implementing the guiding concept – namely to keep surfaces free of visible switches and sockets. At every alternate mounting point, a power outlet integrated in the luminaire's

Title
162 out of 172 Houses Are on the High Street …

Artist
Sofie Thorsen

Curator
Julia Schäfer

Opening
September 17, 2005

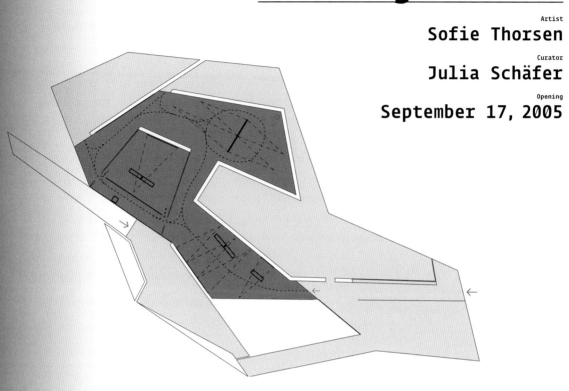

Plexiglas cover supplies electric current. This is also useful in the café, which is refurbished at regular intervals based on the designs of invited artists. If the light tubes need to be replaced with other types of luminaire, current can be drawn from the mounting points by means of the appropriate adapters provided. If no light tubes or spotlights are required, anodized aluminum caps are used to conceal the ceiling mounting points. During planning, the idea of a simple light-emitting tube evolved into a custom-built luminaire whose components are mainly concealed in the suspended ceiling. We commissioned the construction of a preliminary model to test the necessary specifications for technical operation and design before putting the appliance out to tender. To avoid subsequent obligations we made sure to select a "neutral" supplier (not one of the companies invited to tender) for the construction of the prototype. Thus, the sample luminaire could be transferred to the commissioned firm for use as a prototype for production. Due to the technical complexity of this customized unit, potential bidders were limited in number: many of the manufacturers who had been enthusiastic at a preliminary stage did not submit quotes upon tender. After the parties involved agreed to simplify the design somewhat and to actively seek potential small manufacturers, we were able to find a supplier willing to produce the luminaires within the predetermined cost limit. Ultimately, the company Lichtbau

For several years, Sofie Thorsen's drawings and slide series with explana-
tory audio texts have been exploring subjects such as dwelling, the influence of tourism on established village structures, and the formal appearance of detached houses and housing estates in new or older villages.
Indeed, the village is the subject of an entire artistic series, in which
it represents a metaphor for the living conditions and social structures
within particular dimensions and parameters. Local differences are the
result of the inclusion of traditional construction styles and materials
that function as signifiers for the buildings' users. Past and present,
reality and fiction play an essential role in all of Thorsen's projects:
what was, what is, what has changed, and what may happen? In the course
of the artist's investigations, fictional elements increasingly enter her
works. The exhibition conceived for the GfZK communicated Thorsen's view
of the phenomenon of the village since 2001. It achieved this in several
chapters and from different perspectives, making use of a variety of media.
According to context, various aspects of Thorsen's work on this subject
were illuminated, and yet all the individual projects continued to relate
to one another; this relationship was underscored through visual axes and
contrasting "chapter pairs." The exhibition was planned in response to the
architecture of the GfZK-2 and its possibilities in underlining a sense of
thematic overlapping within the works themselves. (Julia Schäfer)

from Berlin was commissioned.
The final specifications of the
luminaire were determined on the
basis of a second sample luminaire.
Built by the manufacturer, this was
further improved to the ends of
optimal clarity and practicality, so
that the final version combining
minimalist design and functional
complexity could be delivered.

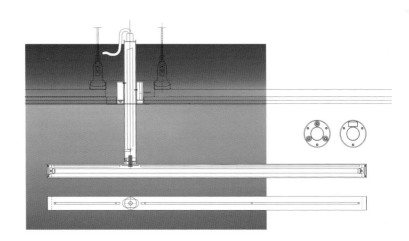

About two years prior to my exhibition, *162 out of 172 Houses Are on the High Street* ..., in the new building of the GfZK in September 2005, I met with Julia Schäfer in Vienna, who was in charge of curating the exhibition. The building was still under construction, but we both knew the general concept of the ground plan – Julia, of course, better than I did from passing by the construction site every day. Julia had unfortunately forgotten the floor plans of the building in Leipzig, but she quickly produced a hand-drawn sketch that successfully showed the entrance to the building and its front area. However, the further the illustration focused on the rear section of the house, the more ambiguous it

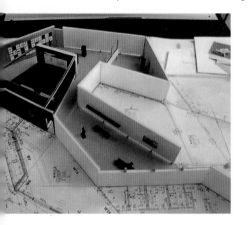

became. The back of the building resembled a white patch – none of us were sure where the walls would be, and, even less, which of them were or were not to be mobile. This was perhaps the first sign that the architecture seemed to demand a different form of analysis. It became clear that we would not be able to work according to the usual strategy of placing works of art into an exhibition space, some variation of the "white cube," which undoubtedly prompted hitherto known responses. Indeed, it became apparent that the way to figure out the building's possibilities and limitations would be through working with it, and that it would not be easy to ascertain how the architecture truly functioned.

I was fortunate to witness several shows in the new building, but obviously never in the form I would be exhibiting in myself, as every show was different. Julia and I discussed the different spatial options at great length, talking about the qualities of the different spaces, possible choreographies and relations to other exhibitions held at the same time, as well as pragmatic questions such as the prospect of darkening the exhibition space. We built a simple model to help us decide which spaces to use, and I later built a more detailed one for the exhibition itself. The models became the site where most of the decisions about the layout of the exhibition were made, and building them

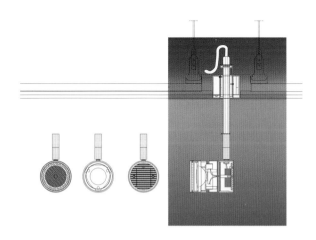

certainly helped me to understand how the architectural spaces worked.

Thinking about the exhibition in the new GfZK building actually helps to draw parallels to the works I showed there together for the first time: a series of pieces, both individual and very different, produced over the course of the four previous years. All worked within the same, clearly defined framework, since they addressed the motif of the village – both an architectural and social space – as a site of desires and projected narrative; certain elements kept reappearing in the works such as the landscape, the house, and its façade. The pieces were closely connected on a formal level. The majority were slide or video projections, and I liked to think of them functioning as one large ensemble in the show.

In that sense, the architecture became a veritable gift once I had figured out how it worked. The impossibility of separating the individual works, the continuation of the landscape-style orientation of the pieces in the horizontal layout of the exhibition, and the odd angles, which promoted views and relations between the pieces, all productively contributed to the dynamics of the exhibition. We decided to increase the dialog between the works by taking down the curtain in the cinema; this enabled more views across the exhibition through the

Construction Management

In order to assess a construction project, ideally it should fulfill three criteria upon completion: firstly, the acknowledged quality of its architectural design and implementation; secondly, budget compliance; lastly, construction schedule compliance. By some unwritten law however, in practice most projects only ever really fulfill two of these criteria. Observing the completion deadline and budget can often be detrimental to the quality of construction. High construction performance, though remaining within budget, often involves exceeding the completion deadline. And observing the deadline while simultaneously ensuring a high quality of construction generally causes construction costs to rapidly increase.

With regard to the GfZK-2 this rule proved true again: we were able to

remain within the construction cost limit computed and specified at the start of the project in 2002 – and a total of four prominent prizes and awards certify the quality of the architectural design. But admittedly, we had to slightly exceed the construction deadline.

The design of the GfZK-2 stood for uncompromisingly cutting-edge architecture – that was one of the challenges. The other challenge was the tight budget – for a technically full-fledged museum building – of EUR 1,800 net per square meter of gross floor area. In what was a truly uncommon experience, each of the participating parties responded to these basic conditions by seeing itself as part of a greater whole and by acting accordingly. Everyone – from the client, her representatives and consultants, to the architects, the architects in charge, specialized planners/designers, expert advisors, and executing companies – actively communicated with one another thus dissolving divisions common within the construction industry. The project manager continually administered planning and implementation. The architects, specialized planners and we, the architects in charge, all brought our experience to bear in the development and realization of the project in a way exceeding what is customary in terms of service and responsibility. The project's success was equally dependent on the commitment and skill of the firms implementing construction, who were often willing to assist far glass walls, often placing several objects into the visual field of the observer. The black walls were all that would be left of the "black box," something that might have been the obvious solution in another kind of exhibition space. In this context, therefore, the pieces did become elements of the same larger piece – more than they already were. In retrospect, I also think that the building somehow defined my understanding of the works, as I was forced to position them in a very direct dialog, thus discovering relations in my own work that I was not entirely aware of before. Although the spaces did demand maximum attention during the preparation stage – at times perhaps more attention than an exhibition space should require – I do, in fact, think that the building was a lucky match for this particular body of works.

Today, I am sure that Julia would be capable of drawing the floor plan of the building in her sleep, in multiple configurations, and I could probably also still produce a pretty convincing sketch … even now, some years after the exhibition.

beyond the call of duty in developing innovative solutions.

As the architects in charge, we were already involved in the planning process comparatively early, that is, from the preliminary design stage onwards. In view of the tight, strictly limited budget, at this stage of the project we prepared unusually detailed construction cost estimates. These were not calculated on the basis of comparing the costs of similar buildings, but rather by defining, in collaboration with the architects, the assumed technical specifications for as many of the construction components as possible, which in turn enabled us to specify costs. During the subsequent stages of planning, tendering, and implementing construction, we regularly updated the assumed costs to control expenditure, especially since the procedures of planning and inviting tenders partly coincided with construction. This also allowed us to revise plans and the related assignments for tender in accordance with the development of field construction costs.

Construction works including the shell, façades, and interior fit-out were individually allocated to only a small number of construction companies. On the one hand, this minimized constraints on the client by reducing the number of contract partners. On the other, in contrast to assigning all construction works to only one general contractor, this gave the client more effective control over the quality of construction.

During construction we were able to communicate closely with the tendered construction firms, allowing us to identify construction problems early on and to trace in detail the development of excess costs.

The aim of staying within budget also influenced planning and construction by engendering customized solutions, sophisticated in terms of design but comparatively cost-efficient. These include the rubber façade cladding, the sliding interior walls, and the base slab featuring in-slab heating and

thin floor coatings. Sample cladding for the façade, as well as a mockup of a complete interior segment, served to visualize and confirm the design, while also greatly simplifying negotiations with the client and the implementing companies. The building's geometric complexity and the subtle interplay between the structural shell and the interior fit-out posed additional challenges during construction. We had to prepare and monitor many of the construction works and custom-fit connections more meticulously than usual. As there are no repetitions or recurring elements in the building, each component within this work of complex spatial geometry reflects our aim to go to technical extremes in implementing innovative designs. Upon critical inspection, the museum does – as might be expected – reveal limitations due to budgetary restrictions. Not everything is perfect. But minor failures by no means cast doubt on the overall achievements of everyone involved in the project. In terms of its functionality and usability, the museum has most excellently stood the test of time since it was inaugurated.

The Aura of the Institution

On Affect, Atmosphere, and Immersion as Problematics in
Contemporary Architecture and Art

Museums and exhibition buildings dedicated to contemporary art have experienced an unparalleled boom in the last few years. It seems that hardly any city can afford to do without a spectacular new museum designed by a star architect. The "success" of a Tate Modern in London, a MoMA in New York, or a Guggenheim in Bilbao, as well as the Museumsquartier in Vienna, sets the standards. If museums were once dedicated to a complex of exhibits and shows,[1] they have now significantly taken over the function of tourist sites, of urban communication centers with a multiplicity of commercial programs. In most contemporary museum conceptions, a significant reversal of conditions can be observed: while in traditional museums, at least two-thirds of the spaces were dedicated to exhibitions and one-third to infrastructural requirements, this relationship is now reversed. Large areas of museums are now designated to commercial ventures such as museum shops, restaurants, and cafés. This growth of multifunctional areas in the museum converges with an increasing economization and commercialization of culture.

Even before the museum boom of the last few years, the "art institution" had already become "the place to be" in the truest sense of the word: ubiquitous lounges with reading areas or social environments, which were meant to generate temporary and local communities within the exhibition context, formed a kind of substitute dwelling in which the art-affiliated urbanite knew he/she could feel at home. These communicative spaces exemplified the characteristics of many artistic and curatorial practices subsumed by the curator and writer Nicolas Bourriaud under the intensively discussed term "relational aesthetics." According to Bourriaud, "relational aesthetics" was no longer about a utopian design based on a prefabricated idea of evolution, but rather about inhabiting the existing world in a "better" way.[2] After a period of sometimes rather moralizing contextual art practices, subsumed under the term "new institutional critique" in the 1990s, the development of "art as a social space"[3] made it possible to feel comfortable again in the institution, while at the same time allowing for reflection and critique, and establishing the "coolness" of the art world as a scene of distinction. The "white cube" debate, a main catalyst for the critical and artistic strategies of the 1990s, had lost its momentum after the potency and "aura" of this hegemonic model for exhibition spaces had been analyzed, deconstructed, and criticized in detail. For the time being, I would like to address Bourriaud's thesis that the production of aura no longer takes place through the artwork (nor, for that matter, through the exhibition space), but instead through the assembly of a micro-community.[4] In his book, *Relational Aesthetics*, Bourriaud describes an increasingly participatory practice that results in more collective and user-friendly exhibition projects, with an atmosphere that is primarily generated by "a momentary grouping of participating viewers."[5] The notion of atmosphere has created a comeback for the concept of the "aura" (whose gradual disappearance under the influence of mechanical reproduction was already stated by Walter Benjamin in 1935), but under changed auspices. The work of art and the white wall are no longer the sources of this aura. Instead, it seems "as if the micro-community gathering in front of the image was becoming the actual source of "aura," the 'distance' appearing specifically to create a halo around the work, which delegates its powers to it."[6]

1 Tony Bennett, "The Exhibitionary Complex," in: Reesa Greenberg, Bruce W. Ferguson, Sandy Nairne (eds.), *Thinking about Exhibitions*, London 1996, pp. 82–109 (p. 84)

2 Nicolas Bourriaud, *Relational Aesthetics*, Dijon 2002

3 Nina Möntmann, *Kunst als sozialer Raum*, Köln 2002

4 Bourriaud, p. 61

5 Bourriaud, p. 58

6 Bourriaud, p. 61

7 See also: *archplus* 178 (Die
Produktion von Präsenz), 2006

8 See also Walter Prigge:
"Atmospheres are constituted in
the gap between the architectural
object world (here, atmosphere
radiates from the arrangement
of things) and subjective space
experience (here, atmosphere is
an effect of subjective tendencies
and affects): The design of atmospheres always acknowledges
individuals as social co-producers
of space and architecture – that
is the point of no return in
postmodern space production
and a critique of the outdated
modernist way of thinking, which
sought to prescribe everyday
ways of life to individuals
through objective spatial
planning." Walter Prigge, "Zur
Konstruktion von Atmosphären,"
in: *Wolkenkuckucksheim* 8, No. 2,
2004 (http://www.tu-cottbup.de/
Theo/Wolke/deu/Themen/032/
Prigge/prigge.htm)

9 See also the chapter "Illusion
gegen Anti-Illusion," in: Jörg
Heiser, *Plötzlich diese Übersicht*,
Berlin 2007

10 Gerhard Schulze, *Die Erlebnisgesellschaft. Kultursoziologie der
Gegenwart*, Frankfurt a.M. 1992

Here, the proximity to the work of art seems decidedly less crucial than the proximity to the processes of the institution, which is perceived as the crystallization of a
lifestyle that promises intellectualism, cosmopolitanism, and cultural distinction. It is
very much about the immersion into the atmosphere associated with these qualities,
an immersion into the perceived "ambient" space of the art institution, which in itself is
thereby aura-fied. Topics and terms such as atmosphere, the production of presence,[7] and
the respective affects on the side of the observers have played a prominent role in the
architecture and art discourse of the last years. But what is the ideological background
of this institutional "ambient"? Which conception of a subject, whose affects thereby
come into focus, and which forms of publicity are thereby addressed? Which role does
the architecture of exhibition spaces play in this relation? Addressing these questions,
I would like to explore some of the paths of the discourse that recognize a new form of
participatory practice in the intentional addressing of emotions and affects in the spatial
arrangement.[8] First, I will deal with specific theories of spatial perception and orientation that address fundamental shifts within the construction of the perceiving subject in
space. This discussion on the meaning of affective perceptions and atmospheric charges
should serve as a basis for the question I want to pose: how and if architecture can
develop a critical agenda in terms of the perceptibility and negotiability of its effects,
particularly for exhibition spaces.

The Esthetics of the Presence and Atmosphere

Most representatives of an esthetics of presence and atmosphere argue for an identity of
being that defines a unity between the body and the spirit, as well as between reason and
emotion. This discussion will thus be about immersion, the dissolution of boundaries,
affect-oriented atmospheres, and the scripting of emotions – all of the topics, which, in
the last few years, have experienced a clearly intensified popularity in everyday culture, as
well as in art-related discussions[9]: from omnipresent shopping malls and their organizational guidelines for atmospherically loaded space scenarios up to Gerhard Schulze's
description of an "experience society."[10] The question is, then, what kind of production of
affect is currently associated with the production of space, and to which forms of subjectivity does it relate?

On a level of subject theory, a shift of paradigm can be observed, which the media
theoretician Marie Luise Angerer addresses in her book, *Vom Begehren nach dem Affekt*
(2007).[11] On the level of discourse history, a reversal of image-oriented visual studies
towards an intensified interest in affect-oriented methods is under way, in which an
"emotional turn" has already been announced. These discourses are about immersion
and involvement, frequently connected with the statement of the end of the theory and
its accompanying distance, as well as the end of the dominance of the visual. Instead,
aspects of sense and perception such as smell, touch, and sound – which have apparently
previously been neglected – are now at the center of the debate.

This shift not only appears in current art and media theories, but most specifically
in architecture and space production: the crisis of critical theory in architecture and
its discursive attachment to poststructural and deconstructive methods, which were
primarily of a representational-political nature, have opened up the field for a post-
critical, so-called projective theory and practice. The call from representatives of critical
architecture (such as Peter Eisenman or Michael Hays) for autonomy in relation to social
conditions and its implied skepticism about its possible effects on society substantially
contributed to an increasing marginalization of this attitude.

On the tails of the American new pragmatism, a set of theoreticians and architects
are now trying to establish an ideology of the postcritical, of the "projective," which relies

primarily on practice, effect, and performance instead of critique, and shifts the focus from representational critique to questions of presence. Key terms for this trend are, in accordance with Robert Somol and Sarah Whiting, who crucially pushed the discussion towards the projective with their essay, *Notes around the Doppler Effect and Other Moods of Modernism*[12]: performance, staging and special effects, mood and ambience, immersion and synesthesia. The primacy of the affective that is enlisted here is accompanied by a rekindled interest in the atmospheric, a term, which, as a displaced and structurally suppressed theme of rationalistic modern architecture, has again been moved to the center by those approaches looking for the possibility of restructuring the hierarchy of architectural tasks with "atmospheric interventions."[13]

The "atmospheric interaction" between subject and object, as designated by Somol and Whiting, seems to be a pre-conscious, pre-linguistic reaction, which is based on intuition and affect, and therefore is most appropriate for a "conceptual inclusion of the perception and the imagination of the observer," as Ole W. Fischer pointed out.[14] Projects such as Diller+Scofidio's *Blur Building*, an architecture for the production of a cloud that makes the building itself invisible, Peter Zumthor's buildings with their aura-loaded light and surface affects, and Phillippe Rahm's projects, which aim at a kind of spatial esthetic of displaced climate conditions, are at the center of this discussion. One theoretician who is especially well-received in the German-speaking countries regarding this discourse is Gernot Böhme, who has already been working on an "esthetics of atmosphere"[15] for a long time. In reference to Hermann Schmitz, Böhme defines atmosphere as a "moving intensity of feeling," or, in terms of architecture, "calibrated spaces."[16] He refers to the already spatial character of atmosphere and describes what its spatiality means, how it "spills indefinitely into the void" and "that it is experienced by people in its physical presence." However, Böhme also points out – apparently in anticipation of the potential criticism of this approach – that the discursive reservations in relation to the term "atmosphere" are based on the idea that the term falls out of the range of the reasonably articulated because it is "neither substance nor accident, neither purely objective nor purely subjective,"[17] and that it is not comprehensive on a scientific level because, above all, it is "only truly defined by the reaction of the subject."[18]

Considering this, an adequate term for subjectivity is necessary in the framework of an affect- oriented aesthetic program – whether it is primarily of an artistic or architectural origin – which Gernot Böhme only offers in a vaguely defined form. Nevertheless, a short passage interestingly appears in this context regarding the "gaze as atmosphere," in which Böhme describes how the viewer of a work of art is pulled into its spell, feels as though he/she is being looked at, and thereby an immersive effect occurs. One is, as it were, pulled over an affective path into the atmospheric space of the work. Along with Hegel, Böhme argues that the atmospheric character of the beautiful is a dialectic of looking and being looked at, and thereby concludes that the observer must give up his/her personal control in order to enter the atmosphere of the work of art[19] – a conception implying the abandonment of a sovereign autonomous observer. In passing, it should be mentioned that this reflects a thesis that already provoked a debate in the 1960s over the status of the autonomy of art versus the observer (versus space), in which Michael Fried accused minimal and conceptual artists of creating a situation of "theatricality" for an observer who consciously recognizes his/herself in space through the "literalness" of their objects and thereby assaulting the sublime autonomy of both the work and the viewer.[20] It is not by chance that this episode counts as a crucial initial spark for the discourse on theatricality and performance, which has become particularly intense in the last few years and has by now also become part of the discourse on space.[21]

11 Marie Luise Angerer, *Vom Begehren nach dem Affekt*. Zürich/Berlin 2007

12 Robert Somol, Sarah Whiting, "Notes around the Doppler-Effect and Other Moods of Modernism," in: *Harvard Design Magazine* 21, 2004, pp. 16–21

13 Ludwig Fromm, "Das Atmosphärische," in: *Ludwig Fromm, Architektur und sozialer Raum. Grundlagen einer Baukulturkritik*, Kiel 2000, p. 73

14 Ole W. Fischer, "Critical, Post-Critical, Projective?," in: *archplus* 174, 2005

15 Gernot Böhme, "Atmosphäre als Grundbegriff einer neuen Ästhetik," in: *Gernot Böhme, Atmosphäre*, Frankfurt a.M. 1995

16 Böhme, *Architektur und Atmosphäre*, München 2006, p. 25ff.

17 Ibid., p. 25

18 Ibid.

19 Ibid., p. 23

20 See Detlef Mertins, "Transparency: Autonomy and Relationality," in: Todd Gannon, Jeffrey Kipnis (eds.), *The Light Construction Reader*, New York 2002, p. 140ff.

21 See also Christopher Dell, "Die Performanz des Raumes," in: *archplus* 183, 2007

22 Silverman introduces the term "gaze," with which she tried to give the (always already existing) social view (gaze) – which is diametrically opposed to the seeing (look) of the subject – a cultural meaning which describes it as a representation of a "dominant fiction" and therefore the predominating cultural narrations and options of identification in each case, thereby embedding the look both historically and ideologically.

23 Silverman locates this meeting at the "cultural screen" following a concept from Jacques Lacan. Lacan defined the screen (écran) as a place in which the subject is constituted. This place, however, is not of an optical nature, nor is it a geometric space, but rather, opaque. It is this interface which functions as a constitutive mediation between the subject and his/her image. According to Lacan, as the subject occupies the place of an image, which is located on the screen, it becomes understood as a product of regimes of vision with social, cultural, and ideological implications. Silverman extended her argument with the cultural specification of the respective "dominant fiction." By referring to the ability of "looks" to always be able to also develop a resistance against the given modes of viewing of the "gaze," she describes a form of identification that withdraws itself from purely apparative description patterns. See also related chapters from Silverman: "The Gaze," "The Look," "The Screen"

24 Silverman, p. 203

25 See also Ilka Becker, "Einblendung. Körper, Atmosphärik und künstlerische Fotografie," in: Tom Holert, Imagineering. Visuelle Kultur und Politik der Sichtbarkeit, Köln 2000, p. 176ff.

26 Ibid., p. 191

27 Böhme, 2006, p. 30

For the time being, what is relevant here is that the dialectic of looking and being looked at is a basic mode of what the film theoretician Kaja Silverman calls "identification-at-a-distance." Silverman introduces the difference between the "look" and the "gaze" in her discussion over the modes of the subjectivity in order to clarify how the self-made internal image of the subject interacts with the exterior image.[22] She uses the model of the camera in order to illustrate how the subject experiences him/herself as always being in the image, but always dependent on the respective social and cultural constructions of the "gaze." Theatricality is structurally implied within this cultural construction, provided that subjectivity is formed through negotiating an offer of identification that is defined from the outside and an ideal image projected from the inside. Silverman calls this procedure "keying in." As an analogy, she uses the "pose" in which the desire to be perceived in a certain way, "to be apprehended", concurs with the prefigured, expectant positions of the "gaze."[23] What Böhme describes as atmospheric radiation in the moment of regarding a work of art, is for Silverman a fundamental ability of the subject to specifically inscribe itself in a certain regime of vision, in order to play with the inscription and its accompanying form of identification. A specific form of spatiality is thereby produced: "The pose is also generative of mise-en-scène. The pose always involves both the positioning of a representationally inflected body in space, and the consequent conversion of that space into a 'place.'"[24]

In this sense, Böhme's dialectic of looking and being looked at would be a fundamental mode of any identification process, however – and this is what Silverman's work ultimately aims at – this identity can never be totally achieved. The identity always remains at a distance. A closure and conclusive identification would mean to postulate a politically questionable essence or substantialization on the part of the subject.

In an essay on the production of atmosphere in recent photography, Ilka Becker argues that Böhme's understanding of atmosphere does not really keep the historical and cultural conventions that are incribed in it in mind.[25] She points out that moods are explainable only through the discourses that frame their respective genres, particularly those that concern artistic production: "The term of atmosphere is therefore productive only to a certain degree if one does not examine to what extent it is tied to questions of agenda and (identity-) politics."[26] Here, one would hope for a productive junction of affect-oriented discourses on atmosphere and critical identity political positions like those of Silverman. It is this crucial point, at which Böhme warns that the "denial of the atmospheric power of feeling" allows us to be "unconsciously influenceable,"[27] which could even support the problematic ideology of the autonomous subject. Thus, a critical argument on the mechanisms of affectation and their respective ideological structures seems inevitable, in order to avoid surrendering the field of the sensuous and the synesthetic to speculative advertising messages from the wellness industry and marketing experts.

Immersion and Deframing

In current spatial production, the mode of immersion is of crucial relevance. Immersion stands for "diving in" and "being sucked in" to virtual worlds or a kind of second nature. The technology of this kind of staging is intended to withdraw, indeed, to remain invisible; the esthetic effect of the constructed atmosphere should remain undisturbed. The above-mentioned gap in the processes of identification should be filled up and made as seamless as possible in order to serve a promise of immediacy. According to Peter Sloterdijk, who has already dedicated several volumes of material to the subject of spheres and interior worlds, immersion is above all a technology of the dissolution of boundaries, of deframing – or more precisely: a process of deframing for images and views that have lost all boundaries in order to become "surroundings."

One domain in which the questioning of spatial framing, including the dissolution of boundaries and its respective ideological structure, is repeatedly played out paradigmatically, is the discourse around the requirements of exhibitions, their spatial parameters, and their forms of display within fine art. With this in mind, let's take a small excursion into the history of the exhibition space. The concepts of space negotiated here can be discussed in the recourse to a central technology of representation in dominant paradigms of the modern art space, namely, the already addressed "white cube" principle. In 1976, Brian O'Doherty discussed the mechanisms of inclusion and exclusion of this spatialized convention of modern exhibition practice in his collection of texts, *Inside the White Cube*.[28] His analysis of the basic ideological structure of the white gallery space, which has become naturalized and therefore invisible over time, exposed the notion of neutrality in the context of art as a highly problematic issue. Historically speaking, the request to present works of art as autonomous objects taken out of their direct temporal and spatial context was once the result of a criticism of the existing conditions of the presentation of art. It was a specific maneuver of deframing. On the one hand, it was about showing the work of art as a unique object opposite to an idealized viewer and, on the other hand, it was about extracting the art from the political and economic grasp of the bourgeoisie and thus creating new forms of presentation for a democratized view of art. The immersion into the "white cube" promised the immersion into the aura of art, which, in the course of the developments of minimal and conceptual art, withdrew itself more and more from its classical status as an object and became increasingly ephemeral.[29] In place of this, the deframing mechanisms of the "white cube" provided for the necessary absorption of the viewer into an environment that clearly signaled that it was presenting serious and important art. The conception of the authority and aura of the art – in a process of naturalization – dissolved into the figure of the "white cube" and its specific atmosphere. Time and space, in the sense of a historical or local context, thereby step into the background and the preconditions of perception are absorbed into the invisibility of the ideological equipment of the institution. As is the case with Foucault's diagrammatic model of the panopticon[30] as a disciplinary apparatus, the concealing and hiding of acts of perception ensure that the powers-that-be become invisible.

We can of course find similar principles that apply to shopping malls and theme parks. The intention of binding a large number of visitors to one place in which the visitors might forget their everyday worries as well as the surrounding city in order to dedicate themselves completely to the "theme," results in these places functioning primarily – and despite their evident effort to incorporate the whole world – due to exclusion mechanisms: the abundance of distractions and options seeks to cover up that which may not find entrance. In this sense, the multimedia manipulation of sensory perception that occurs in theme parks corresponds to a wellness spa. Their success is based primarily, among other things, on the possibility of forgetting and switching off, being able to drift off, or surrendering oneself to a controlled, always safeguarded and secured, loss of control. In order for this program of drifting-off to succeed, the external references must be minimized, and orientability must be gradually reduced.

A crucial aspect of this form of architecture and spatial production is that it wants to create and enhance certain perceptions and sensory affects, but its scope of possible actions lies only within a clearly predetermined range. Affects are increasingly utilized as a commodifiable field of enterprise, the management of which is called "Imagineering" at Disney. The seemingly expanding options within these highly controlled commercial systems correlate however with a general differentiation and heterogenization of lifestyles and identity constructions which grew out of the radical free-market economy's imperative of flexibility and creativity. Yet the principle of immersion expresses itself in

28 Brian O'Doherty, *Inside the White Cube: The Ideology of the Gallery Space*, Santa Monica/San Francisco 1976/1986

29 See also: Lucy Lippard, *Six Years: The Dematerialization of the Art Object from 1966 to 1972*, New York 1973

30 Based on the example of the panopticon, Michel Foucault brought up for discussion the effects of a fundamentally shifting concept of subjectivity on the historical formation of regimes of vision and paradigmatic spaces. This prison concept from the late 18th century is based on the deliberate placement of visual control and monitoring mechanisms. Thus, all single cells in prisons are oriented towards a central tower in the center of the facility, from which the wardens can recognize each prisoner at any time as a silhouette through the outwardly transparent cells and thereby supervise them. See also: Michel Foucault, *Discipline and Punish. The Birth of the Prison* (1975), New York 1977

31 Andreas Spiegl, "Out of Place Revisited," unpublished manuscript of a lecture held at the symposium *Theorie und Affekt* at the Academy of Fine Arts, Vienna, 01.18.2008

32 Tom Holert, "Am Ende des Subjekts," in: *Texte zur Kunst 67*, 2007, p. 212ff.

33 To read more on Michel Foucault's following discourse about his terms bio-power and bio-politics, see for example: Thomas Lemke, *Gouvernementalität und Biopolitik*, Wiesbaden 2006

34 See also: Michel Foucault, *Dispositive der Macht. Über Sexualität, Wissen und Wahrheit*, Berlin 1978, p. 119ff.

a phantasm of coherence, through its exclusion of complexity and contradictions. As the notion of affect is being reassessed, a "fetishizing of the body as a contrasting figure to subjectivity and to a politics of differentiation"[31] is in progress. "Politically, and on a level of theories of action, there is nothing more to gain here,"[32] as Tom Holert somewhat drastically formulated. He further warns, in recourse to the previously mentioned Marie Luise Angerer, that giving up the "psychic dimension" in favor of the inauguration of a "vitalistic power of motivation" might just serve biopolitical instrumentalizations[33] of "undreamt-of magnitudes and undreamt-of consequences." The insularity and coherence of immersive environments always seems problematic on a level of identity politics in this context. The argument for a structural lack of coherence in the processes of subjectivization is, on the one hand, a form of critique of immersion as a problematic mode of closure. On the other hand, if one takes Silverman's argument of the pose as a space-producing figure seriously, the spatial envelope always seems to be relational to a subject whose role within this staging is still self-determined to a certain extent and that can at least choose temporary deframings among various offers in these immersive environments. The popularity of the affective, atmospheric, and immersive will ultimately have to be measured against those modes of subjectivization that they offer.

The Parameters of the Design of the GfZK

Even if the institution has developed an ambient character filled with "aura," as initially formulated, its architecture can still represent a medium that comments on this production of presence and atmosphere through its own means, makes its preconditions visible, and at times, also undermines them. In the conception of the spatial structure of the GfZK-2, the fundamental elements of the exhibition space were treated as negotiable elements of an institutional dispositiv.[34] The spatial parameters in the construction of this institutional atmosphere, this "ambient," are thereby always exhibited themselves up to a certain extent. The concept of a permeable atmosphere was based on defining the elements of the institution primarily as "screens" or "settings," which could be shifted and thus become visible acts of positioning. They can be designated through the requirement of the negotiation of their positioning. But the agenda is not about a maximization of flexibility. More crucial than what the architecture of the GfZK makes possible is what it makes impossible: namely, simple orientation, the option of completely enclosed spaces, the suppression of architecture and its spatial context, and therefore, a successful immersion into the "aura" of the institution. The design poses an argument about factors like the perception of one's own body in space and the associated affects, the architecture of the institution as well as the complex interweaving, and, at the same time, the staging of all these aspects, which are mostly suppressed in the seamless narratives of museum scenographies. The idea of a community that is connected through an atmosphere of artistic aura, as Nicolas Bourriaud's principle of a "relational aesthetics" outlines, is thereby deliberately questioned. The architecture of the GfZK establishes realms that compete with one another, whose relations must be clarified each time through negotiations along thresholds and lines of difference in the space. The establishment of different partial publicities, which may resist closures and homogenizations, is inscribed as aspiration in the architectural program.

Title
Film, Photography, Text, Object, Building

Artist
Josef Dabernig

Curator
Barbara Steiner

Opening
July 02, 2005

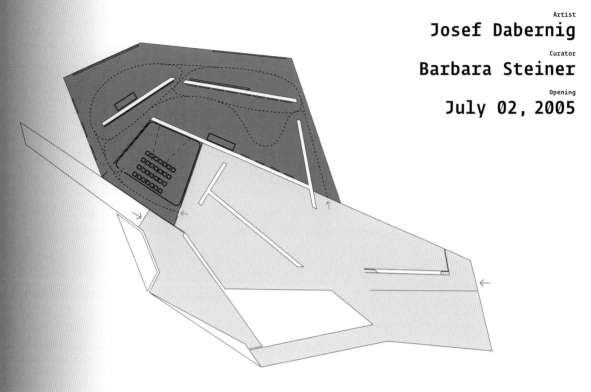

134 ◻▷

Museums with **air conditioning** are inclined towards being climatically and acoustically sealed off from their surroundings in order for the system to function. We wanted to get by with natural ventilation as much as possible in order to maintain climatic and acoustic continuity between the exterior and interior, and to cut down on running costs. A permanent automated ventilation system was only necessary in the café and cinema.

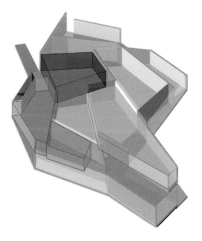

Areas with automated ventilation or air conditioning:

■ Projection space with automated ventilation
▨ Café and service areas with automated ventilation
▨ Areas with optional air conditioning

This exhibition brought together different forms of expressive media – film, photography, text, object, and architecture – and highlighted their contentual-conceptual associations. Through its multifaceted spatiality, the GfZK-2 building provided the ideal preconditions for Dabernig's exhibition, allowing the artist to create contentual links between apparently different media, using the gaps and views throughout the building. Dabernig's works revolve around functionalism, rationalization, perfect organizational schemata, as well as deviations from them, errors, and disturbances. In his films, Dabernig addresses functional processes and social conventions, which have lost their causative foundation only to develop their own intrinsic dynamics. His hand-written extracts derive from books that have a normative function. Thus, Dabernig focuses on subjective attitudes, the personal interests and judgements of various authors, and deviations in the order of the handwriting itself. His photographs explore the incongruities in architecture, urban planning, or its use. Since the late 1980s, Dabernig's sculptures have been based on comprehensible systems of order, and their point of departure lies in the width of the L- and U-shaped profiles and/or in the dimensions of the exhibition space. Formal divergence is either built into the works themselves or arises as a result of a confrontation with their particular architectural context. This also applied to the Leipzig exhibition. The discrepancies that emerged between the building and Dabernig's aluminum grids staked out the conflicts between the artistic object and its surroundings, as the strict formal approach apparent in Dabernig's artworks was transferred to the spatial concept of his exhibition. The objects were positioned in a rhythmical order in relation to the given architectural context. (Barbara Steiner)

Since most of the art shown in the GfZK is relatively unproblematic climatically speaking, we were able to agree on this basic concept. In order to be able to also show climate-sensitive exhibits, an internal area was defined which has the option of being closed off with sliding panels and air-conditioned. This area has two glass walls facing the foyer, through which a visual reference between the air conditioned area and the adjacent exhibition spaces exists. The air conditioned area becomes a display case. The air conditioning system itself was situated outside in a roof recess directly over this space in an easily accessible and cost-efficient manner.

Internal exhibition area with the
option of being air conditioned

1 *Untitled*, 1988, galvanized steel sheets, 190 × 824 × 14 centimeters (from a collection comprising forty-eight objects made of twelve fragmented air ducts in 1988)

2 *Untitled* (in two parts), 1994, aluminum, 354 × 442.5 × 13.5 centimeters and 330 × 406.5 × 13.5 centimeters, courtesy of Muzeum Sztuki Nowoczesnej, Niepołomice

3 *Untitled* (in three parts), 1992, aluminum, 200 × 200 × 34.5 centimeters; *Untitled* (in three parts), 1990, aluminum, 244 × 154 × 47 centimeters

My exhibition *Dabernig, Josef: Film, Photography, Text, Object, Building* was shown on approximately 400 square meters of exhibition space in the GfZK-2. The given architectural context seemed a perfect way to make the relations between inside and outside, as well as the flexibility in spatial configurations and the variations in wall and floor materials available through an open display. The concept of the space may well have influenced Barbara Steiner's curatorial approach when she recommended that I illustrate this web of relations through representational works using the media of film, photography, text, object, and building. At first I saw myself confronted with the task of arranging artworks of various media on the different walls available and in a projection room (or cinema) in such a way as to create a dialog across the lines of sight. I thought that a meta-dialog would thus simultaneously be incorporated into the exhibition through the qualities intrinsic to the architecture and those conveyed by it. Since artistic objects have a strong impact on the space that surrounds them, I thought of works that have such an impact – right from the start. For this reason, I hung a set of six galvanized steel panel sheets[1] and a work

made of aluminum grids[2] across the full length of the wall segment, while two aluminum sets of three parts each[3] were randomly arranged on a third wall.

The accentuated two-dimensionality of the six steel sheets which, rhythmically staggered, simply leaned against the wall contrasted with the linear structure of both aluminum grids – without highlighting this through a direct visual relation. In order to address the variability of a constant and unchanging material, I have, since 1996, only been recycling and reworking elements of previously finished works in my exhibitions. Thus, two works from an exhibition in the Galeria Potocka, Cracow, in

Since the strictly limited construction costs of EUR 1,800 per square meter were tight for such a building, which featured special, demanding structures, we were already looking for suitable construction companies for this assignment during the planning, and examined possible solutions with these companies in order to obtain reasonable offers during the bidding.

Low-priced structural solutions, which had to accommodate a comparatively intense planning process and technical complexity, had to be found. This is a challenging and rather thankless setup for designers and contractors, since in Germany, such additional efforts are not reflected in the cost estimation regulations. During this process of fine-tuning, we were concerned with finding appropriate structural solutions, consciously analyzing and questioning building standards, and cutting back in certain areas as much as possible in order to keep the necessary means available for other areas.

4 *Zalgiris Stadium* (in six parts), 2002, Lambda
prints, framed, each 88.6 × 123.5 centimeters

5 *Interior Design for Depot* (Space for Art and
Discussion), Messepalast/MuseumsQuartier
Wien (MQ Vienna) (in two parts), 1994/95, in
cooperation with Franz Meisterhofer, Lambda
prints, framed, each 88.6 × 123.5 centimeters

6 Design concept on Individual Systems
(curated by Igor Zabel), The Venice Biennale,
50th International Art Exhibition, (in two
parts), 2003, Lambda prints, framed, each 88.6
× 123.5 centimeters

Josef Dabernig   165

1994 – which fully covered two wall lengths each – were ideal for the concrete wall of the GfZK-2, 8.8 meters long and 3.83 meters high. The installation of the same grids on a freestanding wall of the GfZK-2 addressed the idea of the appropriation and exchangeability of time and place. However, the stacked aluminum sets eschewed the question in that they were obviously not installed and simply leaned against a separate wall.

In this way, each of the rooms conceived for my exhibition, with the exception of the cinema, was given a sculptural gesture. The series of six sheets – which, in their staggered rhythm, generated an illusionary effect – found a counter-echo in the wall grids, and the possibility of a "quasi-in-front-and-behind" was enacted by the stacked aluminum sets, which could still be seen on the other side of the wall on the floor.

Embedded as it is in its surrounding space of planes and surfaces, the "object," as an esthetic medium, found a structural extension in the way that pictures were hung on four further walls. Constructed, photographic, or textual works of art were displayed in twenty clip-on picture frames – each 88 × 123 centimeters large, with folding aluminum profiles and a non-reflective protective

film instead of conventional glass. Upon closer scrutiny, a 180-degree panorama in six parts, *Zalgiris Stadium in Vilnius*,[4] continued the cumulative principle of the six sheets. However, the latter's emphatic rhythm was abated in the symmetry of the oval stadium, while a sense of semantic drama seemed to be announced in the heavy storm clouds. Seven further frames were hung on the wall in the largest area of the room – the very wall on the reverse side of which the stacked aluminum sets leaned – and these frames displayed CAD prints and photographs of three

The building does not have a **façade**. The interior spatial configuration reflects itself in the exterior of the building. Its shape is hardly detectable from the outside.

Collage showing a simulation of the
envisioned materiality and visibility, 2003

7 Artistic design *Annex for Lebenshilfe in Ledenitzen/Villach* (in three parts), 1995, Lambda prints, framed, each 88.6 × 123.5 centimeters

8 *Luna Park* (in four parts), 1990, Lambda prints, framed, each 88.6 × 123.5 centimeters/ 123.5 × 88.6 centimeters

9 *Daily Cigarette Consumption 23 09 1979 to 22 09 1980*, Lambda print, framed, 88.6 × 123.5 centimeters

10 *Gas Station and Fuel Statistics for STEYR FIAT CROMA 154 i.e. 22 05 1995 to 27 07 2000*, Lamba print, framed, 88.6 × 123.5 centimeters

11 *Gas Station and Fuel Statistics for LANCIA THEMA i.e. Catalyzer from 20 07 2000*, Lambda print, framed, 88.6 × 123.5 centimeters

12 Handwritten copy of the book by Dr. Franz Xaver Mayr, *Schönheit und Verdauung oder die Verjüngung des Menschen nur durch sachgemäße Wartung des Darmes* (Beauty and Digestion, Or the Regeneration of Man only through the Appropriate Maintenance of the Intestine), 5th edition, 1975, Verlag Neues Leben, Bad Goisern, Upper Austria (first publication 1920), 1977, ballpoint pen, ink on paper, written on both sides, 110 pages, 19.7 × 15 centimeters and 21 × 15 centimeters

13 Handwritten copy of the book by Vittorio Gregotti, *Il territorio dell'architettura* (The Territory of Architecture), Campi del sapere/ Feltrinelli, Milan 1988 (first publication in the series Materiali, 1966), 1999, ballpoint pen on paper, 38 A4 pages.

14 *Lancia Thema*, 2005, 35 millimeters on DVD, color, 17 minutes, production/script/editing: Josef Dabernig, camera: Christian Giesser, sound: Michael Palm, actor: Josef Dabernig

related projects of an "applied" art: *Interior Design for Depot*,[5] *Design Concept on Individual Systems*,[6] and *Annex for Lebens-hilfe in Ledenitzen/Villach*.[7] Four photographs of a Luna Park were shown on the opposite wall.[8] Each of these works referred in different ways to the filmic element which – by displacing semantic and subject-oriented references into ones relating to time and space – mirrored the movement of the object installation. A transposition of this movement into structural relations was shown in three works through tables displayed elsewhere in the exhibition: a list, for example, of my daily cigarette consumption as well as two lists with dates in which gas stations and fuel amounts were recorded.[9][10][11] Furthermore, there were two simple tables – glass slabs on wooden trestles – in the exhibition, with both of

The assembly of spaces was given abrupt edges, which seem to create a "smooth" cross-section through the building's structure. The window openings refer to and interact with the building's immediate surroundings, but there is no explicit design of a façade as a layer around the building. Large wall surfaces are alternated with large window areas, which grant intermittently deep views into the building. Stark contrasts between surface and depth develop, as well as ambiguities between interior and exterior.

their long sides placed along the wall. On the one table in the room with the steel sheets, the book *Schönheit und Verdauung* (*Beauty and Digestion*),[12] which I myself had copied by hand, was presented in a neat and ordered manner – page laid out next to page. The second table was found in the "architectural zone" of the exhibition, an area already coded several times by the grids on the wall, the "applied" projects, and the photos of *Luna Park*. It displayed – page after page, again, in fastidious handwriting – the transcription of the book *Il territorio dell'architettura* (*The Territory of Architecture*).[13] The handwriting of both texts is entirely different, since more than twenty years lie between their execution. But a displacement can also be noticed within the works themselves: line spacing and type size become smaller with each increasing page number. The notion of time is inscribed, entirely without intention, into the leaves of the texts as a form of structural dynamism.

While the rhythm of the aluminum profiles and sheets followed indices that were conceptionally defined, the continuous densification of the typography on the pages of the transcribed book was brought about by the unconscious refinement of the handwriting. Whether these works of transcription are regarded as textual sculptures, post-traumatic activities, or meditations, they are

definitely a formal part of the overarching theme of the exhibition – the grids.

In the only room without a visual connection to the other works, the film *Lancia Thema*[14] could be watched in a glass-encased cinema darkened by curtains. The soundtrack was the only direct connection to the other parts of the exhibition, and it comprised opera arias and Schubert's Die *Nebensonnen* from the *Winterreise* song cycle, which helped to structure the five-part road movie. The protagonist of the film drives a Lancia Thema through an uninviting Italian landscape beyond all clichés, stops his car five times, gets out to photograph it, and promptly continues his journey. Each one of these photo sessions is thematically characterized by a dialectic camera movement: the driver obsessively focuses only on his car while the cine camera – with inserts on the photographer – pans first horizontally and then vertically across those fragments of landscape and architecture in which the photographer is obviously not interested. In this way, *Lancia Thema* crystallizes into an esthetic whole aspects that had appeared in the other works. A structural force was written both into the permutation of the plot and the dramaturgy of the camera. The panorama of the Vilnius stadium returns as a *déjà vu* not only in the Lancia as it stops on a playing field encircled by an

---

We developed the closed external walls as homogenous rectangular planes, which are conceptually a continuation of the display surfaces through other means.

antique wall, but also as a structural repetition in the excessive panning of the camera. Even the structure of the grids recurs in the photos of walls and skeletal cement structures. It might, perhaps, be said that the phantasmatic gaze through the windscreen to the left and right of the street reveals, on a metaphorical level, that which could be seen to the left and right of the cinema room on the gallery walls.

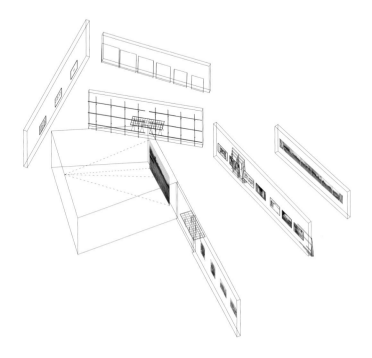

The screening room is conceived as the focal point of spatial relations within and to the outside of the building. On the one hand, this space can be used in the manner of a showcase and remain part of the fluid internal space structure, and on the other hand, it can be used as an external event and cinema space. It can be transparent or blocked off with curtains: creating a space that then seems to penetrate into the structure of the exhibition space, with a strong programmatic and spatial connection to the neighboring café, from which it can also be accessed independently.

Café Neubau/Club Weezie
& Paris Syndrom

With the GfZK-2, a new café also opened its doors in 2004. The concept of having artists create constantly changing interior designs, which was already the case in the GfZK-1, was also retained in the new building. After Anita Leisz, Jun Yang took over the project in 2007.

Steiner   Anita, what were your first thoughts concerning the café?

Leisz   With the move into the new building, the café of the GfZK was able to function autonomously. Its infra-structure as well as its separate entrance allowed opening times that were independent from those of the museum. We could easily count on visitors during the day, but the venue still had to become a popular evening locale. I decided that two types of venue could share one and the same site: a quiet café during the day, perfect for individual customers and guests, and a bar in the evening that would attract groups of people for social gatherings – both without having to make any particular changes or alterations. Both sites were given a name: *Neubau* was the daytime café, *Weezie* the evening bar. The names appeared next to each other in neon writing above the entrance to the premises; and depending on which venue was open, either the one or the other name was alight. As for the design for the interior, I wanted to go into one extreme direction as much as into another: settings, in other words, capable of shifting into their diametric opposite – here during the day, there at night; here one kind of music, there another. And, indeed, it worked. I found the one pole using the fauteuil covered with Scottish tartan fabric and the opposite one through the tables finished in a youthful DIY style. In between them, there were an array of things from various eras and different countries, particular ashtrays, or types of cola.

The tartan material bears a history, a family history, a national history and, for this reason, is most probably valuable and, thus, also "expensive." Placed outside its historical context and reworked in good quality, it embodies a sense of tradition and value. This is the sense in which I used the material – although, in the given site, it at first simply represented itself and was only then seen in relation to the DIY tabletops.

Steiner   Where does the idea of the youthful, DIY-style tables come from?

Leisz   I remember that there is an age when you still live with your family, but when you are slowly becoming more independent. You have a kid's room, perhaps, with which you can no longer properly identify yourself, but you have no money to furnish it according to your own needs and requirements. So you try to alter and rearrange

One could also say that it is here where the final spatial interlocking of the sprawl of exhibition spaces takes place. In order to emphasize the conceptual balance between the interior and exterior, the material used for the exterior walls warps into the interior of the cinema, thereby creating a spatial envelope along the floor, wall, and ceiling.

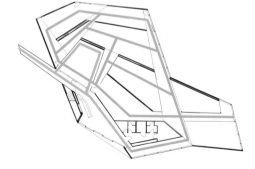

what is already there – "drawing over" works quite well. Whether chairs or shelves are painted green, blue, or pink is simply a matter of personal preference, but the choice of black always signifies resistance. The catch is that it never really looks particularly good: the lacquer does not bond properly to the surface and it peels off through use, ultimately looking quite shabby – all in all, rather charming.

Steiner   And there were also those chairs from the 1960s that you painted beige.

Leisz   Beige was the basic color of the chairs and the tabletops. The tabletops were painted over in black, but the beige was visible in some places through scratches on the surface; these places grew through further use over the years.

Steiner   There were more references, weren't there?

Leisz   Perhaps even repetitions. There was a mirror in the restrooms with sentences engraved in them: "you don't understand me," "I'm a teenager," "I've problems," messages which could be covered by another sliding mirror surface that completely hid them. Furthermore, there was a wall in the locale itself – I called it the anti-graffiti wall – which was three by four meters large and painted with a clear anti-graffiti lacquer used to remove graffiti. The exposed concrete thus turned a shade darker, and the texture became visible. It looked surprisingly good. The area was intended for notices, but actually didn't get used much.

Steiner   Could you tell us a bit about the lighting?

Leisz   Ultimately, the solution was simple: "light bulbs in a holder" that hung on cables from the ceiling. I initially wanted to have drink brands on light boxes above the bar area – those objects that are produced for the catering industry and which breweries, for instance, set up in the bars they supply. Yet the boxes remained empty and were, thus, "dysfunctional."

While looking for a suitable material for these exterior and interior requirements, we finally decided on fine-pored, slate-gray, **rubber granulate mats**. They are suitable for both the exterior and interior, can be seamlessly installed, and have a sound-absorbing surface, which provides an excellent acoustic advantage for the screening room.

Behind the screening room: variations of visibility

Steiner When you speak of two different types of venues in one, then the character of the venue changes according to the particular time and its different visitors. I remember there was this group of children's tables and stools that served an altogether different function in the evenings, with adults sitting around them who found them quite comfortable.

Leisz Yes, I thought that kids would probably tag along during the day and so I wanted something that would suit them but, at the same time, might also work well in the evening. I thought that if children as a "target audience"

would disappear for good, with no sign of ever returning, then this ensemble could still be used in the evenings as adult furniture. I gather that it was rarely used during the day by adults.

Steiner Two venues in one – that is also mirrored in the matches.

Leisz Together with graphic designer Anna Lena von Helldorff, we designed matchbooks as a form of advertising. Using a simple graphic solution, they showed which venue was open when.

Steiner The name *Neubau* never really took off; people always only spoke of *Weezie*.

Leisz I think that has to do with communication. People who live in Leipzig and who met there in the evenings called it *Weezie*, and also did this during the day. Guests who came to the exhibitions and also went to *Café Neubau* probably didn't even mention it. *Weezie* offered events that were announced in the media; *Café Neubau* didn't. So *Weezie* had to become more popular.

Steiner Where did the name *Weezie* come from?

Leisz From a film by the Coen brothers, but the name was written slightly differently.

Steiner Your café successfully demonstrated the building's changeable nature. It was up to the guests to choose what they wished to notice at first sight: either the

conservative elements or those of a youthful resistance, even if the play with various connotations and associations did not, of course, allow for a clear separation between the two. For you tend to be trapped in notions of appropriation very quickly. In other words, elements of youth culture, for instance, suddenly became very trendy or, conversely, you lounged in expensive tartan sofas without really noticing it. Citation and appropriation also play an important role for you, Jun.

Yang I was interested in the use of elements that stand for a certain kind of demand. All the individual pieces are "fakes" or substitutes, as it were. I would like to own

Together with the Keim company, we developed an appropriate wall construction: first, a Keim insulation system was applied on the reinforced concrete walls, which were then covered with hard calcium silicate boards. Finally, the rubber aggregate mats were glued on. This wall structure was tested and approved for application by the Keim company.

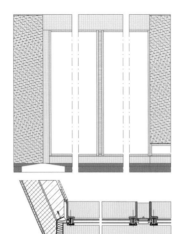

Drawing of exterior wall and glazing: elevation and plan

The rubber mats were available in 1.5 meter-wide sheets. We wanted the rubber surfaces to be seamless and to create the smallest seams possible when adjoined laterally. However, the production of prefabricated parts was not possible: the rubber sheets had to be applied on site on pre-finished wall surfaces. The processing of the mats was simulated on a provided façade sample of full height and 1.5 meters width. This façade sample was then tested on location by being exposed to six months' weather.

something – a Louis Vuitton bag, say, or a designer chair by Charles and Ray Eames – but I can't afford them. So I choose an inexpensive replica instead. This, precisely, was my starting point, although I wasn't interested in the phenomenon of a lifestyle brand, but rather in the question of desire and the fulfillment of an ideal. The fake fulfills the image of the ideal up to a certain degree; that's why it is bought.

Steiner Anita's prosaic neon writing was replaced by "Paris Syndrom" above the entrance. The curvy writing and the color pink give it a gaudy and slightly romantic appeal. Where does the name come from?

Yang It comes from the term "Paris syndrome" which refers to a psychological disorder suffered by female Japanese tourists, in particular, when they travel to Paris and inevitably experience how the city falls short of all their glorious romantic desires. These women – between thirty and forty – have saved money for years and are often abroad for the very first time in their lives. They come to Paris and discover the city of love to be quite loveless and uncharitable. Hitting upon a hard reality that entirely deviates from their preconceptions and idealized images of the city, they suffer from a kind of negative cultural shock akin to traumatization. The Japanese embassy has even set up a twenty-four-hour hotline for these cases.

Steiner So this idea revolves around desire and longing and, at the same time, disillusionment. In this vein, the elements of the interior design are often obviously far away from the originals.

Yang Yes. The chairs are actually upholstered with a kind of tartan fabric that is only vaguely reminiscent of Louis Vuitton. That's why we stitched "Louis Viutton" into it in large letters – a conscious scrambling of letters. I am interested in the paradox between the exclusiveness and the size of the label, as found on white T-shirts with Calvin Klein or Dolce & Gabbana logos. Grandiose chandeliers hang from the room's stucco ceiling. They are clearly low-cost solutions. The chairs bring to mind a design by Charles and Ray Eames; they are a cross between Flötotto school chairs and a frame inspired by Eames. The tables are based on French café tables with cast-iron feet – only in color do they differ, as they have been sprayed entirely brown, like a chocolate glaze. Fans of Viennese coffee-houses will immediately identify the wallpaper with pink and white stripes as a reference to Café Prückel. Finally, the photographs on the wall show famous buildings in the history of architecture that have been reconstructed in various places around the world: the Eiffel Tower, for instance, in Shenzhen, China; Le Corbusier's Ronchamp church in Zhenzhou, China; but also the

---

The building cantilevers over its perimeters in such a way that it seems to float over the area. We wanted it to refer to its surroundings but also to liberate itself somewhat from its direct contact to the ground.

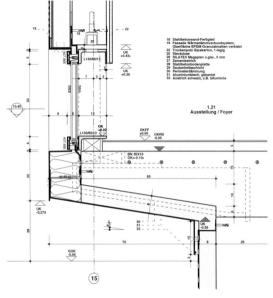

Vertical section of
the base plate

Through the large **glass surfaces**, the exhibitions – as well as the visitors – can be easily observed from the outside, they are further exposed on the slightly raised, floating floor. There is a strong visual interaction between the interior and exterior, but there is also a definitive threshold.

In the development phase, we often spoke with the GfZK about the aim of being a "low-threshold institution" – an institution anchored in everyday life, which invites passers-by to get involved with contemporary art, offering the spatial means to do so. As a result, visitors can slip into the building through a large glass sliding door, immediately finding themselves inside the exhibition space.

Frauenkirche (Women's Church) in Dresden, Germany. With regard to the latter, I was chiefly interested in the phenomenon of resurrecting an entire building. There are entire streets of houses in Dresden that have been reconstructed over the last years; for me, that's as if you were building a city around a specific mental image or even "correcting" it, since, at the same time, other buildings that don't quite fit into the picture disappear. Disney World or Neuschwanstein are conceptionally not so far away. Added to that are photos of "real" buildings, but which are not in their original places – such as the old London Bridge, which was sold to Lake Havasu, Arizona, in 1968 and reconstructed there.

Steiner You also thought of magazines and music: the French edition of *Vogue* or *Wallpaper* are laid out for visitors to read, and cover versions of famous songs can be heard. Often the original song has been so estranged that it can hardly be recognized. Nevertheless, this creates a new quality, which is something I also find is the case with the furniture. Even if the chair is not an original Eames, it is not any old cheap product. If I had the choice, I actually think I would prefer yours.

Yang With regard to the magazines, I found it interesting to think about the fact that a modern museum can also have "other" journals on offer – not just art magazines.

Why no *Vogue* or economic magazines such as *Brand Eins*? If you look at art magazines, they are one-third full of fashion advertisements in any case, so why not have a fashion magazine to begin with? Besides, contemporary art is interested in questions and ideas that are not necessarily addressed in art magazines.

As for the chairs, I did not want to attempt a work of modernist design. It was much more a matter of what constitutes a "copy." Does an "imitation" always have to be substandard and something "negative" merely because the act of copying or replicating is assumed to be negative? Can it not emancipate itself from the original and shed light on something new? Or might one not also regard the "counterfeit" as an expression of a certain desire? Because then the act of copying could have positive connotations. All the elements seen in the café should be recognized, but only upon closer scrutiny should a gap become apparent, a divergence from that which one thought to have in front of one's very eyes.

Steiner We almost forgot to discuss the wallpaper in the restrooms …

Yang It's a typical photo wallpaper that you can order from a catalog, showing the Caribbean, New York by night, or the Alps, as well as many other motifs of longing and desire. The wallpaper fills the wall opposite the mirror

- -

Because of the need for natural ventilation, ventilation openings were also integrated into the curtain wall façade. We experimented at first with window openings between the ceiling-high fixed glass elements, but these were visually unsettling and also did not provide a sufficient amount of security. Ultimately, we decided on narrow ventilation slats, which were located as joints connecting each glass element. We arranged these joints unevenly, with consistently varying distances, which ascend and descend around the building. The consistent variation of these dividers adds an additional dynamic element, thereby heightening the perspectival perception of the building.

in the restrooms so that you can see yourself in front of these familiar landscapes when you gaze into the mirror.

Steiner   In terms of space, you have adjusted yourself to the visitors' movements.

Yang   I had initial problems with the concept of the café. On the one hand, because I liked Anita's café; on the other hand, because it is a complex space – a sort of non-space, in fact, with three entrances. Its transitional atmosphere does not induce a feeling of permanence. But I decided to keep the structure of the space and to respond to it with the furnishing. The arrangement of the furniture is flexible and can easily be changed, something that has already taken place. The café manager broke up the "French rows" – bench alongside bench and table next to table, facing outside – and formed groups of tables and benches instead. Before, of course, everyone wanted to sit on the benches, making themselves comfortable there.

Steiner   You were both keen to investigate functional questions. Why are they so important to you? It is commonplace to assume that artists are not interested in practical things.

Yang   Ultimately, this is a coffee shop and, thus, serves a practical purpose. I approached the whole project as if the coffee shop were a medium akin to film, video, or photography. As a result, the practical aspect was not a compromise, but rather intrinsic to the whole thought process.

Leisz   Questions relating to proportion and material were important for me; I wanted things to feel good. However, I couldn't go so far as to design the furniture myself which is why I had to find another solution. With the bar and some bar tables located at the far ends of the room, a higher level was created. This arrangement gave the rectangular room, accessible from both sides, a middle area where the lower-lying furniture was found. It was important that the chairs were swivel chairs; otherwise it would have been difficult to change and adjust your glance – into the park outside, to your friend, or around the café interior at night. This gave the visitors a sense of freedom.

I mainly worked with furniture that was already present. The core of the fauteuil came from Ikea, the material for the upholstery from Scotland, and the tabletop fixtures are those found in American diners. I had additional footrests made for the bar tables, creating for more seating comfort. I was lucky enough to find just the right amount of chairs at a second-hand dealer; and I designed the bar stools in the style of the chairs, then had them built.

Steiner   It is striking that your work never ended up purely in a rendering of services, but that the parameters of the project became a subject in their own right. In

---

Economical, simple, and industrial materials ended up being combined with high-end and costly materials. The windowpanes had to be as large as possible, but at the same time, their construction had to be simple and economical. On both sides of the ventilation slats – economical, mass-produced products – there were frames made from conventional rolled steel sections applied with a fire-retardant paint. Before them, the glass components measuring up to twelve square meters and weighing up to 700 kilograms were installed. These twin columns are partly structural, in other words, they also carry the weight of the roof edge, which is unusual and only possible because no torque from the roof weight is being transferred onto the glass. As was the case for all the lateral faces of the internal walls, the same material, anodized aluminum sheets, was selected for the subsequent flashing of the parapet, base, and adjoining wall areas.

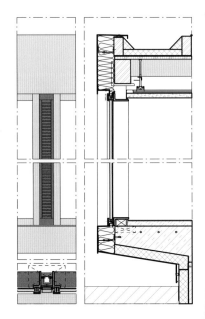

Construction drawing of the glazing, elevation and plan

other words: what does it mean to design a café? What is its intended function? What does a café offer beyond functionality and so forth?

In the meantime, visitors have not simply become accustomed to the changing café concept, but they even like it: they expect a new refurbishment and a new name. We often used to hear that a name change every two years entails the death of public awareness. But the opposite is the case. To all intents and purposes, you also have to admit that every café had and has its own fans. The venue will be returned to you after the two years are up. Anita, what will you do with it?

Leisz   I am waiting for the chance to redesign it – probably in a smaller, more concentrated form. I'm looking forward to it.

Steiner   Jun, do you already have any particular ideas? Yang: Hmm, I haven't actually thought much about it yet. I like the idea that it has a transient nature: a coffeehouse of yearning and desire which will later exist only in the form of a memory. I am also interested in the ways in which the next person will deal with the space, that is, with the "coffeehouse" as a medium.

Materials of the glazing

In November 2004, the building was officially opened with the exhibition project, *Performative Architecture*. The design process of the building was characterized by a fluid transition between variously overlapping interfaces. For example, we designed the café as a space that leaves enough room to be altered and redesigned by artists every two years. A bar counter was designed, but the lighting and the surfaces were kept for the most part alterable. The design of the building's entry area further developed and changed over several years through the cooperation of the GfZK with BLESS and thus, the process of spatial adaptability on the structural level was continued. Just as the spatial variability of the movable elements of the building guarantees that it never arrives at a perfect final state, the process of its planning will continually update itself through the process of the artistic and curatorial negotiations with the building.

AS IF A to Z ...

Architecture – as in the case of the new building of the GfZK – is essentially based in a concept of time. In this concept of time, the only constant is change. Given cultural, social, political, and economic change, constructing a contemporary space means to construct the possibility of spatial change. It seems paradoxical that an awareness of the potential of change anticipates change. The structure within which changes might occur remains as a constant. In this sense, space represents an order and, at the same time, changes providing the spatial order with a program. As the exhibition schedule serves to program time well in advance of each respective change to the space – implying that each spatial alteration may be superseded for each successive exhibition – space appears as a secondary dimension. Space is the medium in which time reveals itself. What emerges as (a) space appears as the bare present, captured here and now as a spatio-temporal aperture for the duration of an exhibition – comparable to photography and its phantasmatic core, capable of purloining a single moment from the flow of time. Thus, the changeability of the space temporarily captured evokes notions of presence, contemporaneity, and the aura of an event. Contrary to expectation, here, the "event" consists of a state in which nothing changes for a specific period of time. In this sense, architecture is a time machine: it represents the constant of change while simultaneously eliciting a hiatus – a moment in time, the architectural "snapshot" of the present.

A

Architektur → Architecture

Visitors are invited to make decisions while on their way through the exhibitions. The building's modifiable internal order is designed to offer a variety of alternative routes through the exhibitions and gallery spaces. The movable walls make it possible to create varying visual axes – thus introducing the option of producing different relationships between the artworks and spaces. As a result, the route chosen by the visitor is decisive for the perspectives and specific ways of perceiving the spaces and works. Like looking, walking is integral to the production of meaning. Regardless of whether we stroll, meander or cover a predetermined distance – walking defines a form of mobility and satisfies a desire for movement. Here, movement implies no more than expressing mastery over time: walking is a form of spending time, and the selected form of ambulation defines the temporal concept from which it departs. Conscious of the fact that the spatial situations may change, the visitor does not know where the way through the spaces and exhibitions will lead him/her. Paradoxically, precisely this lack of knowledge about the spaces demands that we scrutinize them – perhaps only as an expression of that temporary state when, afraid of losing our way, we seek orientation. Basically, the architecture prescribes the routes to be taken, knowing that we may find or leave them.

B

Besucherinnen und Besucher → Visitors

Cafés take into account that institutions, alongside their core tasks, also fulfill functions that are primarily concerned with the institution's cultural embedding. In this sense, the café is also an institution: it is its host institution's alter ego,

C

Cafés

providing a range of hybrid functions from leisure room, restaurant (also with guaranteed restrooms), to public meeting space. Spatially, cafés are integrated in the surrounding institution while also being external to it: the café parasitically feeds on the life of the institution, whilest retaining its autonomy in the cultural and urban environment. One can go to the café without having to visit the institution. Suspended between the institution and its immediate surroundings, cafés always have two entrances and exits; essentially, they are passages, inviting individuals who don't know how else to spend their time to spend it there. Cafés are time machines for spaces of temporal transit. Translating this idea into architectural space implies mediating the impression of an interior space that not only faces outside, but which also represents a paradoxical interior space located within the exterior: sitting in the café, one is still in the city from which one has just departed. Herein lies the reason for the dialectic of glass and concrete, which, incidentally, also extends into areas where there is no longer any mention of institutions and cafés. Contemporary notions of space are constituted by intermediate and hybrid forms of interior and exterior space.

D

Die Orientierung → The Orientation

Architecture's medial orientation is discussed under "M" below.

E

Erinnerung → Memory

Memory plays a key role in architecture, because when we think of architecture we tend to think of a house – as the memory of an archetypal form of architecture. The idea of the house evokes underlying concepts of interior and exterior space. These conceptions of interior and exterior space involve the appropriate mechanisms of inclusion and exclusion, facilitating the divide between occupants and visitors. The paradox of an institutional space lies in the fact that, formally, the latter denotes a specific *interior* space while simultaneously emphasizing that specifically this space cannot be occupied. The acts of visiting and occupying institutionally merge into one another – in a sense visitors to an institution are also its occupants. Aware of the cultural and political problems elicited by the relationship between interior and exterior space, institutions can be seen as representing contemporary living conditions. A primary achievement of institutions is to repeatedly insist on issues concerning the distribution of property and ownership. Even exhibitions that "occupy" the spaces for a certain period of time are merely "visiting." As a consequence, this suggests that architectural concepts for the design of an institution have to reject the typology of the house, in order to propose a spatial order that nullifies distinctions between inside and outside. The aim of this model of architecture is to quash our memory of the house – in terms of its being a paradigm determining conceptions of political and/or cultural space.

F

Feuerlöscher → Fire extinguishers

The fire extinguisher is an unappreciated necessity, for architecture does all it can to prevent the outbreak of fire. The assumption that the fire extinguishers will most probably not be put to use, marks a dysfunctionality that rivals artworks addressing the dysfunctional. Regardless of where they are placed, their position is always wrong. And because their position is always wrong, they are subject to being noticed and consequently in some way in the right place. Considering their "wrong position" evokes contemporary concepts of the subject – an entity, which, in spatio-political terms, is no longer ascribed to a conclusively correct location. From this perspective, the contemporary subject is a spatio-political fire extinguisher, because the subject reminds us of a space that is no longer allowed to exist. Not the fire, but the subject is highly dangerous – seeming to be in the wrong place wherever it appears.

Sometimes there is sufficient reason for no reason at all. Appearing to hover about thirty centimeters above the ground, the architecture seems to defy both gravity and reason. The architecture's purpose does not lie in its foundations: it draws its cause from other vectors – from lines of argument that run through the building, encompass it and connect it with contexts and spaces of different origins. The grounds for this type of architecture are not the ground on which it is built, but rather a heterotopian mesh that confuses and deregulates the geographical location to the ends of revealing a geopolitical task. The reasons lie elsewhere, widely dispersed. Yet they are no less present than the territory concealing the ground – by claiming to be identical with the grounds validating it.

Houses are the *doppelgangers* of a form of architecture that seeks to abandon the – eternally returning – house. As already partly discussed under "E" above, contemporary architecture aims at a form of architecture without houses. As in the case of the GfZK, the building's form adheres to the logics of change and adaptability. That, which appears as the outer form, is the external expression of the structure's intrinsic changeability: sharp angles, shifting perspectives and transparency serve to abandon forms of self-contained house. The house is broken up into fragments of space and architecture. A path remains, defining a circuit around the building – this however, does not necessarily provide better understanding of the edifice. Defying predictability, the architecture appeals to the fragmentary instead. Its esthetic calculates the unpredictable – a principle extended to the interchangeable use of materials, colors, and textures, which are repeatedly employed both on the inside and outside of the building. The spatial concept of the city replaces the house. To navigate through the city streets is akin to navigating within a form of architecture primarily committed to ideas of urbanity rather than to concepts of the house. Thus, this architecture is not conceived of as having a roof, but rather as comprising volumes of varying, limited clear heights – as if the building contains several houses. What appears as the roof is merely the base sheet for a potential terrace, or an additional level of navigation and access. Conceived as pavements and ramps, the entrances to the café and gallery are characteristic features. Thus, the building is not accessed through a door, but rather via pavements as extensions of the street. When one leaves the car, the pavement is that part of the street remaining – with the subject becoming a pedestrian vehicle.

Inside and outside are less dependent on spatial than on political coordinates.

James Joyce's *Ulysses* was not instrumental in planning the architectural design. Still, his translation of Homer's *Odyssey* into the period and course of one day could be seen as a model for the way in which our design translates a highly complex spatial fate of geopolitical consequence into the architecture of a single edifice. In this sense, the architecture of the GfZK is also about an odyssey.

Like "GfZK"

Light is just as crucial for architecture as it is for photography. Beyond color, gradations of light and dark help to define the envisioned image of interior and exterior. It gets light inside when it gets dark outside, and vice versa. If one aims, as this form of architecture does, to minimize the opposites of inside and outside, light is central. Glass surfaces, windows conceived as transparent walls, and intelligent lighting systems in all the galleries, together serve to penetrate the heterogeneous lighting conditions at work in the building. Not only can the light units be rotated to correspond to the respective position of the movable spatial axes, they are also dimmable – in other words, capable of adapting and responding to varying light conditions. The camouflage thus elicited oscillates between adaptation to, and total emancipation from, ordinary sunlight: white box, black box – no box at all. If light suffuses the building without automatically affecting color and luminosity, the interior space appears merely as an architectural membrane in exterior space. Thus, at nighttime the light on the inside shines through the glass walls, extending the architecture outwards and into the nocturnal city. Light in architecture is not only a matter of illumination, but rather of defining a space as interior, exterior, or both at once: light is not about visibility conditions, but rather concerns the specific meaning ascribed to a given space.

M

Medien → Media

To a large extent, the media determine the notion of the present. They impart as the present that which otherwise would not be perceivable, thereby revealing a simultaneity of presence and absence. The ubiquitous desire for mediality suggests a longing for the coexistence of presence and absence: everything should be accessible and perceivable on condition that it be absent, or – put differently – medially present. This simultaneity of absence and presence is therefore constitutive of a perception of space, which inevitably must incorporate both figures. Architecture that faces this relationship inevitably has to invoke space as a medium in its own right – to consequently forward a type of architecture that provides real spaces while simultaneously merely evoking them. Significantly, as a medium, architecture should not convey a message giving information on what it contains; its form should not allow conclusions to be drawn as to the function of the architecture. To define architecture as a medium means to conceive of space as a medial construction – to transform concrete space into the mere image of space. Architecturally, this means linking the notion of constructing space to the projection of space. The use of alternating materials and colors to variegate the floors and walls of the GfZK addresses both the variability of the spatial situations as well as the heterogeneity of the surfaces – to the end of determining the spaces' respective visual layout. It is no coincidence that the only "static" space in the gallery is the cinema, a projection room in the center of the building. Consisting on one side of a load-bearing wall, and of glass partitions on its three other sides, architecturally, the cinema itself is a spatial projection. Reflective, opaque, and transparent at once, it functions as an optical enigma, folding inward from outside. It is a paradigmatic space within the building, providing all subsequent architectural cues. Like the café, the cinema represents both an exterior space shifted inside, as well as an interior space enclosed by the institution external to it. It is simultaneously a real place and an imaginary space. The cinema is designed to be not only a reference to the media of film and video. It is also conceived of as a medial figure, a constructed film that continues to be present even when no film is being screened. In this sense, the architecture already anticipates the intended apparition of the medial.

After the end of modernism and driven by the crisis of teleology, architectural discourse aimed at overcoming the social and cultural goals of modernism – in an attempt to define architecture instead as a cultural response to the crisis. Combining the most heterogeneous array of elements culled from the history of architecture, the forms of architecture referred to by the term "postmodernism" are as familiar as many a new museum building. Such edifices are so popular due to their appealing synthesis of public interest (with the political dimension that this implies) and the rhetoric of a self-referential type of architecture. From a 1980s perspective, "architecture" and "public" are almost synonymous. Let us note at this point architecture's impact as a paradigm in contemporaneous philo-sophical and theoretical discourses. In retrospect, this view of architecture for the sake of architecture proved to be a surrogate action: insisting on architecture's public responsibility is precisely what caused the lack or lacuna associated with notions of the public to be over-hastily compensated and filled. The greater the publicity connected with a given construction assignment, the more attractive the commission was. The implied publicity value of projects related to art meant that, alongside museums, all forms of exhibition hall and art institution that had to be founded, built or extended, were of particular interest architecturally speaking. Constructing architecture for a public institution denoted constructing an image of public aimed at a public for which one could not or did not want to create an image. From this perspective, the tendency towards the spectacular or monumental, as classic figures representing public interest, is self-explanatory. Of course, the architecture inaugurated, as it were, before its inauguration, was architecture for its own sake.

Contemporary architecture should aim to counter the historic purpose of architecture as a substitute act for crisis-ridden concepts of public – even if this means removing the architecture from the image of architecture. In other words, the attempt to challenge existing expectations for architecture – namely archi-tecture's capacity to advocate an image of public – implies refusing to relay this desire. Given that "public" and "architecture" are almost synonymous, this entails the task of reducing the architectural presence of the architecture in order to evoke a space that exceeds, and permeates – or sometimes even ignores or trivial-izes – the architecture.

The architectural design of the GfZK denies a general view of the edifice: angles, edges, and perspectives confuse rather than clarify the architectural object. The design elicits open-sided, negotiable spaces. Rather than prompting architectural constructions or forms, it provides essential architectural props, which, if necessary can be moved and modified as required, so as to render visible sections of space. Rather than staging and displaying an image of public, in the GfZK building, the architecture recoils – functioning as a space machine. This accounts for the mechanics of the sliding walls: the surrogate action represented by architecture is inverted to the physical activity of producing space – thus turning architecture into a public tool.

Surfaces that are suggestive of properties other than the functions concealed by them pursue the principle of the masquerade, and thus abide to a certain extent by illusionism. If surface design is foregrounded as the most predominant feature of a space, one could conclude that the load-bearing elements are intended as secondary and are thus to remain concealed. This dialectic would conceivably produce necessary distinctions between surface and construction, image and architecture. In terms of a form of architecture essentially geared towards the architectural image, space is defined by constructing surfaces. Paradoxically, the surfaces specified in the plans provide the argumentative figures for the construction proper that precede and follow planning. Subsequently, this does not produce a masquerade but rather a specific reality coinciding with the idea of reality, and knowledge pertaining to the imaginary: illusionism does not advocate a false appearance concealing reality, but rather a definition of reality, for which illusionism itself represents a very real figure – thus fulfilling a vital political, cultural, and social function in the process. In architecture, this form of illusionism opposes the illusion of wanting to perceive portions of the unalterable present in constructed manifestations and architectural designs of "versions of reality." Identifying an imaginary figure with reality, this form of Illusionism supports the notion that, in the real building, the preliminary model preceding it should still be discernible.

In this sense, the surfaces deployed in contemporary architecture do not appeal for illusions, but rather for proposals of a model quality. As proposals, they remain virulent and negotiable. As construction guidelines, they insist that the construction itself can merely react to notions of reality in a model way – hence possessing illusionistic traits to some extent. If a construction seeks to disguise this principle by suppressing the surfaces, the architecture becomes all the more of a masquerade concealing its imaginary core.

P

Prinzipiell → In principle

In principle, contemporary architecture has to contend with legal and natural laws.

Q

Quantität → Quantity

At the moment, quantity tends to be used as proof of quality. The economy driving this argument has little to do with the term *oikos* (ancient Greek οἶκος = house) from which it stems.

R

Renderings

Renderings are not only vital for the plans and the property developers' decisions. Above all, they sustain processes of abstraction and virtuality that precede architecture, and that are also associated with it after construction. Simulations of potentially realistic results transform tangible products into pure potentiality, sustainable even after the animations stop moving. In this sense, the virtuality and spatial concepts of rendering are not tools for better clarification, but rather qualities intrinsic to architecture. The effect this has may sound absurd, but in reality it is not: the model is not manifested in the architecture – the model is actually constructed. That which is finalized in the end is the rendering itself – in other words, the architecture is, upon completion, still in a phase of preliminary planning. Significantly, this potentiality by far exceeds possible utility profiles by aiming to fictionalize space. As it was one of the house's primary functions to provide protection, the domestic interior formerly represented resistance against the hostile exterior. In contrast, rendering aims at architecture's new protective function by providing fictions. Perceiving fiction as a form of protection is, as it were, a contemporary translation of the former notion of the interior.

S

Statistisch → Statistically

Statistically speaking, in contemporary architectural discourses the city and urbanism are probably referred to most frequently. In terms of architecture, this requires developing spatial concepts that mediate a consciousness of urbanity even when lost in the depths of the inner corridors and subsidiary rooms of a given building complex. It has become just as popular to incorporate the street in front of the house into the architecture by extending it into the building, as it has to replace doorways and gates with open air corridors and air locks. The literal translation of the urban infrastructure into architectural motifs has a metaphoric quality, proving that, paradoxically, the metaphor of the city precedes the architecture actually producing the city. As demonstrated by the GfZK-2 design by as-if berlinwien, contemporary architecture broadens this perspective by focusing on the concept of the contemporary subject rather than on architectural references. It is the contemporary subject – defined as urban and therefore familiarized with a wide range of social, cultural, and economic contradictions – that provides the coordinates for the spatial concepts. Precisely on the grounds of remaining irreducible to a specific subjective entity, reference to the subject is distinctly urban – insofar as this addresses the anonymity of the subject. In this sense, contemporary architecture and institutions such as the GfZK do not seek to address a public deemed to be represented by them, but rather the concept of a subject conceivable only in a public context. What subsequently appears as architecture is like the contemporary subject's skin – although it is impossible to tell who is inside.

Theory and practice form an inseparable couple. Historically speaking, this mutual relationship resembles a crisis-ridden marriage. By analogy, respective claims to power and related emancipatory ideas were seen to develop within this relationship. At least both have learned from each other that they cannot manage without each other. Both have also learned that it is impossible to leave behind the utopian fusion of their respective histories, methods, and scopes of action. Inseparably conjoined, both theory and practice have at least come to accept and appreciate each other's idiosyncrasies and intrinsic qualities. This is coupled with the realization that, over the years, each side has to a lesser extent come to tolerate the idiosyncrasies and traits of the other – instead, these have literally been appropriated by both in a reciprocal way. In view of this fact, architecture constituted in equal measure by theory and practice is less about buildings or objects but rather about meshes of relationships. Thus, to assess the quality of architecture necessarily entails drawing into consideration the respective way in which theory and practice interrelate in a given work of architecture, and the intensity of this correspondence.

T
Theorie → Theory

Under circumstances

U
Unter → Under

Vectors define quantities, marking both their location and direction. A vector is represented in its simplest form by an arrow defining a specific location within a plane or three-dimensional space. The vector's magnitude and arrowhead provide information as to its direction and scale, necessary to determine the orientation of other reference values. The vector is a central symbol in architectural practice because it is capable of describing a fixed quantity and the latter's directional movement at the same time. By extension, vectorial architecture denotes a form of architecture that is still dependent on movement and aspect/direction after construction is completed. In contrast to orientation based on teleological figures, which, ideologically or esthetically, steer towards a vanishing point or future target, vectors enable more than one vectorial route at any given time, thus also validating the coexistence of varying reference values. Contemporary architecture, as in the case of the GfZK, succeeds in rendering tangible this difference of scale and directional movement to the ends of abstract representations

V
Vektoren → Vectors

and perceptions of space: the architecture does not define itself as the sole point of departure for further developments, but rather also as a direct result of decisive vectors – regardless of whether these were inherently of an economic, cultural, esthetic, or theoretical nature.

W

www.as-if.info and www.gfzk.de

X

Xenophobien → Xenophopia

Xenophobia is inseparable from concepts of space. Xenophobia arises when a space is conceived of as a homogenous entity, in turn challengeable by any form of (cultural or racial) difference. This leads to exclusion strategies solely aimed at achieving a homogenous interior space, thus evoking the exterior environment as inevitably hostile. Architecture that seeks to define exemplary models of space in order to assume a politico-cultural position must necessarily draw into consideration the possible spatio-political effects of xenophobia – even if this entails, as in the case of the GfZK building, tangibly avoiding homogenizing tendencies and suggestions of a clear division between interior and exterior. But this spatio-political issue cannot be resolved simply by utilizing more or less glass, but rather by actively mediating the concept of the non-homogenous subject. Only confronting the contemporary subject with the task of differentiation and having to come to terms with a variety of contradictory demands, can provide the coordinates engendering heterogeneity in the everyday, and of the related forms of spatial politics.

The architecture of GfZK represents a broad spectrum of decisions taking into account the heterogeneous demands made on and by the contemporary subject. This includes problematizing the relationship between inside and outside and the presence of spaces defined by an array of different media – actively fostering variable concepts of space and a polydimensional cartography of the subject. By manifesting in its exhibition program the divergence between concepts of the subject and freedoms of action, the GfZK becomes a space in which the heterogeneity and everyday nature of the unknown represent the legitimate basis for a course of action, for which there are no rules – nor need be.

Y

You

Z

Zuletzt → Ultimately

Ultimately, it is a matter of a drawing being capable of spontaneously outlining an idea, and subsequently of translating that drawing into another medium. If, in the translation of the original idea into a work of architecture, the drawing and its underlying abstraction of space remain perceptible, architecture returns to its point of origin – to the idea, that (constructed) space above all challenges concepts of space and their immediate consequences. But the analysis of this form of abstraction should have figured under "A" above …

Barbara Steiner
Performative Architektur als Grundlage des performativen Museums[1]

Seit 2004 ist die Auseinandersetzung mit Performativität Bestandteil der Programmatik der GfZK. Erstmals benutzten wir den Begriff im Rahmen der Ausstellung *Performative Architektur*, die zusammen mit dem Siemens Arts Program durchgeführt wurde.[2] Konkreter Anlass war der Bau des neuen Ausstellungshauses durch das ArchitektInnenteam as-if berlinwien. Von diesem performativ angelegten Bau ausgehend wurden BLESS, Monica Bonvicini, Angela Bulloch, Oliver Hangl, Jeppe Hein, Olaf Nicolai, Anita Leisz und Pro qm eingeladen, sich mit dem Verhältnis von Architektur und Performativität aus künstlerischer Perspektive zu befassen. Seitdem wurde der Begriff „Performativität" nach und nach auf die Museumskonzeption selbst übertragen. Beide Begriffe, sowohl „performative Architektur" als auch „performatives Museum", scheinen einen doppelten Widerspruch zu provozieren, lassen sich doch weder die statischen Konzepte der Architektur noch des Museums auf den ersten Blick mit Performativität in Verbindung bringen.

Nach John Langshaw Austin ist ein performativer Sprechakt ein Akt, in dem der Sprecher das hervorbringt, was er sagt: Ich äußere mich sprachlich und vollziehe – im Sinne von „saying makes it so" – eine Handlung.[3] Austins Begriff wurde später reformuliert, korrigiert und erweitert, angefangen von den Mustern, Möglichkeiten und Grenzen der Funktionen von Sprache, den Kontexten, Sozialstrukturen und Kompetenzen der SprecherInnen, den Ritualen und Stereotypisierungen, denen performative Äußerungen unterliegen, bis hin zu den Folgen und Wirkungen der wirklichkeitskonstituierenden Macht von Sprache. Einen besonderen Stellenwert nimmt die Geschlechterforschung ein, die Sprechakten im Zusammenhang mit Identitätsbildung nachgeht.[4]

In den 1960er Jahren tauchte der Begriff in der bildenden Kunst als „Performance" auf und meinte in erster Linie ein einmaliges, zeitlich begrenztes Ereignis, oft auch ein situationsbezogenes Ad-hoc-Agieren, das sich – in der westlichen Hemisphäre – vor allem gegen eine Priorisierung des statischen, ästhetischen Objekts und die „Kommodifizierung" von Kunst wandte und neue Produktions- und Rezeptionsbedingungen einforderte.[5] Auch der White Cube, als dominantes Modell des Ausstellens in der Nachkriegszeit, rückte ins Zentrum der Kritik und wurde, wie das Objekt, einer Verzeitlichung unterworfen. Der Ausstel-

lungsraum fungierte nicht länger als repräsentatives Behältnis unverrückbarer Werte und Zuschreibungen, sondern als Ort für temporäre und veränderbare Setzungen: Der Raum selbst transformierte sich in einen Ereignisraum, der einmalige Erfahrungen und Begegnungen in einem Hier und Jetzt versprach.

Diese Entwicklungen hatten auch Auswirkungen auf die Konzeption der Museen: Willem Sandberg, der damalige Direktor des Stedelijk Museums in Amsterdam, überlegte sogar, die alte Idee des Museums mit permanenter Ausstellung völlig aufzugeben. Er wollte, um das Museum zu dynamisieren und zugänglicher zu machen, die Kunstwerke ins Depot stellen und nur zu bestimmten Ausstellungen hervorholen. Dann sollten sie in ein Ambiente mit Freizeitcharakter eingestellt werden, um durch synästhetische Strategien, Kontraste, Überraschungen und Schocks die BesucherInnen aus ihrer Passivität zu holen und zu einer aktiven Auseinandersetzung mit Kunst zu motivieren.[6] Sandbergs emanzipativ gedachter Ansatz vom Museum als einem Erlebnisraum, in dem Raum, Display, Kunstwerke und BesucherInnen zusammengedacht werden, mündete später – wiewohl gänzlich unbeabsichtigt – direkt in eine Eventkultur. Während in seinen Ausstellungen, etwa *Dylaby* 1962, Mechanismen der Inszenierung nachvollziehbar blieben, kam es in späteren Umdeutungen des Sandbergschen Ansatzes zu einer Absorption der BesucherInnen ins Spektakel. Der Einsatz des Performativen bedeutet heute also nicht länger automatisch Emanzipation und Aktivierung oder gar Kritik an herrschenden Verhältnissen, an Materialismus und Konsumismus, sondern mitunter auch Komplizenschaft zwischen Spektakelkultur und Neoliberalismus. Performative Äußerungen können affirmative und emanzipative Funktion besitzen, herrschende Muster und Einstellungen bestätigen, aber auch Abweichungen produzieren, selbst wenn diese nicht unbedingt intendiert sind.

Der Neubau der GfZK von as-if berlinwien basiert auf einem veränderbaren und veränderlich angelegten Raum- und Nutzungskonzept. Teilweise großformatige Schiebe- und Drehtüren sowie Vorhänge erlauben eine wahlweise Verbindung oder Trennung der Räume, um unterschiedliche Raumkonfigurationen, verschiedene Ausstellungssituationen und inhaltliche Verknüpfungen zu ermöglichen. Die Räume erschließen sich über die Bewegung: Dem Blick öffnen sich ständig wechselnde, unvorhersehbare Ansichten und Verbindungen. Ausblicke aus den raumhohen Fenstern auf die Straße, die Nachbarhäuser und die Parklandschaft verankern die Architektur im städtischen

Umfeld; Blickverbindungen, Unterschlitze in den Wänden und die Gestaltung der Oberflächen verknüpfen Räume und Raumteile mit Elementen der Ausstellung. Glaswände, transparente Flächen, Vorhänge und spiegelnde Oberflächen erinnern an großformatige Screens. Die Konzeption des Baus ist darauf ausgerichtet, die Räume immer wieder neu zu definieren und mit unterschiedlichen Funktionen „aufzuladen". So sind verglaste Partien unter anderem als Schaufenster, das Kino als Ausstellungs- oder Vortragsraum, das Café und der Ausstellungsraum als Projektraum oder umgekehrt nutzbar.

Performativität wird hier im Sinne einer räumlichen Praxis verstanden. Die Anlage und die Ausstattung der Räume sensibilisieren für die mögliche Verschiebung der Räume[7] und ihrer Funktionen, aber eben auch für räumliche Limitierungen, gesellschaftliche Verfasstheit und Einbettung. Veränderbarkeit und Inszenierungsmöglichkeiten erweisen sich daher auch als bewusst begrenzt und Transparenz als gesteuert. Nicht alle Wände sind verschiebbar und selbst diejenigen, die es sind, können nicht alle gleichzeitig bewegt werden, sodass sich die KuratorInnen für eine Option entscheiden müssen. Die Wände komplett auszubauen ist technisch unmöglich. Auch können die Vorhänge nur an bestimmten Stellen angebracht werden; in manchen Raumzonen sind Verdunkelungen nicht umsetzbar. „Störungen" der Sichtbarkeit durch Unterschlitze oder Einfall des Sonnenlichts sind mit einkalkuliert. Aussparungen, Öffnungen, Ein- und Ausblicke im gesamten Gebäude und zur Stadt hin lassen Sichtbarkeit und Transparenz deutlich als über Blickregime gesteuert erkennen. Das Subjekt wird in seinem Abhängigkeitsverhältnis zum architektonischen und sozialen Umfeld angesprochen. Der Bau ist kontingent, fluid angelegt. Außen und Innen gehen ineinander über; Grenzziehungen verunklären sich, die Instabilität räumlicher Verhältnisse ist Programm. All diese Faktoren bringen das Konzept von as-if berlinwien in einen direkten Gegensatz zum weißen Ausstellungsraum, der als ein aus einem gesellschaftlichen Zusammenhang herausgenommener (statischer) Raum mit gleichmäßiger (und gleichbleibender) Ausleuchtung und Abschottung nach außen konzipiert ist. In *Inside the White Cube* sprach Brian O'Doherty nicht umsonst despektierlich von der „Ewigkeitsauslage" White Cube.[8] as-if berlinwien bezieht sich auf diesen weißen Ausstellungsraum, klappt ihn buchstäblich auf, perforiert ihn durch Schiebewände, Ober- und Unterschlitze, verschleift Innen und Außen und übersetzt seine Irreversibilität in Reversibilität. Besonders deutlich wird die Bezugnahme zum White Cube in jenen Räumen, in denen eine zweite, zusätzliche Schicht von Gipskartonwänden eingezogen wurde, die von bestimmten Standpunkten aus deutlich als Raum im Raum in Erscheinung tritt. Der White Cube, nun zum Grey Cube verschoben, verliert dadurch seine universell angelegte, ideale Konzeption und auch seine Autorität.

Architektur ist – zunächst sehr allgemein gesprochen – primär dadurch charakterisiert, Raum bzw. das Verhältnis von Innen und Außen zu organisieren. Das liberalbürgerliche Subjekt könnte noch auf einer klaren Trennung von öffentlicher und privater Sphäre beharren – eine Trennung, die seinem Bedürfnis nach Schutz, aber auch nach Separierung und Ausschluss entgegenkam. Doch ist dieses Konzept eines „bürgerlichen Heims", verstanden als spezifische kulturelle Produktion von Grenzen, Raumzuweisungen und Repräsentationen, genauso wie das bürgerliche Subjekt selbst massiv in die Krise geraten.[9] Außen und Innen haben sich verunklärt, sie sind ambivalent geworden; das moderne Subjekt muss mit dieser Verunsicherung leben. Während Le Corbusier das „bedrohliche" Außen noch aus einem sicheren, orientierbaren Innen betrachten lässt, es zum „Bild" macht und damit domestiziert, setzen Vertreter der „nomadisierenden Architektur" mit ihren Mobilitätskonzepten das Subjekt sprichwörtlich in Bewegung. Es lässt sich mit seiner Behausung nicht mehr verorten, ist selbst „ortlos" geworden. Die dekonstruktivistische Architektur treibt die Instabilität des Subjekts weiter und übersetzt sie in die Architektur. Die Instabilität räumlicher Verhältnisse muss dabei in Relation zum „instabilen" Subjekt verstanden werden.[10]

Die Thematisierung und Problematisierung von Subjekt und Raumverhältnissen finden sich jedoch nicht nur in der Architektur, sondern auch in der bildenden Kunst. So geht Dan Graham in verschiedenen Arbeiten der Positionierung des Subjekts im Raum und der Konstituierung des Subjekts nach. In Public Space/Two Audiences (1976), einem durch eine Glasscheibe geteilten Raum, der über zwei Eingänge betreten werden kann, untersucht Dan Graham Prozesse der Subjektbildung, indem er das Verhältnis von Subjekt und Objekt exponiert: Ich blicke und werde angeblickt, bin einmal Subjekt und dann wieder Objekt. Der Einsatz von Spiegeln auf der Rückwand der einen Raumhälfte erlaubt es darüber hinaus, ganz im Lacanschen Sinne, sich selbst – als einen anderen – zu betrachten.[11] Das Verhalten der BesucherInnen, die quasi auf einer Bühne agieren, betrachten und betrachtet werden, ZuschauerInnen und SchauspielerInnen zugleich sind, wird mit ausgestellt. In seinen Pavillonarbeiten versetzt Graham dann das

Subjekt in die Situation, entscheiden zu müssen, ob er den Raum als Außen- oder Innenraum oder als beides gleichermaßen lesen möchte. Er setzt dabei bewusst auf die Konnotationen von Materialien wie Glas, Spiegelglas, Plexiglas oder auch getöntes Thermoglas – Materialien, die traditionell Schnittstellen markieren.

Dieses Interesse an der Interpretationsleistung und damit an der Aktivierung der RezipientInnen findet sich auch bei Jorge Pardo: 4166 Sea View Lane (1994–1998) gibt weder eine klare Auskunft über den Status des „Objekts" – das heißt, ob es sich um ein Haus, eine Skulptur oder um ein Ausstellungsprojekt handelt[12] noch gibt es dabei eine klare Markierung von Innen und Außen. Was innen und außen ist, ist abhängig von der Perspektive des Betrachters. Konnotationen entstehen durch die spezifische, individuelle Aufladung mit Bedeutung, nicht durch visuelle Distinktion. Pardo begreift seine Objekte quasi als in einem Durchgangsstadium von Bedeutungsaufnahme und -produktion befindlich. Seine Objekte, Bilder, Fotos, Bücher sind so platziert, dass „Subjekte durch sie durchlaufen können",[13] je nach den Fragen, Anliegen, Erwartungen, die an die Arbeiten herangetragen werden.

In The Threshold of the Visible World widmet sich Kaja Silverman der psychoanalytischen Politik visueller Repräsentation.[14] Sie verweist auf die entscheidende Rolle des Screens bei der Subjektkonstitution, ein Punkt, in dem sich ihre Interessen mit jenen von Dan Graham und Jorge Pardo kreuzen. In der psychoanalytischen Theorie beschreibt der Screen eine Projektionsfläche, die das Verhältnis des Subjekts zur Realität und damit zu sich selbst reguliert und abbildet. Demnach erscheint uns die Realität nie unmittelbar, sondern immer nur vermittelt: als Bild, als Projektion, die interpretiert werden will. Am Screen zeichnen sich nicht nur gesellschaftliche und ideologische Vorstellungen ab, er bildet auch die Reflexionsfläche für das Subjekt, das sich wie im Spiegel – in diesem Bild von sich selbst – mehr oder weniger zu erkennen und in Übereinstimmung zu bringen sucht. Silverman setzt bei Subjekten an, die sich mehr und mehr über das Image definieren, die durch die Logik der Images, mit der wir Objekte erzeugen und selbst zu Objekten werden, und dadurch, wie wir diese als Werte verhandeln, geprägt werden.[15]

Die Architekten von as-if berlinwien denken in ihrem Konzept das Gebäude als einen architektonischen Screen, in dem sich gesellschaftliche Vorstellungen spiegeln, der die Blicke der BesucherInnen organisiert und ihr Verhältnis zur Realität abbildet, gleichzeitig aber deren Reflexionsfläche bildet. Die Konstitution der Architektur

wird dem Subjekt anheimgestellt, das sich der Veränderlichkeit der Architektur, der eigenen Position, und damit auch der Instabilität der Grenzen, Raumzuweisungen und Repräsentationen in jedem Moment bewusst ist. Außen kann Innen meinen, die räumlichen Schichtungen geben keine Auskunft mehr darüber, wo die eine Schicht endet und die andere beginnt. Die Räume sind nicht mehr nur für eine ganz bestimmte Funktion entworfen, sondern sie beinhalten von vornherein die Möglichkeit ihrer Neuinterpretation und damit auch Umwertung. Das Subjekt wird dadurch in eine aktive Rolle versetzt: zum einen durch die Vergegenwärtigung seiner mehrfach möglichen Positionierung im Raum, als Imago, als Reflexion und als physische Realität, zum anderen durch eine permanente Aufforderung, Bedeutungszusammenhänge herzustellen. Der Raum, seine Funktion und Aufladung sind verhandelbar.

Unmittelbar auf das architektonische Konzept von as-if berlinwien antworteten die Künstlerinnen Anita Leisz und BLESS. Leisz schob in ihrem Konzept für die Neugestaltung des GfZK-Cafés zwei Lokaltypen, das Tagescafé Neubau und die Bar Weezie, ineinander, ohne das Mobiliar zu verändern. Sie bot eine Art Grundvokabular an, dessen Elemente sie zum einen der Jugend- und Clubkultur zuordnete (zum Beispiel schwarz überstrichene Tischplatten) und zum anderen mit tradierter, gehoben-familiärer Wohnkultur verband (mit schottischem Tartan überzogene Sofas). Unterschiedliche Tageszeiten, verschieden sozialisierte Gästegruppen, verschiedene Nutzungen und Angebote führten zu vielfältigen Aneignungsformen und veränderten jeweils die Konnotationen der Ausstattung, von den Möbeln bis hin zum Geschirr. Letztlich verschob sich dadurch auch der Charakter des Lokals – aus Neubau wurde Weezie und umgekehrt. Auch wenn das Café und die Bar jeweils einer bestimmten Tages- oder eben Nachtzeit zugeordnet waren, konnten beide Orte auch gleichzeitig bestehen, bestimmt durch den jeweiligen Gast und seine Erwartungen. So wie im Gebäude von as-if berlinwien und im Café von Anita Leisz Optionen immer wieder von Neuem festgelegt werden mussten und müssen, tragen auch die Objekte in dem von BLESS gestalteten Eingangsbereich der GfZK-2 grundsätzlich mehrere Möglichkeiten in sich und wird auch hier der funktionale (und auch ästhetische) Status der Objekte kontinuierlich verschoben:[16] So liegen etwa die Bücher im Eingangsbereich nicht nur zum Lesen oder Kauf aus, sie transformieren sich (temporär) in Displays und Hocker; funktionale Computer- und Monitorkabel werden sichtbar geschmückt und damit zu

Preziosen (*BLESS N° 26 cable jewelleries*). Die *Perpetual home motion machines (BLESS N° 22)* bieten Ablage- und Präsentationsflächen, eines der Mobiles fungiert hauptsächlich als Garderobe. Manche Elemente geben zunächst keinen Hinweis auf ihre potenzielle Funktion, die Interpretation wird an die NutzerInnen delegiert.

Das Gebäude von as-if berlinwien und die Projekte von Anita Leisz und BLESS sind integraler und programmatischer Bestandteil einer Auffassung des performativen Museums, das räumliche und zeitliche Faktoren gleichermaßen umfasst. Der Aspekt des Performativen meint hier eine Teilhabe an Verhandlungsprozessen über Kunst und über den Ort der Kunst. In den mehrjährigen Forschungsprojekten und den jährlich wechselnden Sammlungspräsentationen der GfZK werden konfliktreiche Konstellationen von Haltungen hergestellt und in der Folge auch ausgestellt, gesellschaftliche und künstlerische Wertesysteme offensiv thematisiert und auch verrückt. Die Gebäude der GfZK-1, eine von Peter Kulka umgebaute Villa, und der GfZK-2 von as-if berlinwien bilden den jeweiligen Vermittlungsrahmen.

Abschließend möchte ich eines unserer Forschungsprojekte erwähnen, das die Prinzipien des „performativen Museums" besonders gut veranschaulicht. Für 2008 und 2009 hat die Galerie für Zeitgenössische Kunst elf Privatpersonen und Unternehmen, darunter auch einen Freundeskreis und zwei kommerzielle Galerien, ausgewählt und eingeladen, ihr Engagement für die Kunst in Form von Ausstellungen zu veranschaulichen und damit auch öffentlich zu machen. Die Beteiligten erhielten eine Carte Blanche, das heißt sie entschieden, was sie zeigen bzw. mit wem sie zusammenarbeiten wollten. Im Gegenzug übernahmen sie alle Kosten für ihre Ausstellung.[17]

Mit der Entscheidung für Carte Blanche öffnete sich die GfZK stark gegenüber Interessen, die von außen an sie herangetragen wurden, und die nicht mit den institutionellen übereinstimmen mussten.

Der konzeptionelle Rahmen des Projekts ließ Haltungen und Präsentationsmodi zu, die denen der GfZK diametral entgegen gesetzt waren und die sich etwa in der Wahl des Ausstellungsgegenstandes, der Art und Weise seines Zeigens bzw. Vermittelns ausdrückten. Rivalisierenden Einstellungen, Ansichten und Haltungen rückten nebeneinander und wurden quasi mit den Werken, über die Werke, über ihre Konstellationen bzw. über das jeweilige Display ausgestellt oder über diskursive Formate bearbeitet. Alle Forschungsprojekte – und Carte Blanche ist davon nur der sichtbarste bzw. offensichtlichste Ausdruck – sind als Instrumente von vornherein so ange-

legt, dass sie nach innen und nach außen potenzielle Reibungsflächen bieten, wobei ein Hauptinteresse darin liegt, auch das Wertgefüge des Kunstbetriebs selbst immer wieder herauszufordern.[18]

Das Gebäude bildete aufgrund seiner Charakteristika eine ideale Grundlage für *Carte Blanche*, ein Projekt, in dem sich private und öffentliche Interessen kontinuierlich überlagert haben, und zwischen verschiedenen Interessen und Erwartungshaltungen innerhalb gegebener Rahmen verhandelt werden musste.

Das Prinzip des Verhandelns und Aushandelns zwischen verschiedenen Interessen und Erwartungshaltungen innerhalb gegebener Rahmen – zu denen auch die Architektur gehört – bildet die Grundlage eines institutionellen Selbstverständnisses. Dabei gilt es von Museumsseite, Position zu beziehen, etwa indem gesellschaftlich/künstlerisch brisante Themen in die öffentliche Diskussion eingebracht, „ausgestellt" und aus verschiedenen Perspektiven bearbeitet werden. Mit anderen Worten: Die eigene Haltung setzt sich anderen Haltungen aus. Und genau dadurch stellt sich die Institution auch immer wieder radikal zur Diskussion; ihre Legitimation und Ausrichtung muss in Auseinandersetzung mit verschiedenen Gruppen und Beteiligten permanent von Neuem erzeugt werden. Die Konzeption der GfZK folgt also weniger dem Verständnis, ein Ort des Bewahrens als ein Ort des Produzierens von neuen Zusammenhängen, Sichtweisen und Bedeutungen zu sein – in dem Bewusstsein, dass das Sprechen über das Museum, also die Sprechakte, letztendlich auch wesentlich das Museum produzieren.

1 Teile dieses Textes wurden unter dem Titel „Performative Architektur" bereits publiziert in: Angelika Nollert (Hrsg.), *Performative Installation*, Köln 2003, S. 180–194; für diesen Anlass modifiziert und wesentlich erweitert.

2 Unter dem Gesamtprojekttitel *Performative Installation* führte das Siemens Arts Program eine fünfteilige Ausstellungsreihe durch, die in verschiedenen Kunstinstitutionen in Innsbruck, Köln, Siegen, Wien und Leipzig stattfand. Alle Stationen behandelten das gemeinsame Thema unter jeweils anderen Gesichtspunkten: *Konstruktion & Situation, Erzählung, Kommunikation, Körper und Ökonomie, Architektur.*

3 Vgl. John Langshaw Austin, *How to Do Things with Words* (1962), dt. *Zur Theorie der Sprechakte*, Stuttgart 1972

4 Judith Butler, „Performative Acts and Gender Constitution. An Essay in Phenomenology and Feminist Theory", in: Sue-Ellen Case (Hrsg.), *Performing Feminism: Feminist Critical Theory and Theatre*, Baltimore 1990, S. 270–282; Judith Butler, *Das Unbehagen der Geschlechter*, Frankfurt a.M. 1991

5 Die Konzentration auf die „materielle"

Substanz des Werkes wurde als verlängerter Arm einer kapitalistischen Logik gesehen, die es zu überwinden galt. Dem autonomen ästhetischen Objekt, gesehen als Kristallisationspunkt eines materialistischen Denkens, sollte die prozesshafte Arbeit gegenübergestellt werden. Siehe: Robert Morris, „Anti Form" (1968), in: *Continuous Project Altered Daily: The Writings of Robert Morris*, Cambridge/London 1993, S. 68

6 Vgl. „Kann man hier Pingpong spielen?", Johannes Cladders über die Funktion des Antimuseums und die Geschwindigkeit einer Institution, im Gespräch mit Hans-Ulrich Obrist, in: *Jungle World* 48, 24.11.1999, S. 2 (siehe auch: http://www.jungle-world.com/artikel/1999/47/29131.html)

7 Dies meint jedoch nicht, dass die Wände wirklich – etwa durch das Publikum – verschoben werden sollen, sondern dass einem die Möglichkeit einer Verschiebung ständig bewusst ist.

8 Brian O'Doherty, *In der weißen Zelle. Inside the White Cube* (1976/1986), Berlin 1996, S. 10

9 Siehe hier vor allem Anthony Vidler, der in *unHEIMlich: Über das Unbehagen in der modernen Architektur* (1992), Hamburg 2002, dem „Unheimlichen" und der „Unbehaustheit" als moderner Verfasstheit nachgeht. In diesem Zusammenhang ist auch interessant, dass zu dem Zeitpunkt, als das moderne Subjekt erstmals in die Krise geriet, das bürgerliche Museum „erfunden" wurde, durchaus als Ausdruck und materielle Manifestation bürgerlicher Identität und bürgerlicher Selbstvergewisserung. Das Museum wurde damit auch ein Stück weit zum Zufluchtsort einer in Gefahr geratenden Identität. Dennoch hat sich der Erosionsprozess nicht aufhalten lassen, wie die Kritik am Museum in den 1910er und dann in den 1960er und 1970er Jahren zeigt. Vgl. Barbara Steiner, „Zwischen Widerständigkeit und Komplizenschaft", in: dies., Charles Esche (Hrsg.), *Mögliche Museen*, Jahresring 54, Jahrbuch für moderne Kunst, Köln 2007, S. 9–21

10 Bei Mark Wigley taucht das Haus als Denkfigur im philosophischen Diskurs auf. Er greift dazu auf Derridas Beschreibung der Dekonstruktion „als ‚heftige Erschütterung' eines Gebäudes" zurück und schreibt: „Dekonstruktiver Diskurs erschüttert in seiner Befragung Strukturen so lange, bis sie ihre strukturellen Schwachstellen zeigen. Er setzt Strukturen unter Druck, er zwingt sie, er treibt sie zur Belastungsgrenze. Unter einem subtilen, aber schonungslosen Druck werden die Grenzen der Struktur deutlich, und sie selbst wird damit als Struktur sichtbar, aber als etwas anderes als das kulturell zugelassene Bild von Struktur." (Mark Wigley, *Architektur und Dekonstruktion: Derridas Phantom* (1993), Basel/Berlin/Boston 1994, S. 47)

11 In manchen Arbeiten, wie etwa *Present Continuous Past(s)* (1976), übernahm die Videokamera eine ähnliche Funktion wie der Spiegel. Zu Jacques Lacan siehe: „Das Spiegelstadium als Bildner der Ich-Funktion, wie sie uns in der psychoanalytischen Erfahrung erscheint" (1949), in: *Schriften I*, Hrsg. Norbert Haas, Weinheim/Berlin 1996; ders., „Das Subjekt und der/das Andere", in: *Die vier Grundbegriffe der Psychoanalyse* (1964), *Das Seminar. Buch XI*, Hrsg. Norbert Haas, Hans Joachim Metzger, Weinheim/Berlin 1996; ders., „Was ist ein Bild/Tableau", in: ebd.

12 Vgl. Barbara Steiner, „What Does this Text Do? About Distortion, Resistance, Dislike and Subjectivity", in: *Jorge Pardo*, Hrsg. Jörn Schafaff, Barbara Steiner, Ostfildern-Ruit 2000, S. 22–33

13 Ebd.

14 Kaja Silverman, *The Threshold of the Visible World*, New York/London 1996, S. 2

15 Vgl. ebd., S. 195

16 Der von BLESS gestaltete Eingangsbereich wird kontinuierlich, nach Vorschlägen unterschiedlicher NutzerInnen, umgebaut und erweitert. Auch die Funktion der Mobiles hat sich in den letzten Jahren mehrfach verändert: So diente eines der Mobiles zunächst als Kassentresen, während es sich heute um eine Kommunikations- und Informationsplattform für interessierte AusstellungsbesucherInnen handelt. Diesen für die GfZK-2 gestalteten Bereich zeigten BLESS als Abbildung in Form einer Wandtapete bei einer ihrer Präsentationen (Booklaunch BLESS, *Celebrating 10 Years of Themelessness*) in Japan im Sommer 2006. Seitdem ist diese Tapete Teil von BLESS N° 29 wallscapes.

17 Darüber hinaus leisteten die Beteiligten einen Betrag für das Gemeinschaftsprojekt, mit dem die Kosten für eine gemeinsame Ausstellung, für Kommunikation und Vermittlung, eine abschließende Publikation, aber auch die Betriebskosten für die genutzten Räume gedeckt wurden. Sie verpflichteten sich ferner, im Rahmen der Gesprächsreihe *Carte Blanche Diskursiv* öffentlich über ihre Motivationen Auskunft zu geben. Für den Fall eines unauflösbaren Konfliktes zwischen den Projektpartnern wurde eine Carte Blanche, das heißt eine letztendliche Handlungsfreiheit, für den Eingeladenen vereinbart. Die GfZK behielt sich allerdings das Recht vor, problematisch oder kritisierbar erscheinende Haltungen öffentlich zu machen und in ihren Auswirkungen zu diskutieren.

18 Neben den temporären Forschungsprojekten, die alle mit dem Kontext der GfZK zu tun haben, sind der Umgang mit der Sammlung und die beiden Ausstellungsgebäude des Museums ebenfalls Instrumente, Reibungsflächen zu erzeugen.

Olaf Nicolai
Neue Räume, andere Sichtbarkeiten[1]

Es hat mich gefreut und auch ein bisschen gewundert, als mich Barbara Steiner darauf ansprach, ob ich zur Eröffnung des Neubaus der GfZK reden möchte. Gewundert habe ich mich, weil es mir ungewöhnlich schien, dass ein Künstler zu diesem Anlass sprechen sollte. Als ich darüber nachdachte, stellte sich mir dann eher die Frage: aber ungewöhnlich warum? Warum soll nicht gerade ein Künstler etwas über jenen Raum sagen, in dem er doch, im weitesten Sinne, auch arbeitet. Warum wird eine Galerie oder ein Museum nur selten als ein Ort verstanden, an dem Künstler Position beziehen? Nicht einfach nur durch die Präsentation ihrer Kunst, sondern darüber hinaus dadurch, wie sie sich bzw. ihre Arbeit zu diesem Ort in Beziehung setzen und dadurch ihre „Zeitgenossenschaft" artikulieren.

Deshalb möchte ich den heutigen Eröffnungsabend zum Anlass nehmen, etwas über „das Zeitgenössische" zu sagen – das dieser Institution auch den Namen gegeben hat: Galerie für Zeitgenössische Kunst. Was eigentlich ist das Zeitgenössische an einer Kunst, und wodurch definieren sich Künstler als Zeitgenossen? Es gibt sehr viele stereotype Antworten darauf. Sie alle kennen sie, sie werden immer wieder zitiert: zum Beispiel diese, dass durch die Avantgarde, durch Künstler andere Räume eröffnet werden, die man im Alltag so nicht kennt und die deshalb neue Sichtweisen ermöglichen. Ich möchte Ihnen eine etwas andere Lesart vorstellen, vielleicht eine etwas Nüchternere, aber ich hoffe, eine deshalb nicht weniger interessante.

Der französische Philosoph Jacques Rancière hat das Museum einmal den Ort genannt, indem das Unsichtbare sichtbar wird. Museen sind für ihn jene Orte, an denen eine Kultur die Grenze definiert, wo Unsichtbares und Sichtbares einander berühren, sich voneinander separieren. Woran hat er bei dieser Formulierung gedacht? Zuallererst hatte er sicher Museen im Sinn, die das Vergangene sichtbar werden lassen, das, was für uns so nicht mehr sichtbar ist, oder solche Museen, die sich auf neu entdeckte, unbekannte Territorien beziehen. Worauf aber Rancière vor allem hinweist, ist die Bedeutung dieses Vorgangs, die Bedeutung dieser Grenzmarkierung. Denn dadurch, wie sich diese Grenzen bilden und wie sie vorgestellt werden, wird die Spezifik einer Kultur definiert. Kulturen sind dadurch beschreibbar, wie sie ihr Verhältnis zum Unsichtbaren definieren, wie sie Dinge sichtbar werden lassen. In dem Sinne ist ein Museum nicht ein Extra, ein Surplus, oder

ein Luxusgut, welches sich eine Gesellschaft leistet, sondern es ist ein Ort ihrer Selbstbestimmung. Ausgehend von dieser These hat Rancière auch formuliert, dass das Museum eben ein Ort ist, an dem soziale Hierarchien konstituiert werden. Es ist ein Ort, an dem gesagt wird: das hat Bedeutung und das hat keine Bedeutung, das ist uns wichtig und das wird uns wichtig werden. Und dieser Konsens darüber, was sichtbar und was unsichtbar ist, der wirkt in die Gesellschaft mehr als nur hinein, er konstituiert und differenziert die Gesellschaft.

Der leider viel zu früh verstorbene Kunsthistoriker Stefan Germer hat dies zugespitzt so formuliert: „Künstlerische wie gesellschaftliche Bildproduktion können wir nicht voneinander trennen." Das heißt, der Künstler ist mit dem, was er tut, immer schon Zeitgenosse und Museen sind Orte, an denen diese Zeitgenossenschaft sichtbar wird. Sie werden sich nun natürlich denken, „das ist doch klar, wenn man sich umschaut und die Bilder hier sieht", aber ich meine das in einem fundamentaleren Sinn: Es geht weniger um Inhalte als vielmehr um den Zusammenhang zwischen der Art und Weise, wie sich Kunst präsentiert und Sie diese als Besucher erfahren, und der Art und Weise, wie Kunst produziert wird.

Ich möchte ein historisches Beispiel anführen, welches das Gesagte nachvollziehbarer macht: Michael Baxandall hat am Beispiel von Piero della Francesca untersucht, welche Konstruktionsprinzipien dessen Malerei auszeichnen. Wenige Leute wissen, dass della Francesca auch Wirtschaftshandbücher schrieb. Er hat Mathematikbücher für Kaufmänner verfasst, in denen vor allem die damals innovative Anwendung der Geometrie zur Mengenerfassung eine entscheidende Rolle spielte. Dieses kaufmännische Grundwissen verschaffte in der Renaissance den Kaufmännern im südlichen Teil Europas einen enormen Vorteil gegenüber dem Norden. Baxandall weist nun nach, dass man die Anwendung dieser geometrischen Formeln auch in den Kompositionsprinzipien von Piero della Francescas Bildern finden kann. Er behauptet nicht, dass der damalige Betrachter schlicht eine Anwendung der Mengenlehre in den Bildern sah. Vielmehr geht es ihm darum zu zeigen, dass die Modi der Perzeption nicht zu trennen sind von den Modi der Produktion, dass die Art und Weise, wie in einer Gesellschaft produziert wird, auch die Art und Weise bestimmt, wie sinnlich wahrgenommen und empfunden wird. Das mathematische Wissen ist in der sinnlichen Präsenz der Bilder wirksam: Die klare Gliederung, die Proportionen, die sehr genau gewählt sind, die Konstruktion von regelmäßigen geometrischen Körpern zu Intervallen – das ist es, was wir dann auf der visuellen Ebene wahrnehmen. Es handelt sich also nicht schlicht um Übersetzungen, sondern um Konfigurationen von Sinn im Sinnlichen.

Bezogen auf die Ende der 1970er Jahre einsetzende Neuorientierung von Museen hat die amerikanische Kunsthistorikerin Rosalind Krauss eine ähnliche Dialektik untersucht. In einer ihrer zentralen Essays spricht sie von der „Logik spätkapitalistischer Museen". Sie beschrieb damit vor allen Dingen die Expansion des Guggenheim Museums von einem singulären Kleinmuseum zu einem weltweit agierenden Konzern. Ihre Analyse dieses Phänomens erörtert den Zusammenhang zwischen den ökonomischen Veränderungen und der einsetzenden Etablierung von Minimal Art und Konzeptkunst im musealen Kontext. Krauss stellt dabei nicht das kritische Potenzial der künstlerischen Arbeiten in den Vordergrund, sondern fragt, inwieweit deren sinnliche Präsenzen auf andere Zusammenhänge hinweisen. Die Minimal Art, nimmt man ihre hervorragenden Vertreter wie Donald Judd und Dan Flavin, hat mit industriellen Materialien gearbeitet. Donald Judd ließ Aluminiumkuben in den Maßen 1 × 1 × 1 Meter bauen und legte sie mit farbigem Plexiglas aus. Dan Flavin verwendete handelsübliche Leuchtröhren, um Räume zu illuminieren. Es handelt sich um industrielle Produkte und Produktionsweisen. Es gibt die saloppe Formulierung vom Verschwinden der Sammlung in den Museen – sie sehen eigentlich nur die Räume. Wenn sich der Betrachter auf diese Erfahrungen einlässt, dann erfährt er, was er so unmittelbar im Alltag nicht kann – nämlich den Raum als ein dreidimensionales, fundamentales, sinnliches Erlebnis. Es ist eine Erfahrung, die man zu dieser Zeit der Arbeitswelt nicht zugeschrieben hat. Rosalind Krauss macht darauf aufmerksam, dass es aber genau in dieser Zeit in der Arbeitswelt ebenfalls zu Verschiebungen kommt, die sich seit den 1960er Jahren abzeichneten und die phänomenologisch wie Parallelismen erscheinen. In den 1960er Jahren fällt zum Beispiel endgültig die Goldbindung des Dollars und das Fernsehen beginnt, die Werbung so zu intensivieren, dass wir heute darüber sprechen, dass ein Produkt sich mehr durch seinen Tauschwert, sprich durch seine werbekräftige Aura auszeichnet, denn durch seinen Gebrauchswert.

Für Krauss deuten die erwähnten künstlerischen Arbeiten sowohl durch ihre sinnliche Erscheinung als auch durch ihre Produktionsweise auf eine neue Ökonomie hin, die eine neue Stufe der Kapitalisierung bedeutete. Und dies nicht nur im Sinne der Umgestaltung von Räumen, sondern auch durch eine neue Form der Produktion:

Sinnliche Erfahrungen, situative Ereignisse erhalten Warencharakter und bilden neue Segmente einer postfordistischen Ökonomie aus. Die Entwicklung, die Rosalind Krauss beschrieb, sah sie sehr pessimistisch als eine Entwicklung hin zur Eventpolitik und Disneyfizierung. Sie sprach davon, dass der Konsument eigentlich nur noch Konsument einer postmodernen Welt auf der Suche nach Erlebnissen ist, um sich intensiv zu erleben. Auch wenn ich diese pessimistische Perspektive nicht teile, finde ich die kritische Befragung des utopischen Potenzials von Kunst durch Krauss bemerkenswert. Die von Künstlern entworfenen möglichen Welten sind weniger Vorbereitungen auf zukünftige Räume im Sinne positiver Utopien, sondern sie verweisen viel wirklicher und unmittelbarer auf Umgestaltungen im Hier und Jetzt.

Die Frage, die sich daran knüpft, lautet: Wo wären vor diesem Hintergrund Ansatzpunkte für einen Künstler, der sich ja nicht einfach nur an der Reproduktion des Bestehenden beteiligen möchte? Dieser Bau ist ein sehr guter Anlass, sich zu vergegenwärtigen, wie das möglich sein könnte. Charles Esche sprach heute zum Anlass der Eröffnung über die Funktion des Museums, Barbara Steiner über die Konzeption dieses Gebäudes. Es ist ein Museum, das den permanenten Dialog ermöglicht, das vielfach neue Einblicke ermöglicht, das verschiedene Blickachsen konstituiert. Die Architekten selbst sehen es als eine Bühne der permanenten Auseinandersetzung.

Ich würde sagen, es handelt sich eigentlich um einen performativen Raum: Es ist der Raum, den Filme konstituieren – Filme mit verschiedenen Kameraperspektiven und Schnitttechniken –, den man in diesem Gebäude allerdings in seiner Dreidimensionalität erfahren kann. Der Raum ermöglicht verschiedene Szenarien, die Fiktion als eine Realität erleben lassen. Auch die Idee der verschiedenen Szenarien taucht bereits in den 1960er Jahren auf. Dan Graham fertigte 1967 eine sehr kleine Zeichnung an, die damals kaum Aufsehen erregte, die aber, wenn man sie heute sieht, sehr prophetisch wirkt. Die Zeichnung zeigt ein Baumdiagramm, dessen Punkte mit Orts- und Zeitangaben versehen sind. Graham hat einfach den Verlauf von Wahlmöglichkeiten aufgeschrieben, die sich aus Entscheidungen mit binärer Logik ergeben. Je nachdem, für welchen Verlauf man sich entscheidet, ergeben sich verschiedene Bewegungsmuster. Am unteren Ende des Blattes steht eine Vielzahl von möglichen Konstellationen, die alle in der an der Spitze des Baumgraphen stehenden enthalten waren. Ort und Zeit beinhalten unendlich viele Möglichkeiten der Bewegung. Grahams Zeichnung ist ein Beispiel

für eine Reflexion über die Multiplizität von Ereignissen und sie meint natürlich auch eine Multiplizität von Ich-Konstruktionen.

Eine bekannte, exemplarische Architektur für derartige Prozesse ist der Spiegelsaal von Versailles. Dieser Saal war nicht nur als ein unendliches Widerspiegelungsszenario des Sonnenkönigs angelegt. Spiegel hatten auch eine eminent koordinierende Funktion für den Hofstaat und die Besucher von Audienzen. Die Zentralisierung des Hofes brachte ein vollkommen neues Phänomen hervor: Der Adlige musste, wenn er Einfluss ausüben wollte, seine eigenen Besitzungen verlassen und an den Hof gehen. Nur dort war es möglich, Einfluss zu gewinnen. In diesen sozialen Spielen und ihrer Kommunikation war es wichtig, dass die eigenen Absichten nicht klar und deutlich nach außen erkennbar wurden, dass man sein Ziel erreichte, ohne dass andere es zu früh bemerkten. Für diese Diplomatie des Verhaltens waren Spiegel unentbehrlich.

In der Malerei des 17. Jahrhunderts in Frankreich stand ein intensives Studium der Gestik, des Ausdrucks im Zentrum. An Akademien wurden Atlanten von Gesichtsausdrücken erstellt – und danach wurde porträtiert. Die Porträtmalerei war geprägt vom Vokabular dieser Musterbücher. Man könnte hier bereits jene Formen von Selbstreflexivität erkennen, deren zeitgenössische Konstellationen Dan Graham in seinen Pavillonarchitekturen thematisiert. Diese Pavillons sind nicht nur kleine Labyrinthe aus Glas und Spiegel, sie werden auch mit Kameras und Monitoren zu aktiv benutzbaren Spielräumen, in denen sich Verhalten in sich wiederholenden Inszenierungen einstudieren, verfremden oder auch perfektionieren lässt. Diese Rückkoppelungsschleifen praktizieren wir auch im Alltag, bloß mit dem Unterschied, dass wir diese nicht wiederholt bewusst durchspielen. Wir haben das Verhalten internalisiert. Das ist es, was ich mit Performance beschreiben möchte und weshalb ich bei diesem Ort, dem Neubau der GfZK, von einem performativen Raum, einer performativen Architektur spreche.

Es ist dies eine Performance, die nicht nur in Museen anzutreffen ist. Das extremste Beispiel dafür ist das gern und häufig zitierte „Big-Brother-Phänomen". Die gleichen medialen Techniken prägen auch alltägliche soziale Beziehungen. Erst in konkreten Situationen, Kontextualisierungen und Verwertungen bilden sich Differenzierungen, die aber nicht getrennt voneinander existieren. Der britische Soziologe Dick Hebdige spricht davon, dass Adaptionsformen nicht einfach *negations* und Widerstandsformen gegenüberstehen, sondern alle miteinander synthetisiert anzutreffen sind. Diese Tech-

niken zu teilen, bedeutet keine alternativ-
lose Unhintergehbarkeit von gegebenen
Standards, sondern meint ebenso die Frage
nach den Optionen, andere Möglichkeiten
mit ihnen und durch sie zu artikulieren.
Das Utopische wäre also nicht erst möglich
durch ein anderes System: An die Stelle
der Forderungen nach der Erfindung neuer
Produktionsweisen tritt die Erkundung
der Potenzialität von gegebenen Produktionsweisen durch andere Anwendungen,
Hybride und Reformulierungen.

Der slowenische Philosoph Slavoj Žižek
drückte dies so aus: Er glaube, heute sei es
wichtiger denn je, nicht ununterbrochen
darüber zu reden, die Welt verändern zu
wollen, sondern diese immer wieder zu
interpretieren. Er ist davon überzeugt, dass
wir nicht wissen, was zurzeit passiert und
dass es an der Zeit ist, sich wieder der Reflexion zu widmen. Wobei er dann den Begriff
der Wiederholung einführt – eine Wiederholung, die, in das Räumlich-sinnliche
übertragen, nicht unähnlich den beschriebe-
nen Szenarien Räume für Reflexionen bildet.
Repeat is not return. In der Wiederholung
öffnen sich Wege, andere Richtungen
werden möglich, die angelegt scheinen,
aber nicht realisiert wurden. Das bedeutet
eine Option, Vergangenes und Gegenwär-
tiges reflektierbar und somit verhandelbar
werden zu lassen. Und das empfinde ich
persönlich als meine Zeitgenossenschaft in
diesen Räumen.

Gewendet auf die eingangs erwähnte
Unterscheidung von Sichtbarem und Un-
sichtbarem könnte man formulieren, dass
Neues nicht durch eine Hinzufügung von
bisher nicht Gesehenem, von Unbekanntem
in das Feld des Sichtbaren entstehen kann,
sondern nur durch eine Veränderung einer
der Sichtbarkeit zugrunde liegenden Matrix.
Eine Arbeit an dieser Veränderung ist es,
worum es geht. Ich hoffe sehr, dass diese
Räume als ein Labor für Zeitgenossenschaft
halten, was sie heute versprechen.

1   Dieser Text folgt der Transkription der Rede,
die am 24.11.2004 anlässlich der Eröffnung des
Neubaus der GfZK gehalten wurde.

Angelika Fitz
Nichts ist sicher im Museum

Kulturbauten, allen voran Museen, boten in
den 1990er Jahren eine der wenigen noch
verbleibenden Nischen für architektonische
Experimente. Die Hoffnung auf den Bilbao-
Effekt lockerte weltweit die Geldbörsen der
Kommunen. Aber kaum waren die neuen
Museumsbauten eröffnet, setzte bereits
heftige Kritik am vordergründigen Spektakel
mancher Formenfeuerwerke ein, die mehr
sich selbst als der Kunst dienen würden. Der
Moment der Restauration war gekom-
men. Kunst und Architektur kehrten im
Gleichschritt zu Modellen einer klassischen
Moderne zurück. Der White Cube, der
mit seinem universalistischen Gestus und
seinem Anspruch auf Neutralität eigentlich
bereits als überholt galt, erlebt seither
eine Renaissance. Die Architektur soll der
Kunst wieder den Vortritt lassen und so den
bereits verloren geglaubten Autonomiesta-
tus des künstlerischen Werkes noch einmal
retten. „Wenn Sie sehr viel Geld ausgeben,
kann ich die Architektur verschwinden
lassen",[1] versprach der Architekt des neuen
MoMA in New York, Yoshio Taniguchi, seinen Auftraggebern.

In der Galerie für Zeitgenössische Kunst in
Leipzig, die eigentlich ein Museum ist, hält
man nicht viel von diesem Trend zur „Moderne light". Anstatt sich in den abgesicherten
Hafen des bürgerlichen Modernekanons
zurückzuziehen, bezieht sich die Arbeit
der GfZK auf noch offene, experimentelle
Stränge der Moderne. Unter der Leitung von
Barbara Steiner stehen kontextspezifische,
ereignisorientierte, politische Kunstprak-
tiken im Fokus. Dazu gehört, dass die
Sammlung laufend in Dialog mit Wechsel-
ausstellungen tritt. Solche Konfrontationen
auch räumlich zu intensivieren, war eines
der Bedürfnisse, das zur Beauftragung des
ArchitektInnenteams as-if berlinwien für
einen Neubau führte. Gleichzeitig sollten
im Stammhaus der GfZK, das erst Ende der
1990er Jahre preisgekrönt von Peter Kulka
um- und angebaut worden war, Kapazitäten
frei werden für den Ausbau von Bibliothek
und Vermittlungsprogrammen. Mit der
GfZK-2 ist ein neues räumliches Gefüge ent-
standen, das dem hohen programmatischen
Anspruch der Institution gerecht wird.

Während Peter Kulka bei seinem Erweite-
rungsbau die Grundstruktur der bestehenden Gründerzeitvilla (GfZK-1) weitgehend
beibehalten hat, setzte as-if berlinwien
einen eigenständigen Baukörper in den
angrenzenden Park, der das bestehende
Ensemble von Museum und Nebengebäu-
den städtebaulich zwingend erweitert,
aber in seiner geometrischen und formalen
Ausprägung auf direkte Bezüge verzichtet.

Das flache, durchgehend nur einstöckige
Gebäude schmiegt sich an die Grenzen des
Baumbestandes, wodurch sich ein unre-
gelmäßiger Pavillon ergibt, der entfernt an
eine zufällige Konglomeration von Kristallen
erinnert. Mit seinem zurückspringenden
Sockelbereich scheint er den Park kaum zu
berühren, scheint mehr wie ein Floß auf
der Oberfläche zu treiben. Die akzidentelle
Außenform lässt den Baukörper unübersicht-
lich und fragmentarisch wirken, was durch
Niveausprünge auf der Dachebene noch
verstärkt wird. Trotz seiner gut 1000 Quad-
ratmeter Grundfläche entsteht der Eindruck
eines leichten Pavillons, der auch temporär
gedacht sein könnte und dadurch einen
wohltuenden Kontrast zur Monumentalität
vieler Museumsbauten bietet. Im Inneren
bereichert die Zersplitterung der Kubatur
die Belichtungssituation der kleinteiligen
und verschachtelten Ausstellungsräume.
Während der Wunsch nach Tageslicht in der
Regel zu großen, durchgängigen (Kunst)
Hallen mit einheitlichem Charakter führt,
will as-if berlinwien möglichst viele unterschiedliche Raumwirkungen erzeugen, die
von intimen Situationen bis zu öffentlichen
Schaufenstern reichen. Durch Oberlichtbän-
der, die an die einzelnen Wände grenzen,
bzw. durch Unterschlitze, von welchen die
Wände hochgehoben werden, erhalten auch
die am weitesten innen liegenden, potenziell
für heikle Sammlungsbestände klimatisier-
baren Räume natürliches Licht.

Die eigentliche Komplexität der Struktur
entfaltet sich von Innen nach Außen.
Polygonale Raumgefüge, von denen keines
mit einem anderen identisch ist, schließen
aneinander an, umschließen sich oder
durchdringen sich wechselseitig. Es gibt
keinen Standpunkt, von dem aus die BesucherInnen den Gesamtzusammenhang der
Ausstellungsräume überschauen könnten.
Hin und wieder, wenn eine Raumfolge an
eine Außengrenze stößt, taucht unvermittelt
ein Stadt- oder Parkausschnitt auf. Subtil
rhythmisierte Glasflächen wechseln in unre-
gelmäßiger Folge mit soliden Abschnitten.
Aus- und Einblicke erhalten ihren Reiz vor
allem durch ihre Unvorhersehbarkeit. Die
Wahrnehmung bleibt frisch, könnte man
in Anlehnung an Le Corbusier bemerken,
der Architekturen in „tote und lebendige"
einteilte, „je nachdem, ob das Gesetz des
Durchwanderns nicht beachtet oder ob es
im Gegenteil glänzend befolgt wurde".[2]

Architektur muss nach Le Corbusier
durchschritten werden, um die Formen und
Linien, die Beziehungen, Rhythmen und
Proportionen für die BenutzerInnen wahrnehmbar zu machen. In seiner *promenade
architecturale* wird die äußere Bewegung mit
der inneren Bewegung, mit den „aufeinan-
der folgenden Erschütterungen",[3] in Korre-

lation gebracht. Der Weg wird zum Symbol für eine mehrschichtige Wirklichkeit. Das entspricht der zentralen Bedeutung des Verhältnisses von Raum und Bewegung in der Moderne. Das moderne Subjekt wird als bewegtes gedacht, sei es im urbanen Raum, der in der technologischen Beschleunigung moderner Fortbewegungsmittel erlebt wird, oder im Innenraum, der in der *promenade architecturale* zur Flaniermeile wird. Das Fenster entwickelt sich vom Belichtungsinstrument zum Bilderrahmen für den Blick, der Innen und Außen in Beziehung setzt, der diese Beziehung inszeniert. Durchlässigkeit, Transparenz und die Schwelle zwischen privat und öffentlich werden zu zentralen Themen. Weiter dynamisiert wird der Blick von den neuen Sehgewohnheiten, die das Medium Film einführt. Beim Abschreiten großzügiger Fensterbänder zeigt sich die in das Zentrum der Aufmerksamkeit gerückte Verschränkung von Innen und Außen als Filmstreifen. Die Kameraperspektive bemächtigt sich des Auges: „The screen undermines the wall."[4]

Dem klassischen räumlichen Erlebnisparcours der architektonischen Moderne erteilt as-if berlinwien mit der GfZK-2 eine Absage. Hier wird kein modernes Subjekt angesprochen, das sich durch „erbauliche" Wege und transparente Durchblicke seiner Position versichern kann, kein Flaneur, der das bunte Treiben, wie einen Film an sich vorbeiziehen lässt. In der GfZK-2 wird das Ineinanderfließen der Räume immer wieder gestört, genauso wie die Kontinuität zwischen Innen und Außen gebrochen bleibt. Es gibt keinen Panoramaausblick in die Landschaft oder auf die Stadt. Und auch im Inneren gibt es keinen Standort, von dem aus die BesucherInnen das Gebäude überblicken oder „durchschauen" könnten. In dem fast labyrinthischen Gefüge kommt nie Selbstverständlichkeit auf. Anstatt sich in der Bewegung seiner selbst zu versichern, wird das Subjekt zunehmend verunsichert.

Anders verhält sich die GfZK-2 in Bezug auf das zweite im Kontext der Moderne diskutierte Paradigma, nämlich das der Medialisierung des Blicks, das as-if berlinwien konsequent ins 21. Jahrhundert weiterführt. Der „Film" spielt sich für BewohnerInnen des 21. Jahrhunderts nicht mehr allein dadurch ab, dass sie Raumfluchten durchschreiten oder ihren Blick über Fensterbänder schweifen lassen, sondern ebenso sehr in der Interaktion mit Bildschirmen. Nicht nur in der kollektiven Black Box des Kinos, auch im alltäglichen, privaten Bereich werden Körper und Blick vor Bildschirmen fixiert, während die Raumerfahrung sich in einer Abfolge von Bildsequenzen verzeitlicht. Ähnlich wie räumliche Erlebnisse in Bildern geschichtet werden, erschließen sich auch Funktionen

nicht mehr allein durch Wegführungen, sondern können auf bildhaften Oberflächen, Interfaces, zugeschaltet werden. Die Welt erscheint am und als Display. Und genau dies führt die GfZK-2 in exemplarischer Weise vor. Dazu gehört, dass die Wand als Träger oder Hintergrund von Kunst selbst zum Thema gemacht wird. Technischer Aufbau, Volumen und verschiedene Materialitäten der Wände werden an den Naht- und Verschiebestellen immer wieder sichtbar gemacht, nicht als Verweis auf die Konstruktion, sondern auf die Aufgaben, auf die „Tätigkeit" von Wänden oder von Boden und Decke im Dispositiv der Ausstellung. Viele Elemente entpuppen sich als großformatige Schiebewände, mit denen Raumgeometrien, Raumgrößen und Raumsequenzen verändert werden können. Durch die mannigfaltige Verschiebbarkeit können sich die Displayteile wie auf einem dreidimensionalen Bildschirm zu immer neuen Konfigurationen formieren. Auf diesem Screen können sowohl neue Blick- und Projektionsbeziehungen als auch alternative Raumprogramme zugeschaltet werden. Ähnlich wie das für viele Optionen offene Betriebssystem am Desktop eines Computers haben die meisten Räume der GfZK-2 kein fixes Programm. Ein Projektionsraum kann von der Black Box zur Vitrine werden, eine Galerie zum Vortragsraum, der Vortragsraum zum Atelier für *artists in residence* und mit wenigen Eingriffen wieder zum Ausstellungsraum.

Diese Flexibilität, die natürlich auch eine ökonomische Funktion erfüllt, indem sie den Aufwand an ausstellungsspezifischen Umbauten reduziert, könnte leicht in eine „Multifunktionalität ist gut für nix" abdriften. Die ebenso beeindruckenden wie verwirrenden diagrammatischen Darstellungen der möglichen räumlichen Konfigurationen und programmatischen Schaltungen, die von den ArchitektInnen erstellt wurden, bringen hier kaum Abhilfe. Die Bandbreite der räumlichen Möglichkeiten vermittelt sich schon eher in einem Video, das as-if berlinwien für die Ausstellung *Ornament & Display*[5] produziert hat: Während Schiebewände und textile Raumteiler händisch hin und her verschoben werden, kann man von einer fixierten BeobachterInnenposition aus die Arbeit des Positionswechselns von Raumelementen verfolgen und die daraus entstehenden unterschiedlichen Raumkonfigurationen auch atmosphärisch antizipieren. Denn die flexible Architektur ist mehr als ein präzises funktionales Instrument. Proportions- und Materialwechsel erzeugen in jeder spezifischen Situation eine Konzentration, bei der nichts an multifunktionale Beliebigkeit erinnert.

Neben Sichtbeton, Glas und verschieden eingefärbten Verkleidungen tauchen auch

ungewöhnliche Materialien auf, wie ein bei Sportanlagen gebräuchlicher Gummibelag, der fallweise an Boden, Decke, Wänden und Außenwänden zur Anwendung kommt. Aus der Entfernung ist die teilweise gummierte Außenwand kaum von Basaltstein, wie er bei traditionellen Museumsbauten gerne eingesetzt wird, zu unterscheiden. Erst wenn man näher herantritt, wird die monumentale Ernsthaftigkeit zum sportiven Augenzwinkern. Dazu passen zahlreiche selbst entwickelte Lowtech-Details, wie die Mechanismen der Schiebeelemente oder die Lüftungslamellen.

Bei aller partiellen Rauheit ist die GfZK-2 ein ausgesprochen nobler Raum, ja eigentlich ein musealer Kunstraum. Trotz der politisch diskursiven Ausrichtung der Institution sind Auftraggeberin und ArchitektInnen nicht der Versuchung erlegen, beim Neubau mit der Ästhetik eines Offspace zu kokettieren. Vielmehr distanzieren sich die differenzierten ästhetischen Oberflächen der GfZK-2 gleichermaßen von der Pseudoneutralität des White Cube wie von der Quasi-Naturalisierung eines „kritischen Displays", wie es sich – markiert durch Versatzstücke wie Tapeziertische, Speditionspaletten oder Zitaten aus Gerüst- und Trockenbau – in den letzten Jahren stillschweigend etabliert hat. Im Gegenteil, die Performativität der Displays der GfZK-2 deckt solche stillen Übereinkünfte auf. So funktionierte die Ausstellung *Schrumpfende Städte*[6] mit ihrer „Ästhetik der Anti-Ästhetik" in den Kunst-Werken Berlin gut. Auch der Ausstellungsteil in der Gründerzeitvilla der GfZK-1 erzeugte einen diskreten Charme. Im Kontext des Neubaus wirkte das gleiche Display „vorgeführt", trat aus seiner Hintergrundfunktion heraus und wurde selbst zum Ausstellungsstück.

Nichts ist sicher in diesem Museum oder besser: vor diesem Museum. Die GfZK-2 ist eine Meisterin der Verunsicherung. Ihre komplexe Performativität bietet Widerstände in verschiedenste Richtungen, lenkt die Aufmerksamkeit immer wieder vom Was auf das Wie der Präsentation. Schon die Oberflächen sind mehrfach performativ, als selbstreflexive Instrumente des Ausstellens, als operative Interfaces für programmatische Schaltungen und als atmosphärische Parameter. Deshalb ist die differenzierte Ästhetik dieses Kunstraums keinesfalls ein Manierismus. Oder wie der Künstler Olaf Nicolai in seinem Essay *Show Case* schreibt: „Fragen nach Formen, Stimmungen, Attitüden und Stil sind kein luxuriöses Spiel mit Oberflächen. Sie sind Fragen nach Organisationsformen von Handlungen"[7] – und somit Fragen, die vor dem Hintergrund des aktuellen Museumsbooms dringend wieder gestellt werden sollten, wenn wir in Zukunft mehr Auswahl beanspruchen wollen, als uns zwischen musealen Erlebniswelten und sakralen Tempeln der Kunst entscheiden zu müssen. Der Neubau für die GfZK weist intelligente Wege aus diesem Dilemma.

1 Zitiert nach Michael Freund, „Die Leichtigkeit eines Monuments", in: Der Standard, Wien 20.11.2004

2 Le Corbusier, An die Studenten. Die „Charte d'Athènes" (1942), Reinbek bei Hamburg 1962, S. 29

3 Ebd.

4 Beatriz Colomina, Privacy and Publicity. Modern Architecture as Mass Media, Cambridge 1996, S. 235

5 Ornament & Display, kuratiert von Angelika Fitz, kunsthaus muerz/steirischer herbst, 29.10.2005–26.02.2006

6 Schrumpfende Städte – Internationale Untersuchung, KW Institute for Contemporary Art Berlin, 04.09.–07.11.2004; Schrumpfende Städte 2 – Interventionen, kuratiert von Philipp Oswalt, Barbara Steiner, Walter Prigge und Nikolaus Kuhnert, GfZK Leipzig, 26.11.2005–29.01.2006

7 Olaf Nicolai, Show Case, Nürnberg 1999, S. 30

Christian Teckert
Die Aura der Institution
Über Affekt, Atmosphäre und Immersion als Problematik zeitgenössischer Architektur und Kunst

Museen und Ausstellungsgebäude, die sich den jüngeren Entwicklungen der bildenden Kunst widmen, erlebten in den letzten Jahren einen beispiellosen Boom. Es scheint kaum eine Stadt zu geben, die es sich noch leisten kann, ohne ein spektakuläres neues Museum mit Stararchitektur auszukommen. Die „Erfolge" einer Tate Modern in London, eines MoMA in New York oder eines Guggenheim in Bilbao, aber auch des Museumsquartiers in Wien haben Vorbildwirkung. Waren Museen einst dem Komplex des Ausstellens und Zeigens[1] gewidmet, so übernehmen sie nun zusehends die Funktion von touristischen Sites, von städtischen Kommunikationszentren mit einer Vielzahl an kommerziellen Nebenaktivitäten. In den gängigen Konzepten der Museumsmacher lässt sich eine signifikante Umkehrung der Verhältnisse herauslesen: Waren in den traditionellen Museen ursprünglich zumindest zwei Drittel der Räume den Ausstellungen gewidmet und der Rest den anderen Museumsaktivitäten, so hat sich dieses Verhältnis mittlerweile umgekehrt. Große Bereiche der Museen sind inzwischen kommerziellen Angeboten gewidmet, werden von Museumsshops, von Restaurants und Cafés gefüllt. Die zunehmende Aufblähung der multifunktionalen Hüllen der Museumsbauten korreliert mit einer zunehmenden Ökonomisierung und Kommerzialisierung von Kultur.

Doch schon vor dem Museumsboom in den letzten Jahren war die „Kunstinstitution" an sich zu einem angesagten Ort geworden, zu einem place to be, im wahrsten Sinn des Wortes: Die allgegenwärtigen Lounges mit Theorieangeboten oder soziale environments, die temporäre und lokalisierte Gemeinschaften im Ausstellungskontext generieren sollten, bildeten gemäß der maßgeblich von Nicolas Bourriaud propagierten „relationalen Ästhetik" eine Art Ersatzwohnraum, in dem sich kunstaffine Urbaniten gut einzurichten wussten. Laut Bourriaud ging es dabei nicht mehr um einen utopischen Entwurf auf Basis einer vorgefertigten Idee von Evolution, sondern darum, sich in der existierenden Welt in einer „besseren" Form einzurichten.[2] Nach den Zeiten einer zumeist etwas aufdeckerisch-moralisierenden Kontext-Kunst der 1990er Jahre war es mit der Entwicklung einer „Kunst als sozialem Raum"[3] wieder möglich, sich bei aller Reflexion und Kritik in der Institution wohlzufühlen und die Coolness der Kunst-

welt als szenetaugliches Distinktionsmotiv zu etablieren. Die White-Cube-Debatte, Auslöser zentraler kritischer, künstlerischer Strategien der 1990er Jahre, war wieder abgeebbt, nachdem die Wirkmächtigkeit und „Aura" dieses hegemonialen Raummodells des Ausstellens analysiert, dekonstruiert und kritisiert worden waren, worauf zu einem späteren Zeitpunkt noch genauer einzugehen sein wird. Vorerst möchte ich die These Bourriauds aufnehmen, dass die Produktion von Aura nicht mehr durch das Kunstwerk stattfindet (und auch nicht mehr durch den Ausstellungsraum), sondern vielmehr durch die Zusammenkunft einer Mikro-Gemeinschaft (micro-community)[4]. Im Kapitel „The Aura of Artworks Has Shifted towards their Public" seiner Relational Aesthetics beschreibt Bourriaud die zunehmende Praxis partizipatorischer, kollektiver und benutzerfeundlicher Ausstellungsprojekte als symptomatisch dafür, dass primär das momentane Zusammenkommen von partizipierenden BetrachterInnen eine Atmosphäre generiert[5] – eine Atmosphäre, die jener ursprünglichen Idee der Aura, deren sukzessives Verschwinden unter dem Einfluss der mechanischen Reproduzierbarkeit Walter Benjamin schon 1935 beklagte, eine Wiederkehr unter veränderten Vorzeichen ermöglichte. Nicht mehr das Kunstwerk und nicht die weiße Wand sind die Quellen dieser Aura, sondern es erscheint, „as if the micro-community gathering in front of the image was becoming the actual source of aura, the ‚distance' appearing specifically to create a halo around the work, which delegates its powers to it".[6]

Doch scheint hier weniger die Nähe zum Kunstwerk entscheidend als die Nähe zu den Prozessen einer Institution, die als Kristallisationspunkt eines Lifestyles wahrgenommen wird, der Intellektualität, Weltoffenheit und kulturelle Distinktion verspricht. Es geht um das Eintauchen in die damit verbundene Atmosphäre, um eine Immersion in den in seiner Wahrnehmung als „Ambient" selbst auratisch gewordenen Raum der Kunst-Institution. Themen und Begriffe wie Atmosphäre, die Produktion von Präsenz[7] und die damit verbundenen Affekte auf Seiten der BetrachterInnen spielen auch nicht zufällig wieder eine prominente Rolle im Architektur- und Kunstdiskurs der letzten Jahre. Doch mit welchen ideologischen Aufladungen ist dieses institutionelle Ambient verbunden, welche Vorstellung eines Subjekts, dessen Affekte damit in den Fokus geraten und welche Formen von Öffentlichkeit sind damit adressiert? Welche Rolle spielt die Architektur von Ausstellungsräumen in diesem Zusammenhang? Dazu möchte ich einige Spuren jenes Diskurses verfolgen, der rund um die gezielte

Adressierung von Emotionen und Affekten in der Raumgestaltung eine neue Form von partizipatorischer Praxis zu erkennen glaubt.[8] Zunächst werde ich hier auf spezifische Theorien der Raumwahrnehmung und Orientierung eingehen, an denen sich grundlegende Verschiebungen innerhalb der Konstruktion des wahrnehmenden Subjekts im Raum erkennen lassen. Diese Diskussion der Bedeutung von affektiven Wahrnehmungen und atmosphärischen Aufladungen soll hier als Grundlage für die Fragestellung dienen, wie und ob Architektur speziell für Ausstellungsräume eine emanzipatorische Agenda im Sinne der Wahrnehmbarkeit und Verhandelbarkeit ihrer Wirkungsweisen entwickeln kann.

Die Ästhetik der Präsenz und Atmosphäre

In den Argumenten der meisten Vertreter einer Ästhetik der Präsenz und Atmosphäre geht es um den Versuch, eine Identität des Seins anzustreben, eine Einheit zwischen Körper und Geist, zwischen Ratio und Emotion zu erreichen. Doch genau das strukturelle Verfehlen einer (geschlossenen, kohärenten) Identität (oder besser: der Empfindung von Identität) ist jenes Motiv, das ich in Bezug auf gegenwärtige Formen der Raumproduktion diskutieren möchte, welche versuchen, genau diese Distanz zu minimieren. Die Rede wird also sein von Immersion, Entgrenzung, Entrahmungsverfahren, affektorientierten Atmosphären und Emotionssteuerung – allesamt Themen, die neben kunstimmanenten Diskussionen[9] auch in der Alltagskultur in den letzten Jahren eine deutlich verstärkte Konjunktur erfahren haben, von den omnipräsenten Shopping-Malls und ihren Gestaltungsleitlinien über atmosphärisch aufgeladene Raumszenarien bis hin zur Beschreibung der „Erlebnisgesellschaft" von Gerhard Schulze.[10] Die Frage wird sein, mit welchen Affektangeboten, Affektsteuerungen und damit verbundenen Formen von Subjektivierung die Produktion von Raum gegenwärtig einhergeht.

Auf subjekttheoretischer Ebene lässt sich hier ein Richtungswechsel beobachten, den die Medientheoretikerin Marie Luise Angerer in ihrem Buch *Vom Begehren nach dem Affekt* (2007)[11] thematisiert hat. Diskursgeschichtlich ist ein Umschwung von den bildorientierten Visual Studies zu einem verstärkten Interesse an affektorientierten Ansätzen im Gange, sogar von einem *emotional turn* war schon die Rede. Ganz entscheidend geht es in diesen Diskursen um ein Eintauchen und Hineingezogen-Werden, nicht selten verbunden mit der Behauptung vom Ende der Theorie, der mit ihr einhergehenden Distanz sowie einem Ende

der Dominanz des Visuellen. Stattdessen werden nun die bisher angeblich vernachlässigten Sinne und Wahrnehmungsfiguren wie Geruch, Haptik oder Sound in den Vordergrund gestellt.

Nicht nur in den Kunst- und Medientheorien der Gegenwart zeichnet sich diese Verschiebung ab, auch und vielleicht sogar vor allem in der Architektur und der Raumproduktion haben die Krise der kritischen Theorie in der Architektur und ihre diskursive Kopplung an poststrukturalistische und dekonstruktivistische Ansätze, die primär repräsentationspolitischer Natur waren, das Feld für eine post-kritische, eine sogenannte projektive Theorie und Praxis geöffnet. Die Forderung der Vertreter der kritischen Architektur (wie etwa Peter Eisenman oder Michael Hays) nach Autonomie gegenüber den gesellschaftlichen Bedingungen ermöglichte zwar ein Kommentieren oder auch Indizieren gesellschaftlicher Entwicklungen, die Skepsis gegenüber unmittelbarer Einflussnahme allerdings trug wesentlich zu einer Marginalisierung dieser Haltung bei, die immer noch sehr stark den linguistischen Leitbildern der 1970er und 1980er Jahre anhing.

Mit dem Rückenwind des amerikanischen New Pragmatism versucht nun eine Reihe von Theoretikern und Architekten eine Ideologie der Post-Kritik, des Projektiven zu etablieren, die statt auf Kritik wieder verstärkt auf Praxis, Wirkung und Performanz setzt und den Fokus von der Repräsentationskritik zur Präsenz verschiebt. Nach Robert Somol und Sarah Whiting, die mit ihrem Essay *Notes around the Doppler-Effect and Other Moods of Modernism*[12], die Diskussion um das Projektive entscheidend angestoßen hatten, sind die Schlüsselbegriffe für diese Strömung: Performance, Inszenierung und *special effect*, Stimmung und Ambiente, Immersion und Synästhesie. Dieses hier eingeschriebene Primat des Affektiven geht einher mit einem wieder erwachten Interesse am Atmosphärischen – ein Begriff, der als verdrängtes und strukturell unterdrücktes Motiv der rationalistischen Architektur der Moderne nun wieder in den Mittelpunkt jener Ansätze gerückt wird, die in der „atmosphärischen Intervention"[13] eine Möglichkeit zur Neustrukturierung der architektonischen Aufgabenhierarchie erkennen.

Die „atmosphärische Interaktion" zwischen Subjekt und Objekt, wie sie von Somol und Whiting bezeichnet wird, scheint als vorbewusste, prä-sprachliche Reaktion, die bei der Intuition und beim Affekt ansetzt, für eine „konzeptionelle Einbeziehung der Wahrnehmung und Vorstellungswelt des Betrachters" bestens geeignet, wie Ole W. Fischer betont.[14] Projekte wie das *Blur Buil-*

ding von Diller+Scofidio (eine architektonische Apparatur zur Erzeugung einer Wolke, die das Gebäude selbst zum Verschwinden bringt), Bauten von Peter Zumthor mit ihren auratisch aufgeladenen Licht- und Oberflächenwirkungen oder auch die Projekte von Phillippe Rahm, der eine Art Raumästhetik der dislozierten Klimabedingungen anstrebt, stehen innerhalb dieser Diskussion im Mittelpunkt. Jener Theoretiker, der im Zuge dieser Diskussion speziell im deutschsprachigen Raum starke Beachtung findet, ist Gernot Böhme, der schon seit längerem an einer „Ästhetik der Atmosphären"[15] arbeitet. Kurz gefasst definiert er Atmosphären im Rückgriff auf Hermann Schmitz als „ergreifende Gefühlsmächte" oder aber in Bezug auf die Architektur als „gestimmte Räume".[16] Er weist auf den immer auch räumlichen Charakter der Atmosphären hin und beschreibt, ihre Räumlichkeit bedeute, dass sie „unbestimmt in die Weite ergossen sind" und „dass sie vom Menschen in seiner leiblichen Präsenz erfahren werden". Böhme betont aber auch sozusagen in Vorwegnahme der potenziellen Kritik dieses Ansatzes, dass die diskursiven Vorbehalte gegenüber dem Terminus der Atmosphäre darauf gründen, dass Atmosphären, weil sie „weder Substanz noch Akzidens, weder rein objektiv noch rein subjektiv"[17] sind, aus dem Bereich des vernünftig Sagbaren herausfallen, also wissenschaftlich problematisch fassbar sind. Und das vor allem auch, weil sie „ihre letzte Bestimmtheit erst durch die Reaktion des Subjekts erfahren".[18]

Exakt deswegen bedarf es im Rahmen eines an Affekten und Intuition orientierten ästhetischen Programms, sei es nun primär künstlerischer oder architektonischer Provenienz, eines adäquaten Subjektbegriffs, der bei Gernot Böhme aber nur in vage definierter Form zu finden ist. Interessant erscheint in diesem Zusammenhang dennoch eine kurze Passage über den „Blick als Atmosphäre", in der Böhme beschreibt, wie der Betrachter eines Kunstwerks in dessen Bann gezogen wird, sich angeblickt fühlt und dadurch ein immersiver Effekt auftritt. Man wird sozusagen über eine affektive Bahn hineingezogen in den atmosphärischen Raum des Werkes. Mit Hegel argumentiert Böhme den atmosphärischen Charakter des Schönen als Dialektik von Anblicken und Angeblickt-Werden und schließt daraus, dass der Betrachter seine Selbstmächtigkeit aufgeben muss, indem er in die Atmosphäre des Kunstwerks eintritt.[19] Damit ist implizit eine Aufgabe des Konzepts des souveränen, autonomen Betrachters verbunden. Nebenbei sei hier erwähnt, dass dies eine These widerspiegelt, die schon in den 1960er Jahren eine Debatte über den Status der Autonomie von Kunst versus Betrachter (versus Raum) auslöste, als Michael Fried den Minimal-Art- und Concept-Art-Künstlern vorwarf, mit der „literalness" ihrer Objekte den Betrachter, als sich bewusst im Raum erkennend, einer Situation der „theatricality" auszuliefern und damit die hehre Autonomie sowohl des Werks als auch des Betrachters anzugreifen.[20] Nicht zufällig gilt diese Episode als eine Initialzündung des Diskurses über Theatralität und Performanz, der speziell in den letzten Jahren wieder an Intensität zugenommen hat und mittlerweile auch den Raumdiskurs erreicht hat.[21]

Hier ist aber vorerst relevant, dass die Dialektik von Anblicken und Angeblickt-Werden ein Grundmodus dessen ist, was die Filmtheoretikerin Kaja Silverman „Identification-at-a-Distance" nannte. Es ist die Differenz zwischen look und gaze, die Silverman in ihrer Diskussion der Modi der Subjektivierung einführt, um zu klären, wie sich das von sich selbst gemachte innere Bild des Subjekts und das äußere Bild zueinander verhalten.[22] Sie verwendet das Modell der Kamera, um zu veranschaulichen, wie das Subjekt sich als immer ins Bild gesetzt erfährt, allerdings immer abhängig von der jeweiligen sozialen und kulturellen Konstruktion des gaze. Theatralität ist in dieser kulturellen Konstruktion strukturell mitgedacht, insofern das Subjekt im Verhandeln zwischen der Einpassung (Silverman benutzt hier den im Englischen sicherlich treffenderen Ausdruck „to key in") in ein von Außen definiertes Identifikationsangebot und ein von Innen imaginiertes Idealbild herausgeformt wird. Sie verwendet als Analogie die Pose, in der das Begehren, in einer bestimmten Art und Weise wahrgenommen, angeblickt zu werden („to be apprehended"), mit den präfigurierten Erwartungshaltungen des gaze zusammenläuft.[23] Was Böhme für das atmosphärische Ausstrahlen im Moment des Betrachtens eines Kunstwerks beschreibt, ist für Silverman eine ganz grundlegende Fähigkeit des Subjekts, sich kulturell je spezifisch einem Blickregime einzuschreiben, mit der Form der jeweiligen Einschreibung und damit auch der Form der Identifikation aber zu spielen. Ganz nebenbei wird dabei eine spezifische Form der Räumlichkeit produziert: „The pose is also generative of mise-en-scène. The pose always involves both the positioning of a representationally inflected body in space, and the consequent conversion of that space into a ,place'."[24]

In diesem Sinne wäre die von Böhme angeführte Dialektik von Anblicken und Angeblickt-Werden ein basaler Modus jedweder Identifikationsprozesse, allerdings – und darauf zielt Silvermans Arbeit letztlich ab – kann diese Identität nie erreicht werden. Die Identität bleibt immer auf Distanz.

Eine Schließung und endgültige Identifikation würde bedeuten, eine subjektpolitisch fragwürdige Essenz oder Normierung zu postulieren.

Hier setzt auch die Kritik von Ilka Becker an, die in Böhmes Atmosphärenbegriff die jeweiligen historischen und kulturellen Konventionen zu wenig mitgedacht sieht.[25] Sie gibt zu bedenken, dass Stimmungen nur über die sie rahmenden Diskurse der jeweiligen Genres, speziell was künstlerische Produktion betrifft, erklärbar sind. „Der Begriff der Atmosphäre ist demnach nur begrenzt produktiv, wenn man nicht untersucht, inwiefern er an inhaltliche oder (identitäts-)politische Fragestellungen geknüpft ist."[26] An dieser Stelle wäre auf eine produktive Zusammenführung von affektorientierten Atmosphären-Diskursen und identitätspolitischen Positionen, wie derjenigen Silvermans zu hoffen. Denn worum es auch Gernot Böhme geht, ist die Warnung, dass die „Leugnung atmosphärischer Gefühlsmächte uns unfrei – nämlich über das Unbewusste beeinflussbar"[27] macht und damit die problematische Ideologie des autonomen Subjekts stützt. Deswegen erscheint eine kritische Auseinandersetzung mit den Mechanismen der Affizierung und ihrer jeweiligen ideologischen Struktur unumgänglich, will man den Bereich des Sinnlichen nicht den spekulativen Werbebotschaften der Wellnessindustrie und den Marketingexperten überlassen.

Immersion und Entrahmung

In der gegenwärtigen Raumgestaltung ist der Modus der Immersion von entscheidender Bedeutung. Immersion steht dabei für das Eintauchen und Hineingezogen-Werden in virtuelle Welten oder in etwas wie eine zweite Natur. Die Technologie dieser Inszenierung soll zurücktreten, ja unsichtbar bleiben, der ästhetische Effekt der je konstruierten Atmosphäre ungestört bleiben. Der zuvor beschriebene Spalt in den Prozessen der Identifikation wird hier möglichst fugenfrei verkittet, um ein Versprechen der Unmittelbarkeit zu bedienen. Immersion ist nach Peter Sloterdijk, der den Sphären und Weltinnenräumen schon einige Bände voll assoziativem Material gewidmet hat, vor allem eine Technik der Entgrenzung, der Entrahmung – oder genauer: ein Entrahmungsverfahren für Bilder und Anblicke, die zur Umgebung entgrenzt werden.

Jene Domäne, in der diese Fragestellungen der räumlichen Rahmung wie auch der Entgrenzung und ihrer jeweiligen ideologischen Struktur immer wieder paradigmatisch durchgespielt wurde, ist die der bildenden Kunst oder besser: die des Diskurses um die Bedingungen des Ausstellens, seiner räumlichen Parameter, seiner Formen des Displays.

Dazu ein kleiner Exkurs in die Geschichte des Ausstellungsraums. Die dabei verhandelten Raumkonzepte lassen sich im Rekurs auf eine zentrale Technik der Repräsentation im dominanten Paradigma des Kunstraums der Moderne diskutieren, dem zu Beginn schon angesprochenen Prinzip des White Cube. Brian O'Doherty diskutierte 1976 mit seiner Textsammlung *Inside the White Cube*[28] die Mechanismen der Inklusion und Exklusion dieser raumgewordenen Konvention modernistischer Ausstellungspraxis. Seine Analyse der im Laufe der Zeit naturalisierten und damit unsichtbar gewordenen ideologischen Grundstruktur des weißen Galerieraums entlarvte den viel beschworenen Begriff der Neutralität im Kunstkontext als höchst problematische Kategorie. Doch auch das Anliegen, die Kunstwerke als autonome, aus ihrem unmittelbaren zeitlichen und räumlichen Kontext herausgehobene Objekte zu präsentieren, war – historisch gesehen – seinerseits einmal das Resultat einer Kritik an bestehenden Verhältnissen der Präsentation von Kunst. Es war ein spezifisches Manöver der Entrahmung. Einerseits ging es darum, das Kunstwerk als einzigartiges Objekt gegenüber einem idealisierten Betrachter zu zeigen und andererseits darum, die Kunst aus der politischen und ökonomischen Umklammerung der Bourgeoisie herauszulösen und damit neue Präsentationsformen für eine demokratisierte Kunstbetrachtung zu schaffen. Die Immersion im White Cube versprach das Eintauchen in die Aura der Kunst, die im Zuge der Entwicklungen der 1960er Jahre hin zur Minimal Art und Concept Art sich dem klassischen Objektstatus immer mehr entzog und zusehends ephemerer wurde.[29] Stattdessen sorgten die Entrahmungsmechanismen des White Cube für die notwendige Absorption des Betrachters in einer Umgebung, die deutlich signalisierte, dass es hier um ernstzunehmende Kunst ging. Die Vorstellung von Autorität und Aura der Kunst ist aufgegangen – sozusagen naturalisiert – in der Figur des White Cube und seiner spezifischen Atmosphäre. Zeit und Raum im Sinne eines historischen oder lokalen Kontexts treten dabei in den Hintergrund und die Bedingungen der Wahrnehmung werden absorbiert von der Unsichtbarkeit der ideologischen Apparatur der Institution. Wie auch bei dem von Foucault selbst so präzise diagrammatisch aufgelösten Modell des Panoptikums[30] als Disziplinar-Apparat gilt auch hier: Das Kaschieren und Ausblenden der Wahrnehmungshandlungen sorgt dafür, dass die Macht unsichtbar wird.

Ähnliche Prinzipien finden wir natürlich auch bei Shopping-Malls oder Themenparks. Wenn wir mit Themenparks im klassischen Sinne den Versuch assoziieren, eine große

Zahl von Besuchern an einen Ort zu binden, der diese in die Lage versetzen soll, ihre Alltagssorgen und die sie umgebende Stadt zu vergessen, um sich voll und ganz dem Thema zu widmen, dann funktionieren diese primär und trotz ihres evidenten Bemühens, sich die ganze Welt einzuverleiben, nur aufgrund von Ausschlussmechanismen: Die Fülle der Abwechslung und Angebote sucht zu verdecken, was nicht Eingang finden darf. In diesem Sinne entspricht die multimediale Bearbeitung der Sinneswahrnehmung in Themenparks einer Wellness-Kur. Ihr Erfolg beruht unter anderem darauf, dass sie vor allem eines erlaubt – zu vergessen und abzuschalten, sich treiben zu lassen oder auch einen kontrollierten, immer abgesicherten und versicherten Kontrollverlust zu begehen. Damit das Sich-treiben-Lassen gelingt, muss die Außenreferenz minimiert und die Orientierbarkeit sukzessive abgebaut werden.

Ein entscheidender Aspekt dieser Form der Architektur und Raumgestaltung ist, dass sie bestimmte Wahrnehmungen und Sinneseindrücke hervorbringen will und dabei Handlungsangebote produziert, die aber üblicherweise in einem immer schon vorgedachten Raum der Optionen liegen. Auch die Affekte wurden als ein kommodifizierbares Handlungsfeld entdeckt, dessen Management zum Beispiel bei Disney *Imagineering* genannt wird. Die sich beständig steigernden Wahlmöglichkeiten innerhalb dieser kontrollierten kommerziellen Systeme korrelieren allerdings mit einer generellen Differenzierung und Heterogenisierung von Lebensstilen und Identitätskonstruktionen, die aus dem Flexibilisierungsimperativ der radikalen Marktwirtschaft erwachsen sind. Das Prinzip der Immersion spricht in seinen Mechanismen der Ausblendung von Komplexität und Widersprüchen einem Phantasma der Kohärenz das Wort. Im Gange ist mit der Aufwertung des Affekts eine „Fetischisierung des Körpers als Kontrastfigur zum Subjekt und zu einer Politik der Differenzierung".[31] „Politisch, handlungstheoretisch ist hier nichts mehr zu holen," hat es Tom Holert etwas drastisch formuliert.[32] Und weiter warnt er im Rekurs auf die schon erwähnte Marie Luise Angerer davor, dass das Aufgeben der „psychischen Dimension" zugunsten der Inauguration einer „vitalistischen Motivationskraft" biopolitischen Instrumentalisierungen[33] „ungeahnten Ausmaßes und ungeahnter Konsequenzen" diene. Die Abgeschlossenheit und inhaltliche Kohärenz immersiver Umgebungen erscheint in diesem Zusammenhang natürlich identitätspolitisch immer problematisch. In dem Argument dieses strukturellen Verfehlens von Kohärenz in den Prozessen der Subjektivierung liegt einerseits die schon beschrie-

bene Agenda begründet, die Immersion als Modus der Schließung zu kritisieren. Andererseits: Nimmt man Silvermans Argument der Pose als raumproduzierende Figur ernst, dann erscheint die räumliche Hülle immer relational zu einem Subjekt, das seine Rolle in dieser Inszenierung immer noch zu einem gewissen Grad selbst definiert und das zumindest zwischen unterschiedlichen Angeboten temporärer Entrahmungen in immersiven Umgebungen wählen kann. Die Konjunktur des Affektiven, des Atmosphärischen und Immersiven wird letztlich daran zu messen sein, welche Angebote der Subjektivierung damit verbunden sind.

Die Parameter der Gestaltung der GfZK

Auch wenn, wie eingangs formuliert, die Institution zu einem mit Aura gefülltem Ambient geworden ist, so kann gerade ihre Architektur ein Medium darstellen, diese Produktion von Präsenz und Atmosphäre mit ihren Mitteln zu kommentieren, ihre Grundbedingungen sichtbar zu machen oder bisweilen auch zu unterlaufen. In der Konzeption des Raumgefüges der GfZK-2 wurden die basalen Elemente des Ausstellungsraums als disponible Versatzstücke eines institutionellen Dispositivs[34] behandelt. Die räumlichen Parameter der Ambient-Konstruktion werden damit bis zu einem gewissen Grad auch immer selbst mit ausgestellt. Es ging um eine durchlässige Atmosphäre, die die Elemente der Institution sozusagen als „Paravents", als „Kulissen" einsetzt. Sie können verschoben und damit sichtbar werden. Sie können entlang der Notwendigkeit von Verhandlungen ihrer Positionierung benennbar werden. Dabei geht es jedoch dezidiert nicht um eine Maximierung von Flexibilität. Entscheidender als das, was die Architektur der GfZK ermöglicht, war in diesem Zusammenhang das, was sie verunmöglicht: die einfache Orientierung, die Option komplett abgeschlossener Räume, die Ausblendung der Architektur und des räumlichen Kontextes und damit die Möglichkeit einer gelungenen Immersion in die Aura der Institution. Vielmehr ging es darum, Faktoren wie die Architektur, die Wahrnehmung des eigenen Körpers im Raum und die damit verbundenen Affekte, die Inszenierung der Institution sowie die komplexen Verwebungen dieser Aspekte darzustellen, die in den bruchlosen Narrativen musealer Szenografien zumeist unterdrückt werden. Die Idee einer Gemeinschaft, verbunden durch eine Atmosphäre künstlerischer Aura, wie sie Nicolas Bourriauds Prinzip einer „relationalen Ästhetik" entwirft, wird dabei ganz bewusst infrage gestellt. Die Architektur der GfZK produziert vielmehr miteinander konkurrierende Teilbereiche, deren Relationen über

Verhandlungen entlang von Differenzlinien im Raum jeweils neu geklärt werden müssen. Die Konstitution von (auch antagonistischen) Teilöffentlichkeiten ist hier als Hoffnung ins architektonische Programm mit eingeschrieben.

1 Tony Bennett, „The Exhibitionary Complex", in: Reesa Greenberg, Bruce W. Ferguson, Sandy Nairne (Hrsg.), *Thinking about Exhibitions*, London 1996, 82–109, S. 84

2 Nicolas Bourriaud, *Relational Aesthetics*, Dijon 2002

3 Nina Möntmann, *Kunst als sozialer Raum*, Köln 2002

4 Bourriaud, S. 61

5 „a momentary grouping of participating viewers", Bourriaud, S. 58

6 Bourriaud, S. 61

7 Vgl. dazu *archplus* 178 (Die Produktion von Präsenz), 2006

8 Siehe dazu auch Walter Prigge: „Atmosphären konstituieren sich im Zwischenraum von architektonischer Objektwelt (hier strahlt Atmosphäre aus dem Arrangement der Dinge) und subjektivem Raumerlebnis (hier ist Atmosphäre Wirkung subjektiver Stimmungen und Affekte): Der Entwurf von Atmosphären erkennt die Individuen prinzipiell als soziale Mitproduzenten von Raum und Architektur an – das ist der „Point of no Return" in der postmodernen Raumproduktion und der Kritik an der veralteten Moderne, die den Individuen alltägliche Lebensweisen durch objektive Raumordnungen vorzuschreiben suchte." Walter Prigge, „Zur Konstruktion von Atmosphären", in: *Wolkenkuckucksheim* 8, Nr. 2, 2004 (http://www.tu-cottbus.de/Theo/Wolke/deu/Themen/032/Prigge/prigge.htm)

9 Siehe dazu das Kapitel „Illusion gegen Anti-Illusion", in: Jörg Heiser, *Plötzlich diese Übersicht*, Berlin 2007

10 Gerhard Schulze, *Die Erlebnisgesellschaft. Kultursoziologie der Gegenwart*, Frankfurt a.M. 1992

11 Marie Luise Angerer, *Vom Begehren nach dem Affekt*, Zürich/Berlin 2007

12 Robert Somol, Sarah Whiting, „Notes around the Doppler-Effect and Other Moods of Modernism", in: *Harvard Design Magazine* 21, 2004, S. 16–21

13 Ludwig Fromm, „Das Atmosphärische", in: ders., *Architektur und sozialer Raum. Grundlagen einer Baukulturkritik*, Kiel 2000, S. 73

14 Ole W. Fischer, „Critical, Post-Critical, Projective?", in: *archplus* 174, 2005

15 Gernot Böhme, „Atmosphäre als Grundbegriff einer neuen Ästhetik", in: ders., *Atmosphäre*, Frankfurt a.M. 1995

16 Böhme, *Architektur und Atmosphäre*, München 2006, S. 25ff.

17 Ebd., S. 25

18 Ebd.

19 Vgl. ebd., S. 23

20 Siehe Detlef Mertins, „Transparency: Autonomy and Relationality", in: Todd Gannon, Jeffrey Kipnis (Hrsg.), The Light Construction Reader, New York 2002, S. 140ff.

21 Siehe dazu Christopher Dell, „Die Performanz des Raumes", in: archplus 183, 2007

22 Silverman führt zur Klärung dieser Bezüge den Terminus gaze ein, mit dem sie versucht, dem (immer schon vorhandenen) gesellschaftlichen Blick (gaze), der dem Sehen (look) des Subjekts entgegengesetzt verläuft, eine kulturelle Aufladung zu geben, die ihn als Repräsentation einer „dominant fiction", also der jeweils kulturell vorherrschenden Erzählungen und Identifikationsangebote beschreibt, den Blick damit also historisch und ideologisch einbettet.

23 Silverman lokalisiert dieses Zusammentreffen am cultural screen in Anlehnung an Jacques Lacans Konzept. Lacan definierte den screen (écran) als Ort, an dem sich das Subjekt konstituiert. Dieser Ort allerdings ist nicht optischer Natur, kein geometraler Raum, sondern opak. Jene Schnittstelle, die als konstitutive Mediation zwischen Subjekt und (s)einem Bild fungiert. Indem das Subjekt bei Lacan den Ort eines Bildes einnimmt, im screen verortet ist, wird es als Produkt von Blickverhältnissen mit sozialen, kulturellen und ideologischen Implikationen begriffen. Silverman erweitert sein Argument um die kulturelle Spezifizierung der jeweiligen dominant fiction. Indem sie auf die Fähigkeit des look verweist, immer auch eine Resistenz gegen die vorgegebene Blickweise des gaze entwickeln zu können, thematisiert sie eine Form der Identifikation, die sich rein apparativen Beschreibungsmustern entzieht. Vgl. bei Silverman die entsprechenden Kapitel „The Gaze", „The Look", „The Screen"

24 Silverman, S. 203

25 Vgl. Ilka Becker, „Einblendung. Körper, Atmosphärik und künstlerische Fotografie", in: Tom Holert, Imagineering Visuelle Kultur und Politik der Sichtbarkeit, Köln 2000, S. 176ff.

26 Ebd., S. 191

27 Böhme, 2006, S. 30

28 Brian O'Doherty, Inside the White Cube: The Ideology of the Gallery Space, Santa Monica/San Francisco 1976/1986

29 Siehe dazu Lucy Lippard, Six Years: The Dematerialization of the Art Object from 1966 to 1972, New York 1973

30 Anhand des Beispiels des Panoptikums thematisierte Michel Foucault die Auswirkungen eines sich grundlegend verschiebenden Begriffs des Subjekts auf die historische Formation der Blickregime und die paradigmatischen Räume. Dieses Gefängniskonzept aus dem späten 18. Jahrhundert beruht auf einer gezielten Installierung von Blickverhältnissen und Überwachungsmechanismen. So orientieren sich sämtliche Einzelzellen des Gefängnisses auf einen zentralen Turm in der Mitte der Anlage, von wo aus die Aufseher durch die nach außen hin transparent gehaltenen Zellen jeden Gefangenen jederzeit als Silhouette erkennen und somit überwachen können. Siehe dazu: Michel Foucault, Überwachen und Strafen: Die Geburt des Gefängnisses (1975), Frankfurt a.M. 1994

31 Andreas Spiegl, „Out of Place Revisited", Manuskript des gleichnamigen Vortrags im Rahmen der Tagung Theorie und Affekt in der Akademie der Bildenden Künste Wien, 18.01.2008

32 Tom Holert, „Am Ende des Subjekts", in: Texte zur Kunst 67, 2007, S. 212ff.

33 Zu den an Michel Foucault anknüpfenden Diskursen rund um seinen Begriff der Bio-Macht und Bio-Politik siehe zum Beispiel: Thomas Lemke, Gouvernementalität und Biopolitik, Wiesbaden 2006

34 Zum Begriff Dispositiv siehe: Michel Foucault, Dispositive der Macht. Über Sexualität, Wissen und Wahrheit, Berlin, 1978, S. 119ff.

Andreas Spiegl
AS IF A bis Z …

A

Architektur – wie im Falle des Neubaus der GfZK Leipzig – basiert wesentlich auf einem Zeitbegriff. Die einzige Konstante, die dieser Zeitbegriff kennt, heißt Veränderung. Vor dem Hintergrund kultureller, sozialer, politischer und ökonomischer Veränderungen bedeutet die Konstruktion eines zeitgenössischen Raums die Konstruktion möglicher räumlicher Veränderungen. Paradox daran erscheint, dass das Wissen um die Veränderung die Veränderung schon vorwegnimmt. Konstant bleibt die Struktur, innerhalb derer sich Veränderungen abspielen können. In diesem Sinne steht der Raum für eine Ordnung und zugleich für eine Veränderung, die für die räumliche Ordnung das Programm liefert. Da die Programmierung der Zeit – in der Figur des Ausstellungsprogramms – der jeweiligen Veränderung des Raums vorauseilt und zugleich impliziert, dass jede räumliche Veränderung mit der nächsten Ausstellung wieder verändert werden kann, erscheint der Raum als sekundäre Dimension. Raum ist das Medium, in dem sich Zeit ausdrückt. Was als Raum erscheint, erscheint als bloße Gegenwart, die hier für die Dauer einer Ausstellung als räumliches Zeitfenster festgehalten wird – vergleichbar der Fotografie und ihrem phantasmatischen Kern, aus der Zeit einen Augenblick entwenden zu können. In diesem Sinne evoziert die räumliche Veränderbarkeit im vorübergehend festgehaltenen Raum eine Vorstellung von Gegenwart, von Gegenwärtigkeit und die Aura eines Ereignisses. Das Ereignis besteht wider Erwarten darin, dass sich für eine bestimmte Zeit nichts verändert. In diesem Sinne ist die Architektur eine Zeitmaschine: Sie repräsentiert eine Konstante der Veränderung und sie evoziert zugleich ein Innehalten – einen Augenblick, die architektonische Fotografie einer Gegenwart.

B

Besucherinnen und Besucher sind eingeladen, auf ihrem Weg durch die Ausstellungen Entscheidungen zu treffen. Die in sich veränderbare Ordnung des Raums ist so konzipiert, dass es immer mehrere Möglichkeiten gibt, sich auf den Weg durch die Ausstellungen und Räume zu machen. Die Verschiebbarkeit der Wände ermöglicht die Gestaltung unterschiedlicher Sichtachsen und damit die Option, verschiedene Bezüge zwischen den künstlerischen Arbeiten und Räumen herzustellen. In diesem Sinne entscheidet die Wegführung der Besucherinnen und Besucher über die je spezifischen Perspektiven auf Räume und Arbeiten. Wie der Blick wird das Gehen zu einem Moment der Bedeutungsproduktion. Unabhängig davon, ob dieses Gehen als Flanieren, als Wandern oder Absolvieren einer Wegstrecke angelegt ist – es markiert eine Form von Mobilität und stillt damit ein ambulantes Begehren nach Bewegung. Bewegung meint hier nicht mehr als den Ausdruck einer Bewältigung von Zeit. Gehen ist eine Form, Zeit zu verbringen, und die Form des Gehens definiert, von welcher Zeitvorstellung beim Gehen ausgegangen werden kann. Im Wissen um die Veränderbarkeit der Raumsituationen weiß man nicht, wohin der Weg durch die Räume und Ausstellungen führen wird. Paradox daran erscheint, dass gerade dieses Nicht-Wissen um den Raum dazu führt, die Räume selbst in Augenschein zu nehmen – und sei es als Ausdruck einer Gegenwart, die nur nach Orientierung sucht, wenn die Gefahr droht, den Weg verlieren zu können. Diese Architektur legt prinzipiell Wege vor – im Wissen darüber, dass man diese finden und verlieren kann.

C

Cafés tragen der Erfahrung Rechnung, dass Institutionen neben ihren Kernaufgaben auch Funktionen haben, die eher mit der kulturellen Einbettung des Institutionellen per se zu tun haben. Cafés sind in diesem Sinne selbst Institutionen, die sich mit ihren hybriden Funktionen zwischen Erholungsraum, Gaststätte, Toilettengarantie, Diskussions- und Kommunikationsraum in die Institutionen als Alter Ego einschreiben. Räumlich sind sie gleichermaßen integriert wie appliziert – parasitär naschen sie am Leben der Institution und halten zugleich an ihrer Autonomie fest, mit der sie sich allein ihrem urbanen oder kulturellen Umfeld zuwenden. Sie sind betretbar, ohne die Institution besuchen zu müssen. Eingespannt zwischen der Institution und ihrem Umfeld haben sie immer zwei Ein- und Ausgänge – im Wesen sind sie Passagen, die dazu einladen Zeit zu verbringen, wenn man nicht weiß, wie man die Zeit verbringen soll. Cafés sind Zeitmaschinen für zeitliche Zwischenräume. Architektonisch ins Räumliche übersetzt bedeutet dies, gleichermaßen den Eindruck eines Innenraums zu vermitteln, der sich nicht nur dem Außen zuwendet, sondern eigentlich ein paradoxes Innen im Außenraum repräsentiert. Wenn man im Café sitzt, sitzt man in der Stadt, die man gerade verlassen hat. Die Dialektik aus Glas und Beton liegt darin begründet und reicht auch dorthin, wo von Institutionen und Cafés keine Rede mehr ist. Das Zwischenräumliche, das Hybrid aus Innen und Außen ist konstitutiv für zeitgenössische Raumvorstellungen.

D

Die Orientierung der Architektur am Medialen wird unter „M" besprochen.

E

Erinnerung spielt in der Architektur eine wichtige Rolle, weil man bei dem Gedanken an Architektur dazu tendiert, an ein Haus zu denken – als Erinnerung an eine Urform von Architektur. Mit dem Gedanken an das Haus wird implizit die Vorstellung von einem Innen- und Außenraum evoziert. Enthalten in diesem Gedanken an Innen- und Außenräume sind die entsprechenden Ein- und Ausschlussmechanismen – die Trennung zwischen Bewohnern und Besuchern. Das Paradox eines institutionellen Raumes besteht darin, dass er formal einen Innenraum verspricht und zugleich betont, dass dieser nicht bewohnt werden kann. In diesem Sinne gehen das Besuchen und das Bewohnen institutionell ineinander über. Eine Institution wird gewissermaßen von ihren Besucherinnen und Besuchern bewohnt. Im Wissen um die kulturelle und politische Problematik von Innen- und Außenbeziehungen repräsentieren Institutionen eine Form zeitgenössischer Wohnverhältnisse. Was sie leisten, ist das Insistieren auf der steten Frage nach den Eigentums- und Besitzverhältnissen. Selbst Ausstellungen, die für eine bestimmte Zeit die Räume „okkupieren", sind nur zu Besuch. Für die Architektur bedeutet dies, bei der Konzeption einer Institution den Gedanken an das Haus zu verwerfen, um eine Raumordnung vorzuschlagen, für die Innen und Außen außer Kraft gesetzt werden. Das Ziel dieser Architektur liegt darin, die Erinnerung an das Haus als Paradigma politischer oder kultureller Raumvorstellungen vergessen zu machen.

F

Feuerlöscher sind undankbare Requisiten, weil die Architektur alles dafür tut, dass nie Feuer ausbricht. In diesem Sinne markieren sie eine Disfunktionalität, die bisweilen mit künstlerischen Arbeiten konkurriert, für die das Disfunktionale wesentlich ist. Unabhängig davon, wo sie stehen, stehen sie immer an der falschen Stelle. Und weil sie an der falschen Stelle stehen, fallen sie auf und stehen damit irgendwie an der richtigen Stelle. Mit ihrer richtigen und zugleich falschen Stelle erinnern sie an die Problematik einer zeitgenössischen Subjektvorstellung – mithin an ein Subjekt, für das es raumpolitisch keinen richtigen Ort mehr gibt. Aus dieser Perspektive ist das zeitgenössische Subjekt ein raumpolitischer Feuerlöscher, weil es an einen Raum erinnert, den es nicht mehr geben darf. Brandgefährlich, nicht das Feuer, sondern das Subjekt, das vermeintlich an der falschen Stelle steht, wo immer es erscheint.

G

Grund genug gibt es, manchmal keinen Grund zu haben. Scheinbar knappe 30 Zentimeter über dem Boden schwebend, entzieht sich diese Architektur der Bodenhaftung und eines Grundes. Der Grund für diese Architektur liegt nicht im Fundament. Ihre Begründung zieht sie aus anderen Vektoren: aus argumentativen Richtlinien, die das Gebäude durchlaufen, umspannen, mit einem Kontext und mit Räumen vernetzen, die anderen Ursprungs sind. Der Grund für dieses Gebäude ist nicht der Baugrund, sondern ein heterotopisches Geflecht, das die adressierte Geografie verunklart, dereguliert und als geopolitische Aufgabe erkennen lässt. Die Gründe liegen anderswo, weit verstreut. Sie sind aber nicht weniger präsent als das Territorium, das den Grund verbirgt, weil es meint, mit dem Grund identisch zu sein.

H

Häuser sind die Doppelgänger einer Architektur, die sich vom Haus verabschieden will, das da immer wiederkehrt. Teils unter „E" wie „Erinnerung" besprochen, zielt zeitgenössische Architektur auf eine Architektur ohne Häuser. Wie in diesem Fall folgt die Form des Gebäudes einer Logik der Veränderbarkeit, der Verschiebbarkeit. Was als Außenform erscheint, ist die Auslagerung der immanenten Veränderbarkeit: das Spitze, die Kanten und Ecken, die Perspektiven, die Ein- und Durchblicke sperren sich gegen den geschlossenen Eindruck eines Hauses. Das Haus wird aufgelöst in Raum- und Architekturfragmente. Was bleibt, ist der Weg entlang einer Strecke rund ums Gebäude, das sich auch dann nicht erschließt: Diese Architektur appelliert ans Fragmentarische, das sich der Berechenbarkeit entzieht. Ästhetisch kalkuliert sie mit dem Unberechenbaren – bis zum Material, zur Farbe und Textur, die gleichermaßen Außen und Innen in ihrer Verschiebbarkeit wiederkehren. An die Stelle des Hauses tritt die Stadt als räumliches Konzept. Der Wegführung durch die Straßen entspricht hier die Wegführung durch eine Architektur, die sich der Urbanität mehr verpflichtet fühlt als dem Haus. In diesem Sinne hat diese Architektur auch kein Dach, sondern eine Grenze der Raumhöhen, die differieren, als wären in dem Gebäude mehrere Häuser enthalten. Was als Dach erscheint, ist nur die Folie für eine mögliche Terrasse, eine weitere Ebene der Wegführung und Begehbarkeit. Charakteristisch sind die Eingänge, die für das Café wie für die Galerie als Wege und Rampen konzipiert sind. In diesem Sinne betritt man die Architektur nicht durch eine Tür, sondern durch einen Weg als Fortsetzung der Straße. Der Weg

Ist der Teil der Straße, der übrig bleibt, wenn man das Auto verlässt: das Subjekt – ein Fußmobil.

I

Innen und Außen folgen weniger räumlichen als politischen Koordinaten.

J

James Joyce' *Ulysses* spielte für die Planung dieser Architektur keine Rolle. Dennoch wäre seine Übersetzung von Homers *Odyssee* in die Dauer und Wegstrecke eines Tages ein Modell dafür, die hier skizzierte Übersetzung eines hochkomplexen geopolitischen Raumschicksals in die Architektur eines einzigen Gebäudes zu beschreiben. In diesem Sinne handelt die Architektur der GfZK auch von einer Odyssee.

K

wie GfZK

L

Licht ist für die Architektur genauso entscheidend wie für die Fotografie. Jenseits der Farben definiert das Spektrum von Hell und Dunkel das Bild, das man sich von Innen und Außen zurechtlegen will. Innen wird es immer dann hell, wenn es Außen dunkel wird und umgekehrt. Will man aber wie diese Architektur den Gegensatz von Innen und Außen minimieren, so spielt das Licht eine zentrale Rolle. Glasflächen, Fenster als transparente Wände und ein ausgeklügeltes Lichtsystem in den Räumen sorgen für ein Durchdringen der heterogenen Lichtverhältnisse. Die Leuchtkörper sind nicht nur in der Lage, sich mit den verschiebbaren Raumachsen zu drehen, sondern auch dimmbar – das heißt dazu bereit, sich den je verschiedenen Lichtverhältnissen anzupassen und darauf zu reagieren. Die Camouflage, die hier evoziert wird, pendelt zwischen der Anpassung an die solare Beleuchtung des Alltäglichen und der vollkommenen Emanzipation davon. White Box, black box, no box at all. Wenn das Licht die Architektur durchdringt, ohne dabei die Farbe und Helligkeit zu verändern, dann erscheint der Innenraum nur als architektonische Membran des Außenraums. Gleichermaßen setzt sich das Licht in der Nacht durch die Glaswände in den Außenraum fort und erklärt die urbane Nacht zur bloßen Verlängerung der Architektur. Aus dieser Perspektive handelt es sich beim Licht in der Architektur nicht um eine Frage der Beleuchtung, sondern um eine Charakterisierung des Raumes als Innen, Außen oder beides zugleich. Licht adressiert nicht die Sichtbarkeitsbedingungen, sondern die Bedeutung, die einem Raum zugeschrieben werden kann.

M

Medien definieren in hohem Maße die Vorstellung, die man sich von der Gegenwart machen kann. Sie erklären zur Gegenwart, was gegenwärtig anders nicht wahrnehmbar wäre und eröffnen damit eine Gleichzeitigkeit von Anwesendem und Abwesendem. Das umfassende Begehren nach Medialität deutet auf ein Begehren nach dieser Koexistenz von An- und Abwesendem. Alles sollte erreichbar und wahrnehmbar sein unter der Bedingung seiner Absenz, das heißt einer bloß medialen Präsenz. Diese Gleichzeitigkeit von Absenz und Präsenz ist damit konstitutiv für eine Wahrnehmung von Raum, der beide Figuren in sich aufnehmen muss. Architektur, die sich diesem Verhältnis stellt, kommt nicht umhin, den Raum selbst als Medium erscheinen zu lassen – mithin als Architektur, die Räume real bereitstellt und diese zugleich nur evoziert. Wesentlich ist daran, dass die Architektur als Medium nicht eine Botschaft vermitteln darf, die Informationen über die Inhalte eines Gebäudes gibt oder über die Form des Gebäudes auf dessen Funktion schließen lässt. Architektur als Medium heißt nicht weniger, als den Raum selbst als mediale Konstruktion zu vermitteln – ihn gewissermaßen in ein Bild zu verwandeln, das den konkreten Raum nur als Raumbild zu verstehen gibt. Architektonisch bedeutet dies, die Konstruktion von Raum an eine Projektion von Raum zu binden. Die alternierenden Materialien und Farben, die in der GfZK den Boden gleichermaßen variieren wie die Wände und deren Zusammenstellung, adressieren nicht nur eine Veränderbarkeit der räumlichen Situationen, sondern appellieren zugleich an die Heterogenität der Oberflächen, die das jeweilige Raumbild erzeugen. Nicht zufällig ist der einzig fixierte Raum in der Galerie das Kino, das heißt ein Projektionsraum im Zentrum der Architektur. Auf der einen Seite eine tragende Wand und die anderen drei Seiten von Glasflächen markiert, wird das Kino selbst zur architektonischen Raumprojektion: spiegelnd, opak, transparent, ein Vexierbild von Innen und Außen – ein paradigmatischer Raum, von dem sich alle anderen architektonischen Überlegungen ableiten lassen. Wie das Café repräsentiert das Kino einen Außenraum im Innenraum oder einen Innenraum, umgeben vom Außenraum der Institution. Ein Raum, der real vorhanden ist und zugleich als imaginärer Raum evoziert wird. Das Kino ist nicht nur einem Medium wie dem Film oder der Videoprojektion gewidmet, sondern es erscheint selbst als mediale Figur, als gebauter Film, der auch dann anwesend ist, wenn gerade kein Film läuft. In diesem Sinne wird das Mediale, das darin erscheinen sollte, schon von der Architektur antizipiert.

N

Nach der Moderne und einer in die Krise geratenen Teleologie strebte der architektonische Diskurs danach, die sozialen und kulturellen Ziele der Moderne zu verwerfen und die Architektur selbst als kulturelle Antwort auf die Krise zu definieren. Die unter dem Begriff der Postmoderne subsumierten Erscheinungen einer Architektur, die sich heterogenster architektonischer Versatzstücke ihrer Geschichte bediente, sind genauso bekannt wie die Museumsneubauten, die deshalb so begehrt waren, weil sie den Charme öffentlichen Interesses und damit einer politischen Dimension mit der Rhetorik einer sich selbst zum Thema erhebenden Architektur verbinden konnten. Aus der Perspektive der 1980er Jahre sind Architektur und Öffentlichkeit fast synonyme Begriffe. Der Einfluss der Architektur als Paradigma für die gleichzeitigen philosophischen und theoretischen Diskurse sei hier nur angemerkt. Retrospektiv betrachtet erweist sich dieser Blick auf die Architektur um der Architektur willen als Ersatzhandlung, die im Insistieren auf ihre öffentliche Rolle gerade dazu beigetragen hat, die Lücke oder Leerstelle, die mit der Vorstellung von Öffentlichkeit verbunden war, vorschnell zu schließen. Je mehr Öffentlichkeit die Bauaufgaben assoziieren ließen, umso attraktiver waren die Aufträge. Der mit der Kunst implizierte Öffentlichkeitswert sorgte seinerseits dafür, dass neben den Museen jegliche Form von Ausstellungshallen oder Kunstinstitutionen, die es neu zu gründen, zu bauen oder zu erweitern gab, für die Architektur von besonderem Interesse war. Eine Architektur für eine öffentliche Institution zu bauen, bedeutete ein Bild von Öffentlichkeit für eine Öffentlichkeit zu konstruieren, von der man sich kein Bild machen konnte oder wollte. Der Hang zum Spektakulären oder Monumentalen als klassische Figuren für eine Repräsentation von öffentlichem Interesse erklärt sich aus dieser Perspektive von selbst. Selbstredend stehen dafür die Eröffnungen von Architekturen, die gewissermaßen noch vor der Eröffnung eröffnet wurden – als bloße Architekturen um ihrer selbst willen.

Für zeitgenössische Architektur gilt es, dieser Geschichte einer Architektur als Ersatzhandlung für einen in die Krise geratenen Öffentlichkeitsbegriff etwas entgegenzusetzen, und sei es, die Architektur aus dem Bild der Architektur wieder verschwinden zu lassen. Mit anderen Worten: Um der Erwartungshaltung der Architektur gegenüber, dass sie ein Bild von Öffentlichkeit suggerieren soll, zu begegnen, gilt es, eine Antwort auf dieses Begehren zu verweigern. In Anbetracht der nahezu synonymen Bedeutung von Öffentlichkeit und Architektur stellt sich die Aufgabe, in der Architektur die Architektur zurückzunehmen und einen Raum zu evozieren, der über die Architektur hinausgeht, sie durchdringt, sie manchmal ignoriert und beiläufig erscheinen lässt.

Die Architektur der GfZK verwehrt sich einem Blick aufs Ganze. Ihre Ecken, Kanten und Perspektiven verunklären das architektonische Objekt. Was sie einfordert, ist ein Erschließen von Räumen, deren Grenzen offen oder verhandelbar bleiben. Anstelle architektonischer Konstruktionen oder Formen entwirft sie architektonische Requisiten, die je nach Bedarf verschoben und verändert werden können, um je ein Stück Raum erscheinen zu lassen. Statt ein Bild für Öffentlichkeit zu inszenieren, zieht sich die Architektur der GfZK auf eine Raummaschine zurück. Darin liegt auch die Mechanik ihrer verschiebbaren Wände begründet. Die Ersatzhandlung, die Architektur repräsentierte, verkehrt sich hier zum Handanlegen, das Räume produziert. Architektur als öffentliches Werkzeug.

O

Oberflächen, die andere Eigenschaften suggerieren als die Elemente, die sie verdecken, folgen dem Prinzip der Maskerade und damit ein Stück weit dem Prinzip des Illusionismus. Wenn die Oberflächengestaltung als prägende Figur für den Raumeindruck in den Vordergrund tritt, ließe sich daraus folgern, dass die sie tragenden Elemente in den Hintergrund rücken und verborgen bleiben sollten. Was aus dieser Dialektik ergäbe, wäre eine Differenz zwischen Oberfläche und Konstruktion, eine Differenz zwischen Bild und Architektur. Für eine Architektur aber, die wesentlich auf ein Bild von Architektur zusteuert, lebt der Raum von der Konstruktion von Oberflächen. Paradoxerweise liefern damit die geplanten Oberflächen erst die argumentativen Figuren für die Konstruktion, die diesen vorausgeht und zugleich folgt. Was dann entsteht, ist keine Maskerade, sondern eine Realität, die mit der Vorstellung von Realität und mit einem Wissen ums Imaginäre zusammenfällt. Der Illusionismus plädiert dann nicht für ein Trugbild, hinter dem die Realität verborgen bliebe, sondern für einen Begriff von Realität, für den der Illusionismus selbst eine reale Figur darstellt und damit eine politische, kulturelle und soziale Rolle spielt. Wogegen sich dieser Illusionismus in der Architektur wendet, ist der Illusionismus, in der manifest gebauten und architektonisch gestalteten Version von Realität ein Stück unveränderbarer Gegenwart zu erkennen. Wofür dieser Illusionismus plädiert, der mit der Realität eine imaginäre Figur identifiziert, ist die Vorstellung, selbst im Anschein des Faktischen noch das

Modell zu erkennen, das diesem vorauseilt. In diesem Sinne appellieren die Oberflächen zeitgenössischer Architektur nicht ans Trugbild, sondern an die Modellhaftigkeit der Vorschläge. Als Vorschläge bleiben sie virulent und verhandelbar. Als konstruktive Vorgaben insistieren sie darauf, dass die Konstruktion selbst nur modellhaft auf eine Vorstellung von Realität reagieren kann und damit selbst ein Stück weit von illusionistischen Zügen geprägt ist. Wenn eine Konstruktion dieses Prinzip maskiert, indem sie die Oberflächen verdrängt, wird sie erst recht zur Maskerade ihres imaginären Kerns.

P

Prinzipiell hat zeitgenössische Architektur mit Gesetzen und Gesetzmäßigkeiten zu kämpfen.

Q

Quantität tendiert gegenwärtig dazu, als Argument für Qualität herangezogen zu werden. Die Ökonomie, die dahinter steht, hat mit dem Oikos, dem sie sich verdankt, nur mehr wenig zu tun.

R

Renderings spielen nicht nur im Entwurf und für die Entscheidungsfindung der Bauträger eine Rolle, sondern sie bestätigen vor allem den Abstraktionsprozess und die Virtualität, die der Architektur vorausgehen und sie nach der Fertigstellung wieder einholen. In ihren Simulationen des möglichst Realistischen verwandeln sie das manifeste Ergebnis in reine Potenzialität, die auch dann noch vorhanden sein sollte, wenn sich nichts mehr bewegt. In diesem Sinne ist die Virtualität der Renderings und ihres Raumbegriffs kein Instrument zur besseren Veranschaulichung, sondern eine immanente Qualität der Architektur. Die Konsequenz daraus klingt vielleicht absurd, aber sie ist es nicht: Der Entwurf wird dann nicht in der manifesten Architektur realisiert, sondern der Entwurf wird selbst gebaut. Was am Ende finalisiert wird, ist das Rendering selbst, das heißt die Architektur steckt auch dann noch im Entwurfsprozess, wenn sie schon fertig ist. Und diese Potenzialität übersteigt wesentlich die möglichen Nutzungsprofile, zielt sie doch auf eine Fiktionalisierung des Raumes. War es eine Funktion des Hauses, Schutz zu bieten, indem es ein häusliches Innen als Widerständigkeit gegen ein feindliches Außen repräsentierte, so zielt das Rendering auf eine neue Schutzfunktion der Architektur, die in der Bereitstellung von Fiktionen liegt. Die Betrachtung der Fiktion als Schutz ist gewissermaßen eine zeitgenössische Übersetzung des einstigen Innen.

S

Statistisch gesehen sind die Stadt und die Urbanität wahrscheinlich die meist genannten Bezugspunkte für die zeitgenössischen Architekturdiskurse. Für die Architektur bedeutet dies Raumvorstellungen zu entwickeln, die das Bewusstsein um das Urbane auch dann noch vermitteln, wenn man sich schon kilometerweit in den Erschließungswegen und Nebenräumen eines Gebäudekomplexes verloren hat. So populär es geworden ist, die Straße vor dem Haus direkt in die Architektur hineinzunehmen und ins Gebäude zu verlängern, so konsequent ist es geworden, die Tür oder das Tor durch Luftkorridore und Schleusen zu ersetzen. Diese Buchstäblichkeit der Übersetzung urbaner Infrastruktur in architektonische Motive hat metaphorische Qualität und belegt nur, dass die Stadt als Metapher paradoxerweise der Architektur vorausgeht, die sie erst hervorbringt. Zeitgenössische Architektur wie der Neubau der GfZK von as-if berlinwien erweitert diese Perspektive, indem sie anstelle der architektonischen Bezugnahmen auf die Umgebung eines Gebäudes die Vorstellung eines zeitgenössischen Subjektbegriffs ins Zentrum rückt. Das zeitgenössische Subjekt, das als urbanes und daher mit allen sozialen, kulturellen und ökonomischen Widersprüchen vertrautes Subjekt gefasst wird, liefert die Koordinaten für die Raumvorstellungen, die damit identifiziert werden können. Urban ist dieser Subjektbezug darin, weil er gerade nicht auf eine je spezifische Subjektivität reduziert werden kann, sondern dessen Anonymität adressiert. In diesem Sinne wendet sich zeitgenössische Architektur und eine Institution wie die GfZK nicht an eine Öffentlichkeit, die hier repräsentiert werden soll, sondern an die Vorstellung eines Subjekts, das aber nur im Kontext der Öffentlichkeit gedacht werden kann. Was dann als Architektur erscheint, ist eine Form zeitgenössischer Haut eines Subjekts, ohne dass man sagen könnte, wer gerade drinsteckt.

T

Theorie und Praxis bilden ein untrennbares Paar. Historisch entspricht das Verhältnis der beiden zueinander einer krisengeschüttelten Ehe. Analog dazu entwickelten sich die jeweiligen Machtansprüche innerhalb dieser Beziehung und die entsprechenden Emanzipationsvorstellungen. Was sie voneinander gelernt haben, ist zumindest der Eindruck ohne einander nicht auszukommen. Was sie auch gelernt haben, ist die Unmöglichkeit, die je eigene Geschichte und die je eigenen methodischen Handlungsspielräume für die Utopie einer Fusion hinter sich zu lassen. Untrennbar aneinander gebunden, haben sie zumindest akzeptiert, die Eigenwilligkeiten und Eigenschaften des Gegenübers zu schätzen. Mit dieser Erfahrung ist die Einsicht verbunden, diese Eigenwilligkeiten und Eigenschaften weniger tolerieren gelernt zu haben, als sich diese buchstäblich zu eigen gemacht zu haben. Architektur, für die Theorie und Praxis gleichermaßen konstitutiv sind, lässt sich vor diesem Hintergrund weniger als Frage nach Gebäuden oder Objekten verstehen, sondern als Beziehungsgeflecht. Die Frage nach der Qualität von Architektur kommt daher nicht umhin, sich an der jeweiligen Beziehung von Theorie und Praxis in der Architektur zu orientieren und deren Intensität zu bewerten.

U
Unter Umständen

V
Vektoren definieren unter Umständen eine Größe, die zugleich eine Orientierung und eine Richtung markiert. Am einfachsten wird ein Vektor über einem Pfeil repräsentiert, der damit eine bestimmte Lage in der Fläche oder im Raum definiert und der über seine Größe und Pfeilspitze auch Auskunft über die Richtung und Maßstäblichkeit gibt, an der sich die anderen Bezugsgrößen orientieren. Vektoren sind für die architektonische Praxis eine zentrale Figur, weil sie in der Lage sind, gleichermaßen eine fixe Bezugsgröße zu liefern und eine Bewegungsrichtung festzulegen. Vektoriale Architektur wäre demnach eine Architektur, für die Bewegung und Ausrichtung auch dann noch eine Rolle spielen, wenn schon alles steht. Im Unterschied zur Orientierung an teleologischen Figuren, die ideologisch oder ästhetisch auf einen Fluchtpunkt und ein Ziel in der Zukunft zusteuern, bieten Vektoren die Möglichkeit, mehrere Vektoren zuzulassen und damit unterschiedliche Bezugsgrößen geltend zu machen. Zeitgenössischer Architektur wie der GfZK-2 gelingt es, diese Differenz der Maßstäblichkeiten und Richtungen für eine Vorstellung und Wahrnehmung von Raum zu vergegenwärtigen und sich in diesem Sinne nicht nur als Ausgangspunkt für weitere Entwicklungen zu betrachten, sondern auch als Konsequenz von Vektoren, die maßgeblich waren: seien sie ökonomischer, kultureller, ästhetischer oder theoretischer Natur.

W
www.as-if.info und www.gfzk.de

X
Xenophobien sind von Raumvorstellungen nicht zu trennen. Sie entstehen dann, wenn ein Raum als homogenisierte Einheit vorgestellt wird, die durch jegliche Form der Differenz – sei sie kultureller oder rassistischer Natur – infrage gestellt wird. Die Konsequenz daraus sind Ausgrenzungsversuche, die allein auf die Herstellung eines homogenisierten Innenraums abzielen und damit zugleich ein feindlich gesinntes Außen evozieren. Architektur, die modellhaft Räume definiert und sich kulturell und politisch positioniert, kann nicht umhin, sich den raumpolitischen Perspektiven der Xenophobie zu stellen – und sei es, wie am Beispiel der GfZK, indem man Homogenisierungstendenzen genauso vermeidet wie die Suggestion einer klaren Trennung von Innen und Außen. Diese raumpolitische Frage kann aber nicht allein durch die Verwendung von mehr oder weniger Glas beantwortet werden, sondern in erster Linie durch die Vermittlung eines Subjektbegriffs, der sich nicht homogenisieren lässt. Erst die Differenzierung und die Widersprüchlichkeit der Anforderungen, die an ein zeitgenössisches Subjekt gestellt werden, liefern die Koordinaten für die Heterogenität des Alltäglichen und eine entsprechende Raumpolitik. Die Architektur der GfZK repräsentiert ein ganzes Spektrum an Entscheidungen, die dieser Heterogenität der Anforderungen an das zeitgenössische Subjekt Rechnung tragen: angefangen von der Problematisierung von Innen- und Außenverhältnissen und der Gegenwart medialer Räume bis hin zu den sich verändernden Raumvorstellungen und einer mehrdimensionalen Kartografie des Subjekts. Die Tatsache, dass die GfZK in ihrem Ausstellungsprogramm zugleich die Divergenz von Handlungsspielräumen und Subjektvorstellungen repräsentiert, macht diesen Ort zu einem Raum, in dem die Heterogenität und die Alltäglichkeit des Unbekannten eine Gesetzmäßigkeit darstellen, für die es kein Gesetz gibt oder geben müsste.

Y
You

Z
Zuletzt ist alles eine Frage der Zeichnung, die in der Lage ist, eine Idee spontan zu skizzieren und die Skizze dann zu übersetzen. Wenn dann in der Übersetzung der Idee in gebaute Architektur die Zeichnung und damit die zugrunde liegende Abstraktion des Raumes noch spürbar bleibt, dann kehrt die Architektur wieder an ihren Ausgangspunkt zurück, der darin liegt, den Raum vor allem als Herausforderung an die Vorstellung von Raum und dessen Konsequenzen zu betrachten. Aber die Analyse dieser Abstraktion sollte unter A …

Exhibitions GfZK-2, 2004–2008

The Second Glance
November 20, 2004 to October 31, 2004
Artists: Volker Eichelmann, Jonathan Faiers,
Janet Grau, Arturas Raila, Evelyn Richter,
Tilo Schulz, Allan Sekula, Roland Rust
Curated by Julia Schäfer

Performative Architecture
September 10, 2004 to September 31, 2004
Artists: BLESS, Monica Bonvicini, Angela
Bulloch, Oliver Hangl, Jeppe Hein, Anita
Leisz, Olaf Nicolai, Pro qm, Heimo Zobernig
Curated by Angelika Nollert (Siemens arts
program) and Barbara Steiner

The Bosnian Chronicle
November 28, 2004 to January 16, 2005
Artists: Mladen Jadrić, Said Jamaković,
Stjepan & Tanja Roš, Mersiha Veledar,
Lebbeus Woods
Curated by Azra Akšamija

The Future Isn't What It Used to Be
November 28, 2004 to January 16, 2005
Artists: Josef Dabernig, Nina Fischer &
Maroan el Sani, Dorit Margreiter, Deimantas
Narkevičius, Olaf Nicolai, Roman Ondák,
Tadej Pogačar
Curated by Barbara Steiner and Igor Zabel

Via Lewandowsky: Homezone*
April 3, 2005 to October 4, 2005
Curated by Heidi Stecker and Barbara
Steiner

The Photographed City*
March 5, 2005 to April 10, 2005
Artists: Sibylle Bergemann, Wiebke Loeper,
Helga Paris, Merit Schambach, Michael
Scheffer, Maria Sewcz, Clemens von
Wedemeyer, Karin Wieckhorst
Curated by Heidi Stecker and Barbara
Steiner

Untitled (City IV)*
March 23, 2005 to June 19, 2005
Artists: Matthijs de Bruijne, Ebru Özseçen,
Tilo Schulz/Sibylle Berg, Wolfgang Thaler
Curated by Ilina Koralova

Sean Snyder*
March 23, 2005 to June 19, 2005
Curated by Ilina Koralova

What If …*
July 2, 2005 to September 4, 2005
Artists: Frisch, Terence Gower, Karsten
Konrad, Anna Meyer, Inken Reinert
Curated by Julia Schäfer

Dabernig, Josef: Film, Photography, Text, Object, Building*
July 2, 2005 to September 4, 2005
Curated by Barbara Steiner

Sofie Thorsen: 162 out of 172 Houses Are on the High Street …
September 17, 2005 to November 6, 2005
Curated by Julia Schäfer

Tina Schulz
(Winner of the Sachsen LB scholarship 2004)
September 17, 2005 to November 6, 2005
Curated by Julia Schäfer

Urban Painting
September 17, 2005 to November 6, 2005
Artists: Rafał Bujnowski, Katharina
Immekus, Johanna Kandl, Verena Landau,
Orsolya Larsen, Anna Meyer, Doris Ziegler
Curated by Ilina Koralova, Julia Schäfer,
and Barbara Steiner

Shrinking Cities 2: Interventions**
November 26, 2005 to January 29, 2006
Curatorial team: Philipp Oswalt, Walter
Prigge, Nikolaus Kuhnert, Barbara Steiner
(BS), Assistant curators: Friedrich von Bor-
ries, Kathleen Liebold, Heidi Stecker

Why Show Something That One Can See?
February 25, 2006 to May 7, 2006
Artists: Knut Asdam, Kaucyila Brooke, Tom
Burr, Valie Export, Marion Porten
Curated by Julia Schäfer

Monica Bonvicini: Spermanent Instability
February 25, 2006 to May 7, 2006
Curated by Ilina Koralova

Archit-Action!
May 20, 2006 to August 13, 2006
Artists: as-if berlinwien, Lina Bo-Bardi, Ines
Dullin-Grund, Anne Lacaton & Jean-Philippe
Vassal, Cedric Price, Richard Rogers & Renzo
Piano, SANAA, 51n4e
Curated by Barbara Steiner and Oana Tanase

Office for Cognitive Urbanism: Last Minute
Sptember 2, 2006 to October 15, 2006
Artists: Sabine Bitter, Andreas Spiegl, Kamen
Stoyanov, Karoline Streeruwitz, Christian
Teckert, Helmut Weber
Curated by Ilina Koralova

Dorit Margreiter: Analog
September 2, 2006 to October 15, 2006
Curated by Julia Schäfer

Anna Meyer: Bad Female Painters Are the Better Artists
October 28, 2006 to January 7, 2007
Curated by Barbara Steiner

Regine Müller-Waldeck: Emotional Security
(Winner of the Sachsen LB scholarship 2005)
October 28, 2006 to January 7, 2007
Curated by Julia Schäfer

Tilo Schulz: FORMSCHÖN
January 19, 2007 to April 9, 2007
Curated by Ilina Koralova

Dora García: Rooms, Conversations
March 21, 2007 to July 1, 2007
Curated by Julia Schäfer

Muntean/Rosenblum: Make Death Listen
July 14, 2007 to October 7, 2007
Curated by Ilina Koralova and Barbara
Steiner

Joachim Brohm: Ohio
October 20, 2007 to January 13, 2008
Curated by Barbara Steiner

Kay Bachmann: Remo Fasani: Novenari
(Winner of the Sachsen LB scholarship 2006)
October 20. 2007 to January 13, 2008
Curated by Julia Schäfer

* The exhibition was part of the project
Heimat Moderne (Heimat Modernism), a joint
initiative of a number of Leipzig institutions
and independent artist groups from various
cultural fields such as fine arts, architecture,
urban and landscape planning, music,
theater, and literature.

** *Shrinking Cities* is a project of the
Kulturstiftung des Bundes (German Federal
Cultural Foundation) in cooperation with
the Project Office Philipp Oswalt (Berlin),
the GfZK Leipzig, the Bauhaus Dessau
Foundation, and the magazine *archplus*.

In 2008–2010 the GfZK held the project *Carte
blanche*. A book will be published featuring
these exhibitions.

Authors

Arnold Bartetzky was born in 1965 in Zabrze, Poland. He studied History of Art, German Philology, and Philosophy in Freiburg, Germany, and Cracow. In 1998 he obtained a doctorate in History of Art. Since 1995 he has been working as a researcher at the Geisteswissenschaftliches Zentrum Geschichte und Kultur Ostmitteleuropas (Center for the history and culture of east central Europe) at the University of Leipzig, where he is currently associated with the project *Imaginations of Urbanity in the 20th Century*. He has published widely on various aspects of architecture and urban planning from the Renaissance to the present.

BLESS, initiated in 1997, is the result of an encounter between two students. **Desiree Heiss** was born in 1971 in Freiburg, Germany. She graduated in Fashion in 1994 from the University of Applied Arts Vienna, and is now based in Paris. **Ines Kaag** was born in 1970 in Fürth, Germany. She graduated in Fashion in 1995 from the University of Applied Sciences and Arts in Hanover, and is based in Berlin. The two designers escape any firm definition of fashion, remaining faithful to their initial concept. Dividing and combining creation between fashion, art, design, and architecture, they pursue an independent work method, which often implements collaborations and interactions with friends, customers, and other contributors.

Monica Bonvinini was born in Venice in 1965. She lives and works in Berlin. She exhibited at the 27th *Bienal de São Paulo* as well as the *Liverpool Biennial and the Gwangju Biennale* in 2006. She also exhibited at the 1st and 3rd *Berlin Biennales*, the 48th and 51st *Venice Biennales*, as well as in Santa Fe, New Orleans, Istanbul, and Shanghai. She participated in group and solo shows at Kunsthaus Zurich; Istanbul Modern; Berlin's Hamburger Bahnhof; Museum Ludwig in Cologne; Castello di Rivoli; Migros Museum, Zurich; New Museum, New York; P.S.1, New York; MIT List Visual Arts Center, Cambridge; MCA, Chicago; Modern Art Oxford; Tramway Glasgow; Secession, Vienna (with Sam Durant); SculptureCenter New York; Bonniers Konsthall Stockholm; Museion Bozen; Kunstverein Salzburg; Kunstraum Innsbruck; The Art Institute of Chicago; Palais de Tokyo, Paris; Kunstmuseum Basel/Museum of Contemporary Art; Lenbachhaus Munich (with Tom Burr); Le Magasine, Grenoble; and KW Institute for Contemporary Art, Berlin.

Josef Dabernig was born in 1956 in Kötschach-Mauthen, Austria. He graduated from the Academy of Fine Arts Vienna in 1981. He held solo exhibitions at international venues including the Grazer Kunstverein (2004); BAK basis voor actuele kunst, Utrecht (2003); Contemporary Art Center, Vilnius (2002); Galerie Display, Prague (2001); Künstlerhaus Bethanien, Berlin (1997); Galeria Potocka, Cracow (1994); and Secession, Vienna (1992). His work has been exhibited in *Manifesta 3*, Ljubljana (2000) and at the *Venice Biennales* in 2001 and 2003.

Jan Dinnebier trained as an architect and founded the Berlin-based studio dinnebier in 1998. studio dinnebier has been involved in projects such as the Jewish Museum Berlin, the Phaeno Science Center, the Astana Peace Pyramid, and the GfZK Leipzig. The studio specializes in museum lighting and product design. Its latest project is the modernization of the Istanbul opera with Tabanlıoğlu Architects and the Deutsche Oper Berlin.

Angelika Fitz was born in 1967 in Hohenems, Austria. She works as a curator and author, and has realized several exhibitions and publications on architecture, urbanism, art, and post-colonial subjects: *LINZ TEXAS. A City Relates (Linz09/AzW)* and *Wann begann temporär?* (with Ch. Feuerstein), *Ornament & Display*, kunsthaus muerz / steirischer herbst, the project series *Import Export* (film program, symposium, exhibitions, publication) in Mumbai, Vienna, and Berlin as well as *Reserve der Form* (with K. Stattmann). In 2003 and 2005 she was commissioner for the Austrian contribution of the 5th and 6th *São Paulo International Architecture Biennales*.

Paul Grundei was born in 1967 and lives in Berlin. He works as an architect and lecturer in Berlin and Vienna. As a co-founder of as-if berlinwien, he develops architectural projects widely ranging in scale and format. He has taught Architectural Design and Urban Design in several positions: as Lecturer in Urban Planning at Technische Universität Berlin (1998–2000), as Assistant Professor in Architectural Design and Building Construction at the same institution (2000–2007), and as Visiting Professor in Architectural Design and Urban Design at the Berlin University of the Arts (2007–2008).

Bernd Hullmann was born in 1964 in Delmenhorst, Germany. He graduated in Architecture from the Beuth Hochschule für Technik Berlin/University of Applied Sciences in 1988, after which he began working in small architectural offices in Berlin. He has been working as a Project Manager at the Project Management Consultancy SMV Bauprojektsteuerung in Berlin since 1993.

Stephanie Kaindl was born in 1966 and lives in Berlin. She graduated in Architecture from the Technische Universität München, and received a Master's degree from the Southern California Institute of Architecture, Los Angeles. She worked as an architect in Germany and the United States. As a co-founder and partner of as-if berlinwien, she develops architectural projects and projects relating to urban planning. From 2004 to 2009, she taught as an assistant professor at the University of Kassel, Germany. She currently held a visiting professorship at the University of Applied Sciences in Augsburg, Germany, from2009 til 2010. She is a member of AIV (Architekten- und Ingenieurverein), n-ails.de (Netzwerk von Architektinnen und Innenarchitektinnen, Landschaftsarchitektinnen und Stadtplanerinnen e.V.), and a jury member of the annual Schinkel Competition.

Ilina Koralova was born in 1974 in Sofia. She graduated in Art History from the National Academy of Art Sofia. She participated in the Curatorial Training Program of the De Appel Foundation, Amsterdam. Since 2002, she has been living and working in Leipzig as a curator at the GfZK Leipzig, where she has curated solo exhibitions by Tilo Schulz, Monica Bonvinini, Sean Snyder, and Jeppe Hein as well the group shows *o.T. [City IV]*, *Noch einen Wunsch?*, and *Introducing Sites*, among others.

Anita Leisz was born in 1973 in Leoben, Austria. She studied art at the Academy of Fine Arts in Vienna. Leisz had solo exhibitions at the Salzburger Kunstverein and at the Studio Sassa Trülzsch, Berlin, in 2007; at the Kunstverein Langenhagen in 2005; and in 2001 at the Secession in Vienna among others and participated in numerous group exhibitions. In 2004 Leisz designed the café Neubau/Weezie of the Museum of Contemporary Art in Leipzig.

Via Lewandowsky was born in 1963 in Dresden. He studied at the Hochschule für Bildende Künste Dresden from 1982 to 1987. Shortly before the collapse of communism, he moved to West Berlin and, in 1992, he took part in *documenta IX*. He was and is represented in numerous exhibitions at home and abroad, among them *Deutschlandbilder* (1997), *After the Wall* (2000), and *Das XX. Jahrhundert. Ein Jahrhundert Kunst in Deutschland* (2000). In 1995 Lewandowsky was the first winner of the Leipzig newspaper LVZ Art Prize.

Dorit Margreiter was born in 1967. She lives and works in Vienna. She held solo exhibitions such as *Locus Remix: Dorit Margreiter*, MAK Center for Art and Architecture, Los Angeles (2009); *Rebecca Baron, Dorit Margreiter*

– *Poverty Housing. Americus, Georgia*, MAK Austrian Museum of Applied Arts/Contemporary Art, Vienna (2008); *10104 Angelo View Drive*, MUMOK Museum Moderner Kunst Stiftung Ludwig Wien, Vienna (2004). She participated in, among others, the following group exhibitions: the Austrian Pavilion at *Biennale di Venezia* (2009); *The New Monumentality: Gerard Byrne, Dominique Gonzalez-Foerster and Dorit Margreiter*, Henry Moore Institute, Leeds (2009); *SynChroniCity*, 11th *Cairo International Biennale*, *The Reality Effect*, Henie Onstad Art Centre, Høvikodden (both in 2008); Bodypoliticx, Witte de With, Rotterdam; and *die stadt von morgen*, Akademie der Künste, Berlin (both in 2007).

Anna Meyer was born in 1964 in Schaffhausen, Switzerland. She studied at design academies in Zurich and Lucerne, and spent longer periods of study in Fujino, Japan, Los Angeles, and Mönchengladbach, Germany, among other places. In her paintings and large-format billboards for public spaces, she is concerned with the global consumer society and the displacement of living conditions resulting thereof. She also creates fashion collections in collaboration with the Tokyo-based designer Edwina Hörl.

Markus Muntean was born in 1962 in Graz, Austria, and Adi Rosenblum was born in 1962 in Haifa, Israel. **Muntean/Rosenblum** have been collaborating since 1992. They live in Vienna and London. They held a solo show at Team Gallery, New York and at 313 Gallery in Seoul in 2009. They have also exhibited in solo shows at Arndt & Partner, Berlin (2008), at Maureen Paley, London (2007), and at GfZK Leipzig (2007). In 2004 they exhibited at Tate Britain, London.

Olaf Nicolai lives and works in Berlin. He studied at the College of Applied Art, Schneeberg, Germany, and German Literature and Philology at the Universities of Leipzig, Budapest, and Vienna. In 1992, he completed a doctoral thesis on The Vienna Group. He has been awarded several grants, including: the Studienstiftung des Deutschen Volkes at the Studies Center for Art and Science in Venice (1993); Villa Massimo, Rome (1996); the P.S.1 Museum Grant, New York (1998); the IASPIS Grant, Stockholm (2000); and the Villa Aurora, Los Angeles (2008). He has participated in numerous exhibitions such as *documenta X* (1997), *Venice Biennale* (2001 and 2005), *Biennale of Sydney* (2002), *Gwangju Biennale* (2002), and *Athens Biennale* (2007). His work is shown in institutions worldwide – for instance, at Migros Museum, Zurich, Museo Serralves, Porto, Museum of Modern Art, New York, Fondation Cartier, Paris, and Lenbachhaus, Munich.

Julia Schäfer was born in 1972. She has worked with the New Museum, New York, and the Kunstmuseum Wolfsburg, Germany. She has been a curator and art mediator at the GfZK Leipzig since 2003, directly integrating – under the motto of "mediation as curatorial practice" – the various forms of artistic mediation into her exhibition concepts. She has realized projects at Kölnischer Kunstverein, Cologne; NGBK Neue Gesellschaft für Bildende Kunst, Berlin; and P74, Ljubljana. She curated and taught at the Academy of Fine Arts Vienna and Burg Giebichenstein/University of Art and Design in Halle, Germany.

Tilo Schulz was born in 1972 in Leipzig and lives in Berlin. He has been internationally exhibited as an artist and curator since the mid-1990s. His work has been shown in group shows such as *Manifesta2*, Luxembourg (1998), *Young Scene* in the Secession, Vienna (1998), or *deutschemalereizweitausenddrei* in the Frankfurter Kunstverein, Frankfurt am Main (2003). His recent solo shows include *FORMSCHÖN* at the GfZK Leipzig (2007), *STAGE DIVER*, Secession, Vienna (2008), *I WAS SHOT IN THE BACK*, Blackwood Gallery, Toronto (2008), and *GHOST RIDER*, Institute of Contemporary Art Dunaújváros (2009).

Manuel Sedeño was born in 1965 in Emmerich, Germany. He studied physics at the University of Manchester and architecture at the Technical University in Berlin. He graduated in 1993. Since 1996 he runs his own office – from 1999 until 2007 together with Georg Kobusch as a partner. His office specializes in site management for projects with highest demands on the quality of architecture.

Andreas Spiegl was born in 1964 in Austria. He studied Art History at the University of Vienna. He lectures in media theory at the Institute for Art Theory and Cultural Studies at the Academy of Fine Arts Vienna, where he is also Vice Dean for Research and Teaching since 2003. He has curated numerous exhibitions and published on media studies, urbanism, and contemporary art.

Barbara Steiner was born in 1964 in Dörfles, Austria. She is curator and Director of the GfZK Leipzig. She co-edited the publication entitled *Possible Museums*, which introduces the art museum as a public institution dealing with education, critical reflexion, and social change. Her interest focuses on the politics of representation (institutional critique and criticality, architecture, and display) as well as economic critique and criticality in the field of art and museums.

Christian Teckert was born in 1967 and lives in Vienna. He produces architectural projects, exhibitions, installations, lectures, and theoretical works in the fields of architecture, urbanism, and visual culture. In 1999 he set up the Office for Cognitive Urbanism with Andreas Spiegl. In 2003 he founded as-if berlinwien together with Paul Grundei and Stephanie Kaindl. He was co-curator of the exhibitions *Studiocity* in Vienna and Wolfsburg, (1999), *Screenclimbing* in Hamburg (2000), and *ManifeSTATION*, Rovereto, Italy (2008), and is co-author of the publications *Prospekt* (2003) and *Last Minute* (2006), both edited by the Office for Cognitive Urbanism. Since 2006 he is Professor for Space/Concept at the Muthesius Academy of Fine Arts and Design in Kiel, Germany, and, since 2005, he also regularly lectures at the Academy of Fine Arts Vienna. He is a former board member of the OEGFA (Austrian Society for Architecture) and the Vienna Secession.

Gerd Thieroff was born in 1955 in Selbitz, Germany. He holds a degree in Civil Engineering from the Institute of Technology, Technische Universität Berlin. Since 1999 he has been associated partner of the engineering office HHT. He was project leader of the Biosphere Potsdam for Barkow Leibinger Architects and of Haerder-Center Lübeck for npp and Auer + Weber architects.

Sofie Thorsen was born in 1971 in Denmark. In 2001 she graduated from the Royal Academy of Visual Arts in Copenhagen and the Academy of Fine Arts in Vienna. Since 1999 she has been based in Vienna, exhibiting internationally in group and solo shows. From 2005 to 2009, she held a teaching position at the Academy of Fine Arts Vienna. Her work focuses on modern and contemporary narratives about architecture and the urban space, with a particular focus on the photographic and graphic documentation of the built environment.

Jun Yang was born in 1975 in Qingtian, China. He lives in Taipeh, Taiwan and Yokohama, Japan, and is represented by Galerie Martin Janda, Vienna and Vitamin Creative Space, Guangzhou and Beijing. He has held solo exhibitions, among others, at the GfZK Leipzig; Index, Stockholm; Galerie Martin Janda, Vienna; Büro Friedrich, Berlin; and Vitamin Creative Space, Guangzhou; Group exhibitions include: *Manifesta 4*, Frankfurt am Main, 51st *Venice Biennale*, *Liverpool Biennial* (2006), and the 2008 *Taipei Biennial*. At the GfZK Leipzig he built the *gfzk garden*, including the shop *Hei Di* as well as the café *Paris Syndrom*.

Planning

Client:
Galerie für Zeitgenössische Kunst, Leipzig

Project Management:
SMV Bauprojektsteuerung, Berlin

Architecture:
as-if berlinwien (Paul Grundei, Stephanie
Kaindl, Christian Teckert)

Construction Management:
Manuel Sedeño in Kobusch + Sedeño
Architekten, Berlin

Construction Planning:
Hörnicke, Hock, Thieroff, Berlin

Technical Engineering:
PHA Planungsbüro für Haustechnische
Anlagen GmbH, Breuna

Lighting Design:
studio dinnebier, Berlin

Fire Protection Engineering:
Peter Stanek, Berlin

Thermal Building Physics, Building and
Room Acoustics:
IB Graner & Partner

Soil Mechanics and Foundation
Engineering: GuD Leipzig, Leipzig

Surveying:
Geokon, Leipzig

Landscape Planning:
inesterni, Milano/Berlin

Graphical Signage:
Studio Koch, Kopenhagen

Building

Building Shell:
Munte, Leipzig

Façade and Steel Construction:
Prüftechnik und Metallbau, Frankenheim
bei Leipzig

Dry Construction and Finishes:
Mänz und Krauss, Berlin

Heating, Air Conditioning, Plumbing:
Lars Wilke, Saara

Electrical Installations:
EMP Mannteufel & Partner, Leipzig

Luminaire Construction:
Lichtbau, Berlin

Fire Alarm and Intrusion Detection System:
Siemens Gebäudetechnik, Dresden/Berlin

Picture Credits

Cover:
Julia Schaefer
Collage for the exhibition "Analog"

Upper track:
Copyright for the works of Via Lewandowsky,
Josef Dabernig, Monika Bonvicini:
VG Bild-Kunst, Bonn and partner
organisations, 2010

Copyright for the works of Olaf Nicolai:
Courtesy Galerie EIGEN + Art Leipzig /
Berlin / VG Bild-Kunst, Bonn 2010

Wolfgang Thaler
p. 1–16, 133

Uwe Walter
p. 97–104

All others:
Andreas Enrico Grunert and GfZK

Lower track:
Studio Dinnebier
p. 137, 141, 142, 144, 145

Enrico Andreas Grunert
p. 96, 99 left, 127

Hörnicke, Hock, Thieroff
p. 129

Frank-Heinrich Müller
p. 120, 121

Prüftechnik und Metallbau
p. 179

All others:
asif berlinwien

Colophon

This book was made possible through the
generous support of the Friends Organisa-
tion of the GfZK.

© 2010 by Jovis Verlag GmbH

Texts by kind permission of the authors and
interview partners.

Pictures by kind permission of the photo-
graphers and artists.

Edited by Barbara Steiner for the GfZK/
Museum of Contemporary Art Leipzig
and Paul Grundei, Stephanie Kaindl, Christian
Teckert for as-if berlinwien

Copy-editing:
Tanja Milewsky, Leipzig

Translated from the German by:
Ariane Kossack, Ahrensburg,
Oliver Kossack, Leipzig,
Janima Nam, Vienna,
and Erik Smith, Berlin

Graphic Design and Setting:
Tom Unverzagt, Leipzig

Lithography:
Carsten Humme, Leipzig

Printing:
Thomas Druckerei, Leipzig

Binding:
Leipziger Kunst-und Verlagsbuchbinderei

Bibliographic information published by the
Deutsche Nationalbibliothek

The Deutsche Nationalbibliothek lists this
publication in the Deutsche Nationalbiblio-
grafie; detailed bibliographic data are
available on the Internet at http://dnb.d-nb.de

Jovis Verlag GmbH
Kurfürstenstraße 15/16
10785 Berlin

www.jovis.de

ISBN 978-3-86859-007-4

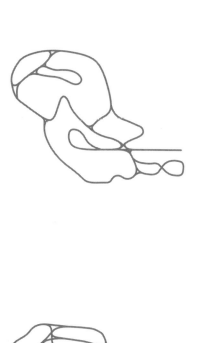

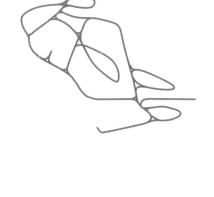

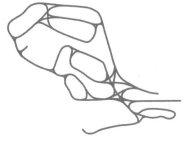